LIBRARY OF LATIN AMERICAN
HISTORY AND CULTURE
GENERAL EDITOR:
DR. A. CURTIS WILGUS

T0347146

South America

on the

Eve of Emancipation

South America

on the

Eve of Emancipation

The Southern Spanish Colonies in the Last
Half-Century of their Dependence

By

Bernard Moses, Ph.D., LL.D.

Routledge
Taylor & Francis Group

LONDON AND NEW YORK

First published 1965 by
Cooper Square Publishers, Inc.

Published 2013 by Routledge
2 Park Square, Milton Park, Abingdon, Oxfordshire OX14 4RN
711 Third Avenue, New York, NY 10017

First issued in paperback 2014

*Routledge is an imprint of the Taylor & Francis Group, an
informa business*

ISBN 13: 978-0-714-62032-9 (hbk)
ISBN 13: 978-0-415-76103-1 (pbk)

PREFACE

IN a book called *The Establishment of Spanish Rule in America*, published in 1898, the present writer gave some account of the origin and earlier history of the institutions framed for the government of Spanish America. This volume aims to present some phases of colonial history and social organization in the last part of the eighteenth century, particularly as they appear in the southern half of South America. The annals of the colonies furnish interesting episodes, but not material for a sustained dramatic narrative. There are periods in the history of some of the colonies, during which one observes few social changes. Men live as their fathers lived and die as their fathers died; and the history of their communities for generations may be told in a few sentences. In attempting to make a connected story of the events of these periods, a writer runs the risk of producing merely a chronicle, or of doing violence to the perspective of time. The task here undertaken is to present certain conspicuous events, institutions, and phases of life, that may illustrate the state of the southern Spanish colonies on the eve of the revolution which gave them independence.

Preface

Many of the statements of these chapters apply generally to Spain's possessions in America. But the physical environment of the colonies within the tropics made prominent certain features of social growth unlike those which appeared in the temperate regions. The state of society in the northern part of South America, during the later decades of the colonial period, is thus a subject by itself, and is put aside for another volume.

B. M.

UNIVERSITY OF CALIFORNIA,
April, 1908.

CONTENTS

v

SOUTH AMERICA ON THE
EVE OF EMANCIPATION

CHAPTER I

THE CAPITAL OF SOUTH AMERICA

THE Spanish colonial settlements established
within the limits of the territory now
claimed by the republics of Argentine, Bolivia,
Chile, and Paraguay, were politically subordinated
to the viceroy of Peru during their first two hundred years. In fact, down to nearly the middle
of the eighteenth century all the territory under
Spanish rule in South America was subject to
this authority. The political centre, the capital
in which resided the government recognized
throughout this vast domain, was the city of
Lima. By the final establishment of the viceroyalty of Santa Fé, in 1739, the northwestern
part of this territory was brought under a new
viceroy. The southeastern part of the continent
continued under the jurisdiction of the viceroy

of Peru, until 1776, when the viceroyalty of
Rio de la Plata was created. This distribution
of territory was modified in 1796, by withdrawing certain districts northwest of Lake Titicaca
from the viceroyalty of Rio de La Plata and
adding them to the viceroyalty of Peru. In
1802 Peru acquired from the viceroyalty of
Santa Fé the districts of Maynas and Quijos,
except the town of Papallacta; and, in 1804, it
was determined that the provinces of Guayaquil
and Chiloé should be subject to the government
of Lima. In 1810 Peru embraced eight intendancies: Lima, Tarma, Cuzco, Huancavelica,
Huamanga, Arequipa, Trujillo, and Puno; its
control extended also over the detached governments of Guayaquil, Chiloé, Maynas, Quijos,
Huarochirí, and Callao. Guayaquil subsequently
became independent and Chiloé was added to the
republic of Chile.

As the residence of the highest political and
ecclesiastical authorities of South America, Lima
acquired many of the features of an old-world
capital. All persons wishing to achieve social
distinction, and all persons who had achieved
such distinction, found it desirable to live in
Lima. The presence of the highest officers of
the government and the dignitaries of the Church
made it the social centre of South America.

In Mexico the Spaniards established their
capital at the centre of the dominant Indian

community. To have followed this example
in Peru would have placed the new city at an
inconvenient elevation, and in a position difficult
of access from the sea. In Mexico the Spaniards
wished to get away from the unhealthful coast.
In Peru the valley of the Rimac near the coast
offered an agreeable and healthful climate and
an abundance of pure water for the uses of a
city and for irrigation in a rainless region. Lima
was, therefore, founded here in January, 1535.
At the close of the eighteenth century, when Tadeo
Haënke wrote his description of the city, it was
surrounded by walls, which had been built as
a means of defence against attacks of pirates.
The inhabitants had been especially aroused
to undertake this work by the report of the
sacking of Vera Cruz, in 1683. Previously they
had exhausted their energies in the fruitless
discussion of various projects; but this event
turned their efforts to practical action. In
October of this year, the viceroy, the Duke of La
Palata, wrote to the cabildo, or ayuntamiento, of
Lima, and asked it to consider the question
of building the proposed wall, and to decide
what means for carrying on the work would be
the least burdensome. He wrote also to the
consulado, the university, the religious orders,
and to various other organizations. After these
negotiations it was finally determined how much
each association should pay, or what part of the

wall it should build, and what tax should be
levied on certain wares in order to secure the
funds necessary for the undertaking.[1] The writer
of *A True and Particular Relation of the Dreadful
Earthquake* of 1746 says that these walls were
between eighteen and twenty-five feet high; that
there was neither ditch nor outworks; and that
they were built by a Flemish priest, whose name
was Don John Ramond.[2]

At the beginning of the eighteenth century
Lima had about 30,000 inhabitants. In 1764
there were 54,000; and the population is estimated
to have increased in the following years so that
it amounted to 87,000 in 1810. Of the latter
number, 20,000 were whites, while the rest were
Indians, negroes, and various classes of mixed
blood. The city was about a mile in extent from
north to south, and about the same extent from
east to west. It was divided into two parts by
the river Rimac. Communication between these
two parts passed over the stone bridge which
was built during the administration of Montes
Claros. At first there was a wooden bridge, and
later the Marquis of Cañete, while viceroy, caused
a bridge to be constructed of brick near the site
of the present stone bridge. This was built
with seven arches, and was subsequently destroyed by the force of the water. After its

[1] *Memorias de los Vireyes*, ii., 365–375.
[2] Ramond died in Lima in July, 1709.

destruction several years passed before the present
structure was undertaken. It was, however,
finally begun in 1608, and completed in 1610.
The plans were made by Friar Geronimo Villegas,
a native of Lima, and the work was carried on
under the direction of Don Juan del Corral. The
expenses of the construction were met in part by a
tax of two reals on every sheep consumed, and by
certain contributions required of other cities in
the viceroyalty. Some of these were unable to see
any evidence of justice in being required to
pay for work that lay entirely beyond the limits
of their jurisdiction; and Quito, in particular,
complained at being compelled to furnish this
assistance. The total cost of the structure,
including the replacing of the arch that was
thrown down by the earthquake of 1746, was
seven hundred thousand pesos. The bridge rests
on five stone arches.

The principal plaza, which is now only a breath-
ing place for the citizens, a place of rest and
recreation, appears to have been used as a market
at the end of the eighteenth century, and was
supplied abundantly with products of Europe
and America, which were generally sold by
negresses, "and judging from their good clothing
and the manner in which they conduct themselves
one may conclude that many of them pass a life
of comfort and the most of them acquire wealth." [1]

[1] Haënke, *Descripcion del Peru*, 3.

The principal streets were broad and straight, dividing the city into blocks one hundred and fifty yards square, and were paved and kept notably clean. Many of the houses were large, built about one or more patios, or courts, and were constructed of adobes and of studs interwoven with cane or bamboo, and covered with plaster or stucco. The roofs, in the absence of rain, were of little importance, except to keep out the sun, and were in many cases formed of a framework of timber and reeds covered with earth. This form of construction, particularly the basket-work walls covered with plaster, were thought to be well adapted, by their lack of rigidity, to withstand the shocks of the frequent earthquakes. There were, in the last decade of the eighteenth century, 3641 houses in the city, which was divided into thirty-five wards, in each of which there was an *alcalde* elected to watch over the particular interests of his ward, and who was subject to the central authority.

The inhabitants of Lima entered upon the second half of the eighteenth century with the task of reconstructing the city only partially accomplished. The earthquake of 1746 had transformed a large part of the buildings into masses of ruins, and those persons who had occupied the houses destroyed had sought safety in the public squares and in the suburbs. At the time of the earthquake, after the first stupefying effect of the shock had passed, and the inhabitants had learned that a tidal wave had completely destroyed Callao, and even carried ships from the harbor directly over the town, they were seized by an unreasonable fear that the same calamity might overtake them. A rumour was spread through all the city that the sea was rising and advancing towards Lima. Apparently forgetting that the city was six miles from Callao and five hundred feet above the level of the sea, they were seized by a panic that prevented all sober reflection, and sent them in wild confusion towards the neighboring mountains.

"The hurry with which every one pushed forward was so irresistible, that even those who, from the circumstances of the report which rendered it incredible, and the knowledge of much such another incident which had happened in the year 1686, did not believe it, suffered themselves, however, to be carried on; or rather were impelled by the general torrent, which formed a kind of sea, while the people, who resembled rolling waves, went on almost dead with fright and fatigue. In reality some of them actually died, notwithstanding the daylight, which yet remained, might have convinced them of their error." [1]

Important features of the social character of Lima were due to the fact that it was the residence of the viceroy of Peru, who was the highest civil

[1] *A True and Particular Relation of the Dreadful Earthquake.* London, 1748, 175-181.

and military authority, and the "supreme judge of all the tribunals who aided him in the administration of justice and the conduct of affairs." [1] He was appointed by the king, and the king also fixed the term of his service. In the last decade of the viceroyalty the sum of all the revenues that constituted his salary amounted to $60,500. Representing the king, he maintained much of the style of royalty. He was attended by two companies of guards, one of cavalry and one of halberdiers. Before 1784 the cavalry company contained one hundred and forty-seven men, but in that year it was reduced to a captain and thirty-four men, and the halberdiers were reduced to a captain and twenty-four men. When the viceroy drove out, four of the cavalrymen preceded him and four followed.

The viceregal court was made to resemble that of a European monarch by the presence, in Lima, of a considerable number of noble families whose wealth and privileges gave them a distinct position in the society of the capital. The highest title created was that of duke, which was conferred upon Don Formin de Carvajal y Vargas, who was born in Chile in 1722, his father being Don Luis de Carvajal, a *regidor* of Concepcion. Don Formin was later an *alcalde* of Lima, a familiar of the inquisition, and the incumbent of other important offices. With the office of *correo*

[1] Haënke, *Descripcion del Peru*, 11.

mayor he received the revenues of the post-office, and when these were resumed by the crown, in 1768, Charles III. granted him as compensation an annual income of fourteen thousand dollars. Eleven years later, in 1779, he was made Duke of San Carlos, a grandee of Spain of the first class, and field marshal. In 1791 he received the Grand Cross of the Order of Charles III.

Some of the other institutions of the capital were the following:

1. The royal Audiencia which was established in 1546 was the most conspicuous of these institutions. This court at the period in question was composed of a regent, eight judges, four *alcaldes de corte*, and two prosecuting attorneys. The viceroy was the president. For the administration of justice, the audiencia was organized in three divisions. Two divisions, composed of the judges (*oidores*), considered civil cases, while the third division, composed of the *alcaldes de corte*, dealt with criminal cases. The annual expense of maintaining the audiencia was $90,900.

2. There was also the Superior Council of the Royal Treasury, composed of the viceroy, as president, and five members, including the regent of the audiencia. This body was created in 1784. Its principal object was to supervise the government and the administration of justice in the provinces, with reference to the affairs of the treasury and the economical affairs of the

department of war.   According to law its sessions
were held one day in each week.

3. Another tribunal was a Court of Accounts,
which examined the accounts of the royal treasury.
It was properly a bureau of auditing.   It consisted of three principal accountants and such
others, with various other officials, as might be
necessary.   The annual expenses of this bureau
amounted to $42,692.

4. There was also a bureau charged with
making a census of Indians.   It was composed of
a judge, an attorney, an accountant, and various
other officials whose salaries amounted to $13,083.
This court held a fund which yielded an annual revenue of $44,287.   From this sum the salaries were
paid, and the balance was reserved for additions to
the fund, and to meet contingent expenses, such as
assisting the Indians to pay their tribute, furnishing succor to the Indians, and rebuilding churches.

5. A commercial tribunal known as the Consulado had existed in Lima since 1613.   It was
supported by one per cent. of the import duties.
The ordinary expenses of this tribunal amounted
to $36,443, and $18,676 were set aside for extraordinary expenses.

6. There was a Court of Mines which was created
in Lima in 1786.   This tribunal was composed of
a judge of appeals, an administrator, a director,
a secretary, and a bureau of accounts.   Its
expenses amounted to $17,913.   It had various

agencies in the mining districts, as at Huarochirí, Huallanca, Pasco, Huancavelica, and at other places.

7. There was, moreover, the Commission of the Royal Physicians, for examining and licensing students of medicine, which was composed of one chief physician, an assistant, two examiners, an attorney, and a secretary.

8. The Royal Mint was founded in Lima in 1565, and was incorporated in the crown in 1753. It employed a superintendent and the necessary subordinates, the annual salary roll amounting to $48,000.

Besides these, there were in Lima various other offices or institutions, the presence of which helped to give to the city the appearance and character of an important capital. Among these were the University of San Marcos and various colleges, the central post-office, the commission for managing the royal monopolies, the custom-house, and the commission for managing the royal monte de piedad, or pawnshop.

At the close of the eighteenth century the religious orders in Lima had acquired a large amount of property, and were receiving extensive annual revenues. The following tabular statement presents the religious houses in Lima at the period in question, together with the numbers of the members and the amounts of their annual revenues stated in dollars:

	No. of members	Revenues.
DOMINICANS:		
Convento grande del Rosario .	146	$35,389
Santa Rosa	9	2,519
Magdalena	19	8,869
Santo Tomás	30	6,802
FRANCISCANS, three monasteries:		
Convento grande de Jesus . .	161	
College of San Buenaventura de Guade-		
lupe	20	
Recoleccion	33	
AUGUSTINIANS, three houses.		
Casa grande	129	34,150
Recoleccion de Guia . . .	9	1,928
University of San Ildefonso . .	30	4,104
MERCEDARIOS, three houses:		
Casa grande	140	19,922
Recoleccion de Bethlem . .	16	2,945
College of San Pedro Nolasco .	34	3,900
Order of San Francisco de Paula .	42	7,139
Hospitalarios de San Juan de Dios	43	4,561
AGONIZANTES, two houses:		
Convento de Nuestra Señora de la Buena		
Muerte	53	19,724
Santa Liberata	5	2,500
Oratorio de San Felipe Neri . .	41	3,283
Hospitium of St. Benedict . .	2	1,630
BELETMITAS, two houses:		
Casa grande . . .	22	3,640
Casa de Incurables . . .	2	1,630
Fourteen Convents of Nuns . .	572	119,504
BEATERIOS, or houses inhabited by pious		
women:		
Real Casa de Amparados de la Purisima		
Concepcion	210	5,300
Nuestra Señora de Copacabana .	12	

	No. of members	Revenues
Santa Rosa de Viterbo . . .	12	1,141
Patrocinio	11	
Camilas	5	
Real Casa de Ejercicios, retreat for religious women		1,200

Besides these houses devoted exclusively to the life of the religious, there were also many hospitals and other institutions having charitable or public purposes, the revenues and expenditures of which were controlled by the Church.

The large amount of wealth held by the religious orders may not be taken as evidence that the King of Spain and the Council of the Indies favored the accumulation of real property in the hands of the Church. There are, in fact, certain indications that they opposed this policy. The following extract from the Laws of the Indies points to such opposition:

"Let the lands be distributed reasonably among the discoverers and colonists, and their descendants, who may remain in the country, and let them not be able to sell them either to the Church or to a monastery or to any other ecclesiastical person, under pain of the lands reverting to the King and being conferred upon other persons."[1]

This law, however, like many others made for the Indies with excellent intentions, was not effective; for the real property was brought into

[1] *Leyes de Indias*, lib. 4, tit. 12, ley 10.

the hands of ecclesiastics to such an extent that
"secular persons came to be mere administrators
of estates possessed by the Church."[1]   In Lima
and some other cities the monasteries had a
very large part of all the real estate, and
the laity were reduced to movable property; and
in the middle of the eighteenth century it was
said "there are but few who do not pay rent to
the Church, either for their houses or farms "[2]

The Tribunal of the Inquisition had its most
important colonial seat in Lima.   It was established here under a decree issued by Philip II.,
in 1569.   It embraced twelve familiars in Lima
and one for each town with Spanish inhabitants.
The Indians were exempt from its jurisdiction.
Its annual revenue in the last decade of the
eighteenth century amounted to $93,917, which
was produced by a fund granted by Philip II.,
and by the suppression of a canonicate in each
of the eight cathedrals of Lima, Quito, Trujillo,
Arequipa, Cuzco, La Paz, Chuquisaca, and Santiago de Chile.[3]   The first *auto-de-fé* in Lima was
celebrated in November, 1573.   Another was
celebrated in 1578.   On this occasion, as it was
customary later, the viceroy and the judges of the
audiencia were present.

---

[1] Oliveira, *La Politica Economica de la Metropoli*, 27, 28.
[2] *A True and Particular Relation of the Dreadful Earthquake*,
279, 280.
[3] Haënke, *Descripcion del Peru*, 10.

"There was a procession of sixteen victims with ropes around their necks, including six priests, a lawyer, and a merchant, the sentences being two hundred lashes on some, burning on others, confiscation on all. The next *auto-de-fé* was in 1581, when there were twenty victims; and so the ghastly work continued during the centuries of Spanish domination, creating a sensation of terror through the land, spreading misery and sorrow broadcast, benumbing thought, and gradually, but very surely, exciting hatred and repulsion."[1]

The Tribunal of the Inquisition, as organized in Lima, was composed of three inquisitors, two secretaries, bailiffs, and porters.

"The inquisitors were secular priests, and distinguished from the others by wearing a pale blue silk cuff, buttoned over that of the coat. They were addressed as lords spiritual, and when speaking, although individually, used the plural pronoun *we*."[2]

There were also certain lay brothers of the order of Dominicans, called brothers of punishment, whose duty it was to attend when requested and inflict corporal punishment when it had been prescribed by the inquisitors. In addition to these there were brothers of charity of the order of San Juan de Dios, who cared for the sick. In order to be able to obtain information from all quarters, the inquisition had a large number of

[1] Markham, *History of Peru*, 172.
[2] Stevenson, *Twenty Years' Residence*, i., 185.

commissaries in the larger towns of its jurisdiction. There were in the service of the inquisition a number of persons, called qualifiers, who were required to examine books, prints, and images, with the view of finding whether they contained any passages or had any features that might make them offensive to the Church. The qualifiers were required also to report to the tribunal their opinion on new books and other publications.

The sessions of the inquisition were secret, and all persons who attended them were sworn not to divulge any knowledge they had of the proceedings. The tribunal could impose fines, confiscate goods, and condemn to banishment or the flames. During the period of its activity, between 1570 and 1761, it caused forty persons to be burned; and three times this number escaped this fate by recanting. The portraits of those who had suffered death in the flames were exhibited, with their names attached, in the passage leading from the Cathedral to the Sagrario. The names of those who had recanted were also placed there, but instead of the portrait over the name, the panel contained a large red cross. This exhibition was continued until 1812.

The inquisition held its sessions not only at Lima, but also at Mexico and Carthagena; and in the later decades it maintained rigid supervision over the introduction, publication, sale, and use of all forms of literature. Every bookseller was required to furnish lists of books offered for sale by him, and to take a solemn oath that he had no others than those named in the lists. He was obliged to own and have in his shop a catalogue of the works condemned by the inquisition, and he was forbidden to purchase or sell any of them. For the first offence his business was suspended for two years; he was, moreover, banished for the same period, and required to pay to the profit of the inquisition a fine of two hundred ducats. For later offences he was punished with increased severity. He was not permitted to offer a private library for sale without furnishing the inquisition lists of the titles of the books, of their authors, and of the dates and places of publication. No person was allowed to import books or to take them from the custom-house without permission from the officers of the inquisition. If books were smuggled into the colonies, they were liable to be discovered on domiciliary visits which the commissioners of the inquisition were free to make at any time. It was, however, conceived that there were some persons whose principles were so unalterably grounded that they might be safely permitted to read books prohibited to others. Priests and monks were assumed to be of this class; but there were certain books on the prohibited lists which even priests, except in very rare instances, were not permitted to read. In case only a few passages were found to be objectionable, these were removed, and the work was thus rendered innocuous.

An instance of the malevolent activity of the inquisition in the later decades of Spanish rule is found in the persecution of Francisco Moyen, who was born in Paris in 1720. His father and grandfather had been musicians attached to the French court. His education had given him a knowledge of music, mathematics, architecture, and drawing and painting. For a number of years he supported himself by his teaching and his music in various cities. On the death of his grandfather in 1742, he was enabled by his inheritance to purchase goods costing three thousand dollars, which he took to the Indies, and thus gave up the life of a wandering teacher and became a merchant. He remained, however, an artist in temperament; and although accepting his proper place in the Church he had little sympathy with the gloomy views of many of the devotees among his associates. He had read Voltaire, and many phases of the awakening spirit of France appealed to him. Going from Buenos Aires to Potosi, in 1749, with a number of companions, one of them, José Antonio Soto, a devoted servant of the Church, was careful to make note of any frivolous or liberal utterances made on the long journey. Four months after leaving Buenos Aires, the little caravan of mer-

chants arrived at Potosi, March 27, 1749. Two
days later Soto reported his list of heretical
propositions to the commissary of the inquisition.
Moyen having been thus denounced, other de-
nunciations followed; and these latter came from
persons who had not, as well as from persons who
had, known him. Then, on May 14, 1749, after
he had resided two months in Potosi, a warrant
was issued for his arrest and imprisonment.[1]

For two months Moyen had enjoyed the hospitality extended to him in the city, and carried on
his work and studies; then suddenly the warrant for his arrest was presented and he was
conducted to a dungeon and kept in strictest
confinement. In the course of time a few persons
were allowed to visit him, but their principal
object was to lead him into discussions and to
draw out from him expressions that might be
made the basis of further charges. He was
furnished with brandy, and the hypocrites who
drank with him carried utterances from the

[1] The warrant issued was in the following terms:
"We, Doctor Joseph de Lizarazu Beaumont y Navarra,
Senior Rector of the Holy Metropolitan Church of this city,
and commissary of it and the jurisdiction of its district, in
the absence for cause of sickness of the proprietor. For
the very Illustrious Señores Apostolical Inquisitors who
reside in the city of the kings of Peru; we command you
Don Bernardo Barragan, Alguazil of this Holy Office, that
immediately this mandate is delivered to you, to go to the
house of the Colonel Don Antonio Rodriguez de Guzman,
or to others in whatever places, that is, or may appear to be

heated debates to the authorities of the inquisition. A year had passed and still his request to be informed of the cause of his imprisonment had not been answered. In 1750 the commissary of the inquisition at Potosi made arrangement to transfer Moyen from Potosi to Lima, and deliver him into the hands of the Holy Office in that city. Amuzquibar, the inquisitor at Lima, in a letter to the commissary of Cuzco, dated February 17, 1752, directed that he should be brought in irons but Moyen had left the city before the arrival of this message. This journey, including the delays by the way, lasted about two years, and on March 26, 1752, a muleteer delivered Moyen to the authorities of the Holy Office at Lima. The muleteer, Ventura Bejar, received sixty-five dollars for conducting him from Cuzco.

necessary within or without this city, and take into custody the body of Don Francisco Moyen, native of Paris, of France, and residing in this city, wherever he may be found, although it may be in a church or other sacred place, fortified or privileged, and as a prisoner and well secured, take him to the public prison of this said city, and deliver him to the chief Alcalde Alguazil, whom we command to receive him from you in the presence of the notary of this Holy Office, and keep him confined and well secured, and not to let him go free, not even with a bond of security, without our license and mandate. And you will cause that the said Don Francisco Moyen leaves his goods with the care necessary for their safety and guard, giving them in charge to the person whom he may choose, and by an inventory before the notary of this Holy Office, that from them he may be maintained. And for the better execution and compliance

At Lima, Moyen was shut up in the vaults of
the inquisition. The persecution of the three
years that had passed since his arrival at Potosi
had broken his body and his spirit. Though
young in years, the marks of age were already
upon him. On the fourth of May, 1752, Moyen
was brought to trial. With postponements and
delays of every sort, the case was kept undecided
for twelve years; and during this time the accused
was wearing chains in one of the miserable
dungeons of Lima. His emaciated body covered
with filth and vermin, and afflicted with sores
caused by his chains, made him an object of pity

with the contents of this our mandate, should you require
favor or help, we exhort and request, and if necessary in
virtue of holy obedience, and under the penalty of excom-
munication major, *late sententie, trina canonica monitioni*
and one thousand dollars essayed, for the extraordinary
expenses of this Holy Office, we command all and whatever
judges and justices, whether ecclesiastical or secular of this
city, or of any other places of the kingdoms or dominions
of his Majesty, that being by you required, they give and
cause to be given to you all the favor and help that you demand. Should you have need of men for a guard, or beasts to
carry the aforesaid, and his bed and clothes with the fetters or
chains, and maintenance of which you may require at the
current prices of their value without making them dearer.
Given in the Imperial City of Potosi, the fourteenth of the
month of May, of the year one thousand seven hundred forty
and nine.

 "JOSEPH DE LIZARAZU BEAUMONT Y NAVARRA,
  "by command of the Holy Office.
 "MANUEL ANTONIO GALVETE Y VARELA,
  "Familiar and Notary of the Holy Office."

and horror. During the first part of his persecution he had not been informed of the charge
against him; but finally, in 1752, he was accused
of being "a heretic, formal, obstinate, and sequa-
cious of the sects of Luther, Calvin, Jansenius,
Quesnel, Manichæus, and Mohammed, and most
vehemently suspected of Judaism, and an ap-
prover of other errors and heresies."[1]

Nine years later, on the eighteenth of February,
1761, the Council of Qualifiers of the Inquisition
pronounced their definite and final sentence.
This sentence was in the following form:

"*Christi nomine invocato.* We find, taking into
consideration the acts and merits of the said process,
that the said Promoter-Fiscal *has not proved his
intention*, according and as it ought to be proved
for the said Don Francisco Moyen to be declared a
heretic, but for the fault which results against the
said Don Francisco Moyen, and we desiring to act
favorably and mercifully towards him, and not with
the rigor of justice, being moved thereto by certain
reasons and motives, in penalty and punishment
for what he has done, said and committed, we order
and command that he present himself in a public
auto-de-fé, if there is shortly one to be celebrated, and
if not, in a particular *auto* in a church, or in the hall
of this tribunal, in the form of a penitential, with
a sambenito, on which is half a cross, a cap on his
head, a rope round his neck, a gag in his mouth,

[1] Vicuna Mackenna, *Francisco Moyen: or the Inquisition
as it was in South America*, 112.

and a taper of green wax in his hand, and thus our
sentence is to be read; and for the vehement sus-
picion resulting against this criminal of the said
process, we command him to abjure, and that he
abjure publicly and vehemently the errors of which
by the said process he has been accused and witnessed
against, and from which, and being gravely suspected, he is absolved *ad cautelam*, and also gravely
advised, censured and threatened, and we condemn
him to the confiscation and loss of half his goods,
and which we adjudge to the Royal Fiscal of his
Majesty, and in his royal name to the Receiver-
General of this Holy Office, and we banish him per-
petually from both the Americas and the Islands
adjacent, subject to the crown of Spain, and from
the city of Madrid, the court of his Majesty, for the
term of ten years, which time must be passed in one
of the garrisons of Africa, Oran, Ceuta, or Melilla,
or else in the penitentiary-house of the tribunal of
the Holy Office of the Inquisition at Seville, at
the discretion of the illustrious Señor Inquisitor-
General, and of the Señors of the Supreme Council
of the Holy General Inquisition, to whose disposal
he be remitted, duly registered, and for the space
of the said ten years he must confess and receive
the sacrament at Easter, on Whit Sunday, and Christ-
mas day, and also repeat a part of the rosary to the
most Holy Mary. And the day following the said *auto*,
he must go out to be disgraced in the public streets,
placed upon a beast of burden, and with the same
marks of infamy as in the said *auto*, and the voice of
the crier is to make public his crime, and although
we have condemned him to receive two hundred

lashes, we command that they be not given, in consideration of the complaint he suffers, and that this sentence be executed notwithstanding any supplication, and for this it is our definite sentence, and so we pronounce it, and command it in these writings and by them."[1]

After twelve years of imprisonment Francisco Moyen was formally tried by the inquisition, but was not found guilty of the charges brought against him. He was consequently absolved, but the members of the Holy Office refused to abandon their suspicions, and these suspicions remained as the only ground for this far-reaching condemnation.

In Peru, the cruelty and inhumanity of the authorities, moreover, found expression in the construction and use of horrible subterranean dungeons in Lima. They were built "in such a manner that a man could not place himself in any natural position whatever. Many persons, victims of despotism, were confined in these holes for years; and when at length let out, it was only to bewail their existence, being rendered useless and helpless for the rest of their lives." These dungeons, popularly known as little hells (*infiernillos*), were maintained as long as Lima remained under the rule of Spain, but were abolished by San Martin, in 1821.[2]

[1] Vicuna Mackenna, *Francisco Moyen*, 168.
[2] Hall, *Journey*, ii., 250–253.

From contemporary records we are able to derive a sufficiently clear idea of the personal qualities of the inhabitants of Lima as well as of their general activity, during the last years of Spanish rule. They were generous, and spent their money lavishly, often going beyond reasonable limits even to their ruin. This was particularly true of the creoles, who, perhaps recognizing their social inferiority, sought to overcome this prejudice by extravagant display. There was little crime among them, but, when a crime had been committed, their inclination to mercy led them to seek to protect the culprit. This humanity was manifested also in their treatment of their slaves. It was very rare that slaves complained of severe treatment by their masters. Living in a society dominated by the viceroy, the inhabitants of Lima acquired somewhat of the refinements and formality of manners characteristic of dwellers near a royal court. Their desire for wealth and its uses led even members of illustrious houses to oppose the prejudices that existed in Spain, and engage openly in trade. They possessed a peculiar pride, or vanity, which tended to manifest itself in extravagant sentiments and statements concerning their surroundings. In their language every white man was a *caballero;* every instrumental concert was an *opera;* every man with the elements of education was a *savant;* and any one showing any evidence of devotion was

a *saint* or an *angel*. They were given to pleasure
and gambling, and in general to a life of entertainment and idleness. Idolizers of women, they
almost always held their own wives in little esteem.
The youth were easily corrupted, and the luxury
of the demi-monde indicated that a large number
of contributions were made to their wealth.

"Lima," says Haënke, "like the cities of Spain,
has its bull-ring where bull-fights are held at appointed
times. The bull-fighters, the most active and daring,
have the custom of hamstringing the bull if he will
not attack. The people of Lima count among their
public amusements the drama, for the representation
of which they have a sufficiently capacious theatre.
Good order and neatness are maintained in the
theatre in spite of the fact that the spectators smoke
during the play. The decorations are mediocre,
and the actors are ordinary. Generally no other
plays are given than those which we call magic or
religious plays. The public applauds them heartily,
and the time appears still very remote when these
coarser productions will be driven from the stage,
which, far from instructing, vitiate the understanding
and confirm bad taste.

"Before the year 1771 cafés were not known in
Lima. To-day there are several, and they are much
frequented early in the morning and at noon. All
kinds of drinks and ices are found in them, and each
has its table for trucks or billiards.

"There is also a public place for the playing of
pelota, or hand-ball, where much money is risked;

but among all the diversions cock-fighting is that which most attracts the attention of the people of Lima, and may be regarded as the favorite amusement of the natives."[1]

The city was, moreover, enlivened by balls and church processions, and the conspicuous activity of the brotherhoods established in connection with churches or monasteries. But perhaps the greatest public ceremony was that attending the reception of a newly arrived viceroy.

"As soon as the viceroy lands at Payta," says Ulloa, "two hundred leagues from Lima, he sends a person of distinction as ambassador to inform the preceding viceroy of his arrival in Peru. The Corregidor of Piura receives the viceroy at the port, furnishes him with whatever may be necessary for his journey, and accompanies him to the border of the neighboring Corregidor's district, constructing temporary structures for sheltering him in the uninhabited country where it may be necessary for him to stop. He finally arrives at Lima, and, without stopping, passes incognito to Callao, where he is received with all possible ceremony by one of the ordinary alcaldes of Lima, appointed for this purpose, and by the military officers.

"The next day all the courts, secular and ecclesiastical, wait on him from Lima, and he receives them under a canopy in the following order: the audiencia, the chamber of accounts, the cathedral chapter, the magistracy, the consulado, the inqui-

[1] *Descripcion del Peru*, 29.

sition, the tribunal de crusada, the superiors of the religious orders, the colleges, and other persons of eminence. On this day the judges attend the viceroy to an entertainment given by the alcalde: and all persons of note take a pride in doing the like to his attendants. At night there is a play, to which the ladies are admitted veiled, and in their usual dress, to see the new viceroy.

"The second day after his arrival at Callao he goes in a coach provided for him by the city, to the chapel de la Legua, so called from its being about half-way between Callao and Lima, a league from either city, where he is met by the late viceroy, and both alighting from their coaches, the latter delivers to him a truncheon as the ensign of the government of the kingdom. After this, and the usual compliments, they separate.

"If the new viceroy intends to make his public entry into Lima, in a few days he returns to Callao, where he stays till the day appointed; but as a longer space is generally allowed for the many preparatives necessary to such a ceremony, he continues his journey to Lima, and takes up his residence in his palace, the fitting up of which on this occasion is committed to the junior auditor, and the ordinary alcalde.

"On the day of public entry, the streets are cleaned and hung with tapestry, and magnificent triumphal arches erected at proper distances.[1] At two in the

---

[1] It is reported that when the Duke de la Palata entered Lima as viceroy the merchants caused the streets through which he was to enter the plaza to be paved with ingots of silver for two squares. These ingots or bars were between

afternoon the viceroy goes privately to the church
belonging to the monastery of Montserrat, which is
separated by an arch and a gate from the street
where the cavalcade is to begin. As soon as all
who are to assist in this procession are assembled,
the viceroy and his retinue mount their horses,
provided by the city for this ceremony, and the
gates being thrown open, the procession begins in
the following order:

"The militia; the colleges; the university with
the professors in their proper habits; the chamber of
accompts; the members of the audiencia on horses
with trappings; the magistracy, in crimson velvet
robes lined with brocade of the same color, and a
particular kind of caps on their heads, a dress only
used on this occasion. Some members of the corporation who walk on foot support the canopy over
the viceroy, and the two ordinary alcaldes, which
are in the same dress, and walk in the procession, act as equerries, holding the bridle of his
horse.

"This procession is of considerable length, the
viceroy passing through several streets till he comes
to the great square, in which the whole company
alights, and is received by the archbishop and chapter.
The Te Deum is then sung before the viceroy, and the
officers placed in their respective seats; after which he
again mounts his horse and proceeds to the palace gate,
where he is received by the audiencia, and conducted
to an apartment in which a splendid collation is

twelve and fifteen inches long, four or five in breadth, and
two or three in thickness. One writer estimates that the
value involved was eighty millions of crowns.

provided, as are also others for the nobility in the antechambers.

"On the morning of the following day, he returns to the cathedral in his coach, with the retinue and pomp usual on solemn festivals, and public ceremonies. He is preceded by the whole troop of horse-guards, the members of the several tribunals in their coaches, and after them the viceroy himself with his family, the company of the halberdiers bringing up the rear. On this occasion all the riches and ornaments of the church are displayed, the archbishop celebrates, in his pontifical robes, the mass of thanksgiving; and the sermon is preached by one of the best orators of the chapters. From thence the viceroy returns to the palace attended by all the nobility, who omit nothing to make a splendid figure on the occasion. In the evening of this, and the two following days, the collations are repeated, with all the plenty and delicacy imaginable. To increase the festivity, all women of credit have free access to the halls, galleries, and gardens of the palace.

"To all this ceremony follow bull-fights which last for five days. The first three days are in honor of the viceroy; the last two are for the ambassador sent to announce his arrival. After the bull-fights come the ceremonies of reception by the university, the colleges, and all the religious communities, with addresses and disputations which are subsequently published. The rector gathers those delivered by members of the university into a volume, which, bound in velvet and gold, he presents to the viceroy, accompanied by a piece of jewelry that is never of less value than eight hundred or a thousand dollars.

Essentially the same procedure as that of the university is followed by the colleges and religious houses in the order of their establishment, and when the viceroy goes to visit them, they present him with the most notable things made by them." [1]

After all this ceremony the viceroy entered upon the routine of his administration, which was continued during the pleasure of the king. The average term of the later viceroys of Peru was seven and a half years.

[1] Ulloa, *Voyage to South America*, ii., 46–50.

CHAPTER II

THE VICEROYALTY OF RIO DE LA PLATA

LIMA was not only the social and governmental centre of South America, but, for the greater part of the colonial period, it was also the commercial centre; and the interests of the south-eastern colonies were sacrificed to the privileges of the Peruvian merchants. The beginning of the last quarter of the eighteenth century witnessed, however, a significant revolution in the affairs of these colonies. The most important events of this revolution were the foundation of the viceroyalty of Rio de la Plata, in 1776; the introduction of a large measure of commercial freedom, in 1778; and the reorganization of the administration by the publication of the Ordinance of Intendants.

At this time the two original viceroyalties of Mexico and Peru retained their rigidity of form and rule, but certain signs of territorial disintegration had already appeared. These consisted in demands for an increase in the number of audiencias, or supreme courts; in the establishment of the viceroyalty of Santa Fé; and in the pretension of the captaincies-general to be independent of the viceroys. The growth of the population in the different quarters of the continent, and the development of local interests and local ambitions, made necessary a more effective administration than could be furnished from any single centre. This difficulty found its normal solution in the division of the original South American viceroyalty. This division was first carried into effect, as already suggested, by establishing a separate viceregal government for the territory now embraced in the republics of Colombia and Ecuador.

In the southern part of the continent the need of a new administrative organization had become imperative. There was wanted a more effective agency not only for the better management of internal affairs, but also for repelling foreign encroachments, particularly those of the Portuguese from the side of Brazil. As a capital for the new government, Buenos Aires had the great advantage of its geographical position. It was near the southern coast, where the Spaniards were attempting to plant colonies: and it was the gateway to the interior of the continent, which was reached by the great rivers of Paraguay, Paraná, and Uruguay. The Cordillera, impassable during a large part of the year, made it necessary that the eastern and western shores should have different centres of governmental

3

authority. The province of Cuyo, east of the Andes, formerly attached to Chile, had more intimate geographical relations with the provinces of Rio de la Plata than with the territory of the Pacific coast, and, therefore, needed to be politically united with the provinces of the southeast.

The viceroyalty of Buenos Aires, when created, was in all its legal features like those that had been previously established in Mexico, Peru, and the present territory of Colombia and Ecuador. In Mexico and Peru, at the beginning of the last quarter of the eighteenth century, the succession of viceroys already extended over more than two hundred years. A complex social organization had grown up in their capitals; elaborate forms and ceremonies were observed both in the government and in private life; and the class distinctions that were recognized gave the society an appearance of maturity. But in Buenos Aires, a frontier town, there was comparatively little wealth, less recognition of forms and ceremonies, and, in every respect, a simpler mode of existence. While the viceroy of Buenos Aires stood under the same law as the viceroy of Mexico or Lima, his real position was widely different from that of the viceroy in either of the older capitals.

The powers and duties of a viceroy were in general such as devolved upon him as the immediate representative of the king. He considered petitions of all sorts addressed to him, and in this he was assisted by a legal adviser, called *asesor general*. The *asesor* prepared the decisions, or replies to the petitions, and submitted them to the viceroy for his signature. From these decisions there was an appeal to the audiencia. The viceroy stood at the head of both civil and military affairs. He was the commander-in-chief of the colonial military and naval forces, but in emergencies he was assisted by a council of war. He called courts-martial, and reviewed for confirmation the sentences imposed by the courts before they were carried out. As president of the audiencia he might attend its sessions, and he had the power of veto over all its decisions.[1] In this capacity he made an annual report to the king through the Council of the Indies, and took this occasion to give the king all necessary information concerning the public and private characters of the members of this court. His conduct was, however,

[1] Sometimes the viceroy attended the meetings of the audiencia in state. The ceremony of these occasions in Lima has been described by a contemporary observer. When it had been announced that the viceroy would thus be present, a deputation of the judges "attended him from his palace to the hall; on his arrival at the door, the porter called aloud 'the president!' when all the attorneys, advocates, and others met him and conducted him to his chair; the judges continued standing until he was seated and nodded permission for them to resume their seats." At the end of the session all the members of the audiencia "accompanied him to the door of his apartment in the palace, the regent walking on his left, and the other members preceding him two and two".— Stevenson, *Twenty Years' Residence*, i., 175.

subjected to restrictions. He was forbidden to marry within the limits of the viceroyalty without the express permission of the sovereign. He might not engage in commercial affairs, acquire property, become a god-father to an infant, or visit a private family. He was the royal vice-patron. All appointments to benefices in the Church required his confirmation. In exercising his power with reference to these appointments, he selected one of three persons proposed by the archbishop. The viceroy of Peru was governor-general of Callao, and twice every year he visited the fortifications, receiving for each visit an addition to his salary of five hundred dollars.

The creation of the viceroyalty of Buenos Aires was the most important act of the Spanish authorities in the later decades of the century. A step towards this event is seen in the king's declaration of 1766, that the governor of Buenos Aires should have supervision over the eastern shore, including the Straits and Cape Horn.[1] Another step was taken by the fiscal of the royal audiencia of Charcas, Tomás Alvarez de Acevedo. He foresaw the necessity of a change, and urged that the government of a province as far away as Buenos Aires was from the centre of power would, almost of necessity, be inefficient and expensive. In spite of the great difficulties of

[1] Quesada, *Vireinato del Rio de la Plata*, 38.

communication, the supreme tribunal for the province of Buenos Aires had its seat nearly two thousand miles away, in the city of Charcas. In order to remedy the evils and promote the public welfare, it appeared to Acevedo imperatively necessary to create a viceroyalty and audiencia at Buenos Aires. The audiencia of Charcas adopted this view, and on the 12th of January, 1771, made a report, and sent it to the king, advising the creation of a new viceroyalty, urging that the province of Cuyo should be separated from Chile, and united with the provinces of Tucuman, Buenos Aires, and Paraguay and the whole be made to constitute the territory of the new viceroyalty of Rio de la Plata.[1] The prompt action that was taken in this case was in a large measure due to the hostility that had broken out between the Spaniards and the Portuguese. The king of Spain determined not only to meet the hostile Portuguese with an effective force, but also to create a new centre of viceregal power. Both the viceroy of Peru and the governor of Buenos Aires favored the project; and in July, 1776, Ceballos was informed that he would be placed in command of the military expedition against the Portuguese in the Rio de la Plata, and that he would be entrusted with the superior authority over this district and all the territories under the jurisdiction of the audiencia of Charcas,

[1] Quesada, *Vireinato*, 40.

as well as those of the cities of Mendoza and San
Juan del Pico; and that there would be conceded
to him the status of viceroy, governor, captain-
general, and president of the audiencia, with all
the powers and duties pertaining to this status.
Ceballos was then governor of Madrid, and the
king provided that this office should be held for
him, in order that he might return to it when
the object of the expedition should have been
attained.

Under the date of August 1, 1776, the king
issued to Ceballos his commission in the following
form:

"Whereas, being well satisfied with the repeated
proofs which you have given me of your love and
zeal for my royal service, and having appointed you
to command the expedition that is made ready at
Cadiz for South America, instructed to obtain satisfaction for the insults offered by the Portuguese, in
my provinces of Rio de la Plata, I have appointed
you my viceroy, governor, and captain-general of the
provinces of Buenos Aires, Paraguay, Tucuman,
Potosi, Santa Cruz de la Sierra, Charcas, and of all the
districts, towns, and territories, to which is extended
the jurisdiction of that audiencia, over which you
will preside when present, with the appropriate
powers and privileges which the other viceroys of my
dominions in India enjoy, according to the laws of
the Indies, thus embracing under your command and
jurisdiction the territories of the cities of Mendoza,
and San Juan del Pico, which at present are depend-

ent on the government of Chile, with absolute independence of my viceroy of the kingdom of Peru,
while thus you remain in those countries, with respect
to the military as well as to the civil government, and
the general superintendency of the royal treasury,
in all its branches and products; wherefore I command
the said viceroy of Peru, the presidents of Chile
and Charcas, the ministers of their audiencias, the
governors, corregidors, alcaldes, ministers of my
royal treasury, officers of my royal army and navy,
and other persons whom it may concern, that they
may have, recognize, and obey you as such viceroy,
governor, and captain-general of the provinces mentioned, in virtue of this my order and testimonial of
that which you will be obliged to direct on your
arrival, to the chiefs, tribunals, and others who may
be concerned, so that without the least reply or
contradiction they may comply with your orders and
that they may comply with them punctually in their
respective jurisdictions, which is thus my will,
and that as soon as you are prepared to leave
Cadiz you make yourself known as viceroy and
captain-general to all persons on all the warships
and transports, in order that they may act in accordance with this knowledge and may be under your
orders when they embark, and to the effect that you
may not be placed in embarrassment in the absolute
service and authority, and with regard to the high
character of my viceroy, governor, and captain-
general, in virtue of this my royal decree, I excuse
you from all the rest of the formalities of other
expeditions, oath, payment of half-year annats,
assuming possession, judgment of *residencia*, and

of whatever other requisites are customary and prescribed by the laws of the Indies, in case of the
appointment of viceroys to those dominions, for
thus entering my royal service; and I command
equally the officers of the royal treasury of Buenos
Aires and the rest of the districts of your government,
that they may pay you punctually from the funds
of my royal treasury to the amount of forty thousand
pesos current in America, which I assign to you in
Cadiz, in virtue of your receipts, or letters of payment
which will serve for them, of proper date without
any other security whatsoever.

" Given in San Ildefonso, August 1, 1776."

The king's instructions concerning the government to be established were issued under date
of August 15, 1776. The new viceroyalty was
independent of that of Peru, and the power conferred upon Ceballos was the absolute power of
the king. At this time the governor of Rio de
la Plata was Juan José de Vertiz, who, having
handed over to the new viceroy the command of
the troops and the superior authority over all the
cities and territory under his control, was ordered
to remain as governor of this province, subordinated to the viceroy as the viceroy was subject to
the king. The sixteenth article of the instructions
commands the viceroy to raise all the militia
possible in the "district of the new viceroyalty,"
to commission officers, and to make effective
regulations for clothing, arming, and disciplining

the troops to be maintained; and at the conclusion of the expedition to make arrangements
under which the established armed force may
be continued. It was not difficult to foresee that
the irritation caused by Spain's commercial
policy was destined, sooner or later, to make a
considerable military force needed to ward off
foreign encroachments.

The fleet appointed to carry the nine thousand
soldiers placed under the command of Ceballos
left Cadiz in November, 1776. After crossing the
Atlantic, it assembled at Montevideo. Ceballos
did not go to the colony of La Plata as to a strange
country. He had been governor of Buenos
Aires for a period of ten years, from 1756 to 1766,
and in his military expeditions to Missiones and
against Colonia he had become familiar with the
country over which he was to rule as viceroy. He
knew, moreover, the territory in dispute between
the Spaniards and the Portuguese, as well as the
merits of the pretensions of the parties involved.
He landed his forces at Montevideo, and led them
along the shore to Colonia. At the same time he
sent some of his war-ships to command that town
and fort from the river. Beset by both the land
and naval forces, Colonia surrendered on the
fourth of June, 1777. One hundred and forty
pieces of ordnance and a large quantity of arms and
munitions fell into the hands of the Spaniards.
The officers were sent to Rio Janeiro, while the

common soldiers and the colonists were transported to Mendoza. The colonists and common soldiers had been brought to America from the Azores, the Portuguese government expecting that their experience in the vineyards of their native islands would be utilized in developing the culture of the vine in the region about the mouth of the great river. But the climatic conditions there had been found unfavorable to this undertaking. In the interior of the country at the foot of the Andes there was a better prospect, and the later important development in the cultivation of the grape in that region was furthered by the prisoners of war from Colonia.

The continuance of the war against the Portuguese was prevented by despatches from Madrid, announcing that, by an agreement with Portugal, hostilities had been suspended. Portuguese diplomacy had put an end to the military undertaking. These despatches also brought to Ceballos the information that he had received military promotion. Under these circumstances, the only course open to him was to return with his army to Montevideo. Here he placed General Vertiz in immediate command of the forces, and went to Buenos Aires.

The cessation of hostilities was followed by the treaty of San Ildefonso, October 1, 1777, which aimed to establish a line of demarkation between the Spanish and Portuguese possessions in this part of America. Colonia passed into the hands of the Spaniards, who remained in exclusive control of the Rio de la Plata. The line of separation having been described, it was provided that the Portuguese inhabitants of all territory ceded to Spain should be at liberty to withdraw or remain, and the same privilege was extended to Spaniards resident on territory transferred to Portugal; and all persons were to enjoy equal freedom with reference to the disposition of property.

The navigation of the rivers was to be in common when the boundaries of the two nations lay in them, but the use of the rivers when both shores belonged to one nation was private and belonged to the nation owning the banks. In order that this rule might be observed, monuments with proper inscriptions were required to be placed where the boundary lines came to the river. The islands should belong to the nation holding the nearer shore. But in case the islands were equally distant from the shores, they should be neutral, unless they were very large, in which case they should be divided. For the purpose of fixing the line of demarkation, provision was made for the appointment of expert commissioners by the two governments, under such conditions that the work of actually fixing the boundary might be carried on at different parts of the line at the same time. Moreover, inasmuch as the wealth of the country depended upon the slaves who cultivated the lands, the governors were required to agree on a method of returning them in case they ran away from their owners, so that the fact of passing under foreign dominion might not give them their liberty.

The enemy against whom the king had made war was, after all, the most beneficent factor in the life of the colony of Rio de la Plata; for smuggling by the Portuguese had relieved the inhabitants of that colony, in a large measure, from the consequences of Spain's commercial restrictions. Not only Portuguese wares, but also wares from other countries were smuggled over the border to Buenos Aires. English goods, received at Colonia under relatively low duties, were smuggled across the river and brought to the Spanish settlers. The low prices at which they could be obtained naturally diminished the importations by the overland route from Peru. When Charles III. became aware of the deplorable state of things that had prevailed in this southern colony, he was convinced that the fundamental error lay in the economic legislation to which the colonists had been subjected. Under this conviction he issued the commercial code of 1778. [1] This applied alike to all the Spanish colonies in America. It had been preceded by a decree issued by Ceballos, in 1777, making free the trade

[1] *Reglamento para el comercio libre de España á Indias de 12 de Octubre de 1778.*

of Rio de la Plata with Spain and the rest or
the colonies. This act was approved by the
king and prepared the way for the more general
law of the following year, the commercial code
of 1778.

Hitherto Seville and Cadiz had held the monopoly of Spain's commerce with America. The
advantages of this trade were now extended to the
principal ports of Spain and of the Canary Islands.
In Spanish America practically all of the important ports, including Buenos Aires and Montevideo,
were admitted to the privileges previously enjoyed exclusively by Vera Cruz and Porto Bello.

The war between England and Spain, which
broke out in 1779, prevented the full realization of
the expected results of the enlarged commercial
freedom. This commercial emancipation, moreover, came too late to revive the loyalty of the colonists of Buenos Aires. They were well aware that
they had been neglected for decades, and that this
neglect had been permitted in the interests of the
residents of other ports. They were now free from
the commercial as well as the political domination
of Lima. Seville's monopoly was broken, and the
rich products of Upper Peru, Chile, Paraguay, and
the provinces of the interior were brought to
Buenos Aires, and shipped thence to Cadiz, Barcelona, Malaga, Santander, Vigo, Gijon, San Lucar,
Havana, Lima, Guayaquil, and Guiana; and
these ports sent back to Buenos Aires whatever

wares were demanded to further the advancement and well-being of that colony.

From San Lorenzo, October 27, 1777, the king issued an order declaring the viceroyalty permanent. By this order General Vertiz was appointed to succeed Ceballos, but it was left to Ceballos to determine when this appointment should become effective. This order, moreover, introduced an important reform, by creating the office of General Superintendent of the Army and the Treasury, the occupant of which was to have general direction and management of all the departments of the treasury. The creation of this office fixed a limitation on the power of the viceroy which had not existed during the administration of Ceballos; for he had performed the functions of general superintendent of the royal treasury, and "to him was subordinated the intendant appointed for the military expedition and all his subordinates of the auditor's office and the treasury." [1] The intendancies were made to embrace all the inhabited districts of the viceroyalty and all those that might be inhabited in the future, and the power to be exercised by the intendant under the new viceroy and his successors was in some sense a counterpoise to the authority of the viceroy; for in the order appointing Vertiz the king informed him that while he had made him viceroy, governor, and captain-

[1] Quesada, *Vircinato*, 134.

general, he had left the supervision and regulation of the royal treasury in all its branches and proceeds to the care, direction, and management of the intendant of the army whom he had appointed. [1]

During the administration of Vertiz settlements were made on the southeastern coast, in the region formerly known as Patagonia, and these were recognized as part of the viceroyalty of Buenos Aires, and thus under the jurisdiction of the viceroy. But these establishments were found to cost the government large sums, and, with the exception of that of Rio Negro, were later abandoned by the authority of the king. At the same time the king directed that a column should be left there, on which should be fixed the royal arms and an inscription affirming the Spanish sovereignty over the region; and that this territory should be visited or otherwise recognized every year. [2]

At the head of the political hierarchy stood the viceroy, governor, and captain-general; under him the secretary of the viceroyalty; and there were the following provinces with civil or military governors: Montevideo, Tucuman, Paraguay, Charcas, Potosi, Paz, Chucuito, Santa Cruz de

---

[1] The list of viceroys of Buenos Aires with the periods of their service is given in *The Establishment of Spanish Rule in America*, 218.

[2] *Informe del Virey Vertiz, para que se abandonen los establecimientos de la Costa Patagonica*, Angelis, v., 122-127.

la Sierra, Mojos, Chiquitos, Missiones de Indios Guaranies. The coast of Patagonia was under the immediate direction of the commissary-superintendent, Francisco de Viedma, as *Comandante de Armas* in Rio Negro, and Antonio de Viedma, as *Gobernador de Armas* in San Julien.

In Peru and New Granada, the viceroy on retiring from office was required to make, for the benefit of his successors, a somewhat detailed account of his administration, and of the questions, solved and unsolved, that had engaged his official attention. This practice was introduced into the viceroyalty of Buenos Aires, and General Vertiz at the close of his term prepared such an account for the use of his successor, the Marquis of Loreto. [1]

Throughout the eighteenth century it was generally known that the Spanish colonial system had failed to reach the ends for which it was designed by the king and his council. The Indians suffered a barbarous and destructive oppression at the hands of practically irresponsible officials. Yet before the middle of the century the Spanish king had in his possession the *Noticias Secretas de America*, which left no ground for doubting the necessity of reform. The establishment of the liberal commercial code of 1778 magnified the difficulties of administering the colonies under the old organization; and in the presence of the complicated and difficult problem

[1] Quesada, *Vircinato*, 160-170.

the monarchs before Charles III. had been helpless, and their helplessness made more evident the need of a modification of the existing system.

In the governmental reform introduced by the appointment of Ceballos, there was established the single authority of the viceroy for the whole viceroyalty, while subordinate governors remained in the several provinces. This was an adaptation of the order prevailing in Spain. There Ceballos, as governor of Madrid, held the position of a local governor, under the central or national authority. In Buenos Aires as viceroy he held the central power, while Vertiz then held the position of a local or provincial governor. The viceroy was, however, always under the laws of the Indies, and such other orders as might be issued by the king and his Council of the Indies. These constituted the supreme law under which the viceregal government existed. Notwithstanding this distribution of power, the several political entities remained only parts of an absolute monarchy; and all power exercised by any government of whatever grade descended to it from the single source of absolute power—the king of Spain. The viceroy was not assisted by ministers, but there was a secretary of the viceroyalty.

The several provinces, such as Cuyo and those formerly constituting Upper Peru and Paraguay, after the organization of this viceroyalty sent their accounts to the auditor's office and the tribunal of accounts, of the capital of the vice-royalty. In this respect the form of government was assimilated to that of any well-organized state. In the beginning, the viceroy was the single superior, in whom all the authority of the viceroyalty was centred; but when it had been determined to make the viceregal organization in this part of the continent permanent, it was thought advisable to create a general superintendent of the treasury with important powers, and representing, in matters relating to the treasury, the supreme authority in Spain. This order became effective with the appointment of Vertiz to be the viceroy. At this time Manuel Ignacio Fernandez was made general intendant of the army and the royal treasury in the provinces of Rio de la Plata and all other provinces subject to the viceregal government. There was thus introduced a form of dualism, the inconveniences of which showed themselves very early. Under this system the viceroy's government was without a revenue which it could control; and the intendant lacked the power necessary to give his orders executive force. But all doubts or confusion with respect to the jurisdiction of these two functionaries were set aside by the publication of the *Ordenanza de Intendentes.*[1]

---

[1] The complete title of this law was, *Real Ordenanza para el Establecimiento é Instruccion de Intendentes de Exercito y Provincia en el Vireinato de Buenos Aires. Año de 1782.*

By this law the viceroyalty of Buenos Aires was divided into eight intendancies, each to take the name of its principal city. The territory of each was, moreover, with certain exceptions, made to coincide with that of the bishopric in which lay the capital city. These exceptions refer to certain districts that were parts of a bishopric but not subject to the corresponding intendant. Mojos and Chiquitos were included in the diocese of Santa Cruz de la Sierra, but were military governments in immediate subordination to the viceroy. Montevideo and Missiones were other exceptions of a somewhat similar kind.[1] They were in the bishopric of Buenos Aires, but not under the intendant of Buenos Aires or any other intendant. On the other hand the bishopric of Paraguay had the same limits as the intendancy of Paraguay

The capitals named in the ordinance were Buenos Aires, Asuncion, Tucuman, Santa Cruz de la Sierra, La Paz, Mendoza, La Plata, and Potosi. The powers of the viceroy were not to be curtailed, except that the supervision and control of the royal treasury was to be under the general intendant, who in this matter was to act with absolute independence of the viceroy.[2]

[1] Quesada, *Vireinato*, 574.

[2] Lopez, *Historia Argentina*, i., 403; *Ordenanza de Intendentes*, Art. 2; Quesada, 387–519; for the dates of the establishment of the bishoprics and the territory of each see Zinny, *Gobernadores*, i., xcvi.

The next year, in 1783, the audiencia of Buenos Aires was created. It embraced within its jurisdiction the provinces of Buenos Aires, Tucuman, Paraguay, and Cuyo. The inhabitants of the viceroyalty were thus subject to the superior authority of the viceroy, which reached every part of his kingdom; to the authority of the governors-intendants, limited to their several intendancies; to the authority of the audiencia of Buenos Aires, which was exercised in the provinces of Buenos Aires, Tucuman, Paraguay, and Cuyo, and to that of the audiencia of Charcas, which was exercised in the provinces of Upper Peru. To these several civil authorities must be added the ecclesiastical authority of the bishops, whose respective jurisdictions had in general the same territorial limits as the authority of the intendants.

Under this organization the officers of the viceroyalty may be considered as apportioned to two departments under the king, the heads of which were made responsible to him. These might be called the department of the interior and the department of the treasury. At the head of the first stood the viceroy. At the head of the second stood the general intendant of the army and the treasury. In each of the eight intendancies the chief official had the double title of governor-intendant; for he was subordinated to the viceroy in affairs relating to the police, instruction, worship, and the judiciary, while he was the agent of the general intendant in his province, or intendancy, with reference to revenues, expenditures, and all other fiscal matters.

This distribution of power did not create local governments, as that term is applied to a constitutional state. The divisions of the viceroyalty were merely administrative districts; and the officers who exercised power in them did not derive their authority from local constituents, but from the king. They were not parts of a federation, but agents of an absolute centralized superior, or rather of two superiors that were expected to work along different but parallel lines; and "what made the application of the ordinance of intendants, of 1782, inconvenient and impossible in practice was the hierarchical administrative subdivision which it introduced. A viceroy of the treasury and a viceroy of political government were two incompatible terms." [1] The inconvenience of this bifurcated administration was soon set aside, and the two functions which the ordinance had separated were united in the viceroy. This was done by suppressing the independence of the general intendant and making him subject to the viceroy. The chiefs remained independent of one another only during the administration of Vertiz, and while Fernandez was general intendant. On the appointment of Francisco de

[1] Lopez, *Historia Argentina*, i., 408.

Paula Sanz, as general intendant, he was subordinated to the viceroy, and became at the same
time governor-intendant of the province of
Buenos Aires, and in this capacity he exercised
the same functions as the governor-intendants
of the other provinces; but in his character as
general intendant, sub-delegate of the treasury
and the army, he had general jurisdiction in the
whole territory of the viceroyalty, and as governor-
intendant of Buenos Aires, his jurisdiction was
limited to the territory of the bishopric, coextensive with the intendancy.[1]   This organization of
the intendancies of the royal treasury of the viceroyalty of Buenos Aires was not confined to this
political division.   These high functionaries
had the same powers and duties in Peru and
Mexico.[2]

It was natural that there should be many
changes in the law of the Indies, since it required
only the will of the king and his council to amend
or abrogate any existing law.   From the beginning
to the end of Spanish rule in America, therefore,
the laws controlling the colonial administration
were constantly undergoing changes.   The ordinance relating to intendancies furnished no
exception.   The organization and procedure established by the royal Ordinance of Intendants
of 1782 was modified by the General Ordinance
of 1803.   The full title of this ordinance was:

[1] Quesada, *Vireinato*, 449.   [2] *Ibid.*, 464.

Ordinanza General formada de orden de S. M. y mandada imprimir y publicar para el gobierno é instruccion de intendentes subdelegados y demas empleados de Indias.
The later ordinance superseded the earlier, and the first article of it declared that each province should be in charge of a single person with the title of intendant, reuniting the political with the military government. It also provided that the intendant should be appointed by the king. The fourth article designated the intendancies constituting the viceroyalty. They were Paraguay, Cordova del Tucuman, Salta, Cochabamba, La Paz, La Plata, and Potosi. The province of Buenos Aires does not appear in this list; but provision was made for establishing in Mexico, Lima, Bogotá, and Buenos Aires *intendentes de provincia*. The viceroy in no case acted as governor of a province or the governor of a province as a viceroy. By this ordinance it was established that the viceroy should exercise his functions under the laws and the royal instructions. This ordinance appears as a constitution for the colonial governments in America, and embraces the superior government, the subordinate governments, and the whole hierarchical order of employees, pointing out to each one his powers and duties, and in a word, his jurisdiction.[1] It provides for the establishment of superior councils in all of

[1] Quesada, *Vireinato*, 486.

the capitals of the viceroyalties and the captaincies-general. One of these superior councils, or
courts, with the title of *contensiosa*, took account of
private cases, everything that involved a point
of law that could be settled by a trial; the other,
the *junta superior de gobierno*, of which the
intendant of the capital was an *ex-officio* member,
rendered opinions in cases involving governmental matters, everything relative to the revenues, the method, manner, and time of collecting
them, as well as to the employees and their powers
and obligations. In so far as the members of
these two courts were in sympathy with the inhabitants of the capital where they resided and
shared their aspirations with respect to local
affairs, they formed a counterpoise to the centralized power exercised by the viceroy. But
all of these functionaries of the capitals were
under the superior jurisdiction of the audiencias,
whose powers lay above the range of these reforms
and who still were authorized to assume the viceregal functions in case of the death of the viceroy
without provision made for an immediate successor. Subject to the viceregal superiority and
the jurisdiction of the audiencia, the intendants,
as provincial governors by royal appointment,
continued to exercise those large powers which
naturally devolved upon them as the agents of
the viceroy and as important members of an
administrative hierarchy, where the head was

absolute and the other members too isolated to be effectively under practical control.[1]

[1] For a general statement concerning the condition of affairs in the viceroyalty at the end of the eighteenth century see the *Memoria* of the viceroy Avilés addressed to his successor, Joaquin del Pino, dated at Buenos Aires, May 21, 1801, and printed in Zinny, *Gobernadores*, i., xlvii–xcvi.

CHAPTER III

IT is noteworthy that while the English colonies of North America were preparing for an independent national life, the Spanish colonies were drifting toward social anarchy. In one case the colonists were passing to a new phase of political organization under the inspiration of the principles of liberty that had their origin in the mother country. In the other case, the colonists, incapable of self-reformation, were reorganized by a power that shaped their destiny without consulting their will. The new organization of the southern colonies, which created the intendancies, took account of certain political entities that had been maintained during the two centuries and a half of colonial existence. The ancient province was the historical antecedent of the intendancy, although the limits of the two political divisions may not have been the same in all cases. In fact, the territorial limits of the old provinces were not carefully established. The settlements in the heart of the continent, including the cities of Cordova, Tucuman, and

Santiago del Estero, might very well be treated as a province without fixing a definite boundary line through the vast unoccupied regions that separated them from the settlements of Paraguay and the Rio de la Plata. There was no need of definite boundaries when it was a journey of many weeks from one centre of population to another. But since certain groups of provinces have become independent and self-conscious nations, this lack of definite boundary lines has given rise to numerous international controversies respecting territorial limits. Those countries that lay on the shore of the Atlantic or the Pacific were sure of their boundaries on at least one side; and that was about the extent of their certain knowledge concerning the lines that limited their territorial possessions.

The province of Tucuman, as we have seen, became an intendancy under the ordinance of 1782. Twenty-one years later, in 1803, a new ordinance was issued that modified somewhat the distribution of the territory of the viceroyalty. The ancient province of Tucuman was divided by this later ordinance between two intendancies. These were the intendancies of Cordova and Salta, the former embracing the southern part of the province, and the latter the northern part. This organization lasted till the overthrow of the colonial régime. The thirty years that cover the history of the intendancies have been described as a period of incubation, a period of peaceful internal development. Through the opportunities offered by the freedom of trade established in 1778, the province increased in wealth and social importance, but Buenos Aires, favored by its situation, had outgrown the interior cities, and assumed the political leadership of the south-eastern settlements.

A glance at the history of the province of Tucuman reveals some of the difficulties that attended the development. The first European to take formal possession of the territory was Nuñez de Prado, who received his commission for this purpose from Pedro de la Gasca, after the suppression of the rebellion led by Pizarro. Subsequently Nuñez de Prado was compelled to recognize the jurisdiction of Valdivia, and the province was thus nominally brought under the government of Chile. But the inclination of Prado to be loyal to Peru rather than to Chile led Valdivia to seek to make Chilean authority effective in Tucuman. To this end Valdivia sent Francisco de Aguirre to supersede Nuñez de Prado. It had been the policy of Prado to seek to bring the Indians to civilization by peaceful means, but the coming of Aguirre was the beginning of a reign of terror. " The Lules Indians in the province, forty-seven thousand in number, were distributed among fifty-six encomenderos; that is to say, each one of these adventurers, by the fact of having landed on the continent, claimed and realized the right to deprive more than eight hundred of his fellow-men of their lands, their homes, and their liberty " [1] an act of tyranny and injustice that introduced a long series of crimes. For the Indians rose in rebellion against the cruelty of their new masters, destroyed the Spanish town of Barco de Avila, and compelled the inhabitants to retire beyond the river Dulce, where they founded the town of Santiago del Estero. Hostile relations once established between the Spaniards and the Indians, there appeared to be no alternative to the arbitrary exercise of force, and the Spaniards very naturally adopted the policy of repression that had been carried out elsewhere. There appeared to be little prospect of peace or progress under the jurisdiction of Chile, and Peru was persuaded to assert its supremacy and assume control over the province. The advance of the Spanish arms was now followed by the extension of settlements. The towns that were here organized were established under a more or less close adherence to the legal regulations governing this act. The first step in establishing jurisdiction was the erection of a gibbet (*picota*), or tree of justice. Then the streets and squares and lots were marked out in accordance with a plan the main features of which were fixed by law. The point of beginning was the principal square.

[1] *Memoria de la Provincia de Tucuman*, 39.

Around this sites were set apart for the erection of the church, the town hall, and other public edifices. The lots not required for public buildings were distributed among those who were to become the inhabitants. The plans of the towns as originally formed were often retained permanently without essential modification. The plan of the present city of Tucuman, with respect to the width of the streets and all other essential features, is that in accordance with which the ancient town was laid out.

The houses in the provincial towns or cities were generally large, with two or three *patios*, or courts, in one of which the horses and other working animals were kept. The laborers employed in their construction were for the greater part Indians, and more stress was laid on rapidity of the work than on the beauty or convenience of the structures. The walls were generally of adobe and the roofs were covered either with straw or palm leaves, the places of building determining which should be employed. "Later, certain features of luxury were added to what was strictly necessary: a cornice of clay was constructed; the grating for the windows was made of turned pieces of wood; flat stones or tiles were laid for the sidewalk in front; and the walls were whitewashed."[1] Lest some one with a little invention might arise and introduce modi-

[1] *Mem.*, 63.

fications in the style of building, it was provided by law that houses "should be of one form for the adornment of the town." Through adherence to this paternal advice the builders of the old cities of Spanish America gave them a wearisome monotony.

It became early evident to the settlers in Tucuman that precious metals were not to be found there, and that most of their Indian dependents must be turned to agriculture. In this occupation they were driven like slaves, and "the encomenderos refused to the Indians even the smallest part of the harvests of grain, which with the sweat of their brows they had drawn from the land. They were obliged to gather *algarrobas* as their only means of support; it might even be said that they were pastured in the mountains like animals."[1] They were not only driven to agricultural work, they were also required, under severe penalties, to gather the products of the forests, such as pitch, honey, and wax. Others were employed in harvesting and weaving cotton. They were, moreover, held to a strict account, and

"whoever failed to perform exactly what was required of him was whipped or put in the stocks for his neglect; and in inflicting these punishments the majordomos and their assistants were horribly cruel. They had charge of the workshops where the Indians lived

[1] *Mem.*, 71.

deprived of their liberty, without being able to control their property, or even to care for their own children and wives. . . . And the wretched creatures had no one to whom they could look, since all persons, the judges as well as the encomenderos, were united in these extortions. . . . And at the same time numberless Indians were perishing, worn out with work merely to satisfy foreign avarice,"[1]

doomed to slavery and deprived of all advantage of their labor and the fertility of their country.

Although the Indians as a class derived little or no profit from their work, they furthered cultivation in the province and helped to build up certain primitive industries; and it was largely through their efforts that the province was advanced from the barbarism of the early decades to a social state having many of the features of civilization. The towns of Salta, Tucuman, and Cordova increased in population, and became the more important centres of provincial trade, while Santiago del Estero, the ancient capital, declined. With the establishment of the College of Monserrat and the University at Cordova, that town began to assume the character for which, as a centre of learning, it later became famous. The instruction here, as in all the higher educational institutions of South America, was almost entirely devoted to ecclesiastical subjects. In the University of Buenos Aires, even as late as

[1] Lozano, i., 3; see *Mem.*, 72.

1871, two thirds of all the professorships were foundations for teaching the *ciencias eclesiasticas*. The earthquake of 1692 also contributed to change the relative importance of the provincial towns. Santiago del Estero was destroyed, and it is reported that two-thirds of the inhabitants were buried beneath the ruins. The survivors, instead of attempting to reconstruct their dwellings and business houses, abandoned the wreck and joined the inhabitants of the more prosperous towns of the province.

The governor of the province was practically an absolute ruler. Paul Groussac says:

"The governors acted with entire independence within and without the sphere of their prerogatives. The Audiencia of Charcas seldom interfered effectively, and with regard to the decrees of the Royal Council of the Indies, there was invented this exquisite formula, which, when these decrees were not agreeable to the governors, was gravely placed on the margin of the document: '*Se obedece, pero no se ejecuta.*' "

This absolute power of the governor rendered his character a factor of vital importance for the welfare of the province. When he was strong and wise and patriotic, the province flourished and the people enjoyed peace and hopeful prospects. When he was weak or unscrupulous in the pursuit of his own pecuniary advantage, he interfered seriously with the prosperity of his subjects. Gaspar de Baraona became governor in 1700.

5

He abandoned the policy of his predecessors, who had sought to maintain peaceful relations with the Indians, and "entered Tucuman like a pirate in a galleon. " [1]   He had a salary of six thousand dollars a year, yet in five years he accumulated three hundred thousand dollars. He was removed from office in 1707. But during the term of his service the affairs of the province fell into disorder. The Indians, knowing the inefficiency of the government, became bold enough to attack the towns, and it is affirmed that they "were accustomed to go through the streets sacking and killing with impunity."[2]

It was clear that governors of another sort were required to insure the peace and prosperity of the province. Fortunately Baraona's successor, Estéban Urizar Arespacochega, possessed the qualities needed, but the conduct of the Indians, grown accustomed to making depredations, imposed upon him a difficult task. He raised an armed force of fifteen hundred men; and to maintain the security of the eastern frontier provision was made for a permanent body of militia.

This last measure involved heavy expenses, and led the provincial government to impose a certain duty on articles exported to Peru, particularly on mules. The administration of Estéban Urizar Arespacochega proved to be so satisfactory that Philip V., in 1724, made him governor of

[1] *Mem.*, 98.   [2] *Ibid.*, 98.

Tucuman for life. In this respect and with reference to the wisdom and honesty of his administration he was an exception among the governors of Tucuman. He was succeeded by Isidoro Ortiz, Marquis of Aro, whose administration was of such a character that it was said of it, "the excesses of Governor Baraona appeared like puritanism by the side of the corruption now erected into a system." [1] The cabildo of Salta resented the outrageous conduct of the governor, and demanded and obtained his dismissal. His immediate successor was Baltazar de Abarca, a man of unobjectionable character, but a weak administrator, and unable to prevent the ravages of the Indians.

Hitherto the campaigns against the Indians had been carried on with large bodies of troops, whose movements were necessarily difficult and slow and expensive. They were, moreover, generally fruitless, since the savages, with no provision train or heavy equipment, were able to keep out of reach, and gather where they were not expected. Felix de Avache, who became governor in 1730, introduced a system of guerilla warfare, which, considering the character of the enemy and the circumstances under which the fighting had to be done, was much less expensive and much more effective than the system that had been employed hitherto. The effective-

[1] *Mem.*, 100.

ness of this system is seen in the fact that the province was kept free from invaders and its prosperity restored. But the alternation of efficient and inefficient governors brought evil times again with the appointment of Ivan de Armasa. The civilized inhabitants were again affected by the encroachments of their savage neighbors. In fact, the Indians of the Chaco were for the province of Tucuman what the Araucanians were for Chile; they were never overcome or destroyed by force of arms, but in the course of time they were weakened and decimated by the vices and diseases which they acquired by their contact with civilization.

The points of contact between the civilized inhabitants of the province and the Indians of the Chaco were increased during the last half of the eighteenth century by the various expeditions which penetrated that region with the view of exploring the course of the river Bermejo and of finding a way out to the Atlantic coast easier than across the dreary plain of the Argentine.

The most notable event in the province during the last half-century of the southern colonies was the expulsion of the Jesuits. The decree of expulsion was executed in Tucaman in August, 1767, by Juan Adrian Cornejo. It was expected that this act would reveal large accumulations of wealth, and that some part of it would come to the secular uses of the province. It was found, however, that the Jesuits had regularly sent the money and precious metals that had come into their hands to Europe under the pretence of paying for articles of European manufacture needed in the *reductions*, and that what had been retained had been successfully concealed.

It might well have been supposed that the Jesuits in the province of Tucuman had much wealth; for the legitimate acquisition of property was not in opposition to the pretensions of the society. "The renunciation of the members was absolute; but the company had not taken a vow of poverty." They were neither agents bestowing charity, nor beggars. They received compensation for their instruction, and payment for the products of their estates, their factories, or their mines. The inventory of their property confiscated included a number of valuable estates, with mills and slaves. Although the furniture of their houses was not especially valuable, their books and manuscripts, considering the time and place, were important. The schools which they had established and conducted passed into the hands of the Franciscans.

The province of Tucuman during the last decades of the eighteenth century derived great profit from the enlarged commercial freedom which Spain had granted to her American dependencies. Tobacco and sugar-cane became more

[1] *Mem* , 119.

extensively cultivated and brought increasing
wealth; and this wealth made itself manifest in the
improvement of the cities, noted especially in the
construction of better public and private buildings,
and in the establishment of public schools for secondary education. The province enjoyed, moreover, a certain advantage from its position on the
great overland route between Buenos Aires and
Upper Peru. Besides furnishing places for the temporary deposit of wares passing over this route, it
had also, among other manufactories, important establishments for making carts that were used in
this transportation. That there must have been
a considerable and persistent demand for these
carts may be inferred from the extent of the overland trade and from the fact that even those of
the best construction lasted only two years, that
is to say, they served for only two round trips.

The trip with these great ox-carts from Salta
to Buenos Aires took usually three months, and
a little less to return. This period in almost all
cases was extended by delays in loading and by
the necessity of making frequent repairs. Fourteen or fifteen carts usually went together, and
the arrival of the caravan in the province, at
Cordova or Tucuman, from Buenos Aires, was the
chief event of the year. By it the inhabitants
received news from Paraguay, Buenos Aires, and
Spain, but the most recent of the events referred
to were already several months past. It also

brought information of attacks of brigands or Indians on the road, and these incidents, discussed and retold a hundred times around the camp-fires on the journey, lost nothing by repetition; and, when they were finally told in Tucuman, they had grown into elaborate chapters of an unwritten history. The peons, or drivers, of the caravan who had been involved in these encounters became heroes in the eyes of the *cholas* of the province. The coming of the caravan was thus anticipated with popular interest, and its arrival was remembered as an event by which the province had been placed temporarily in touch with the world beyond its borders.

But in the north, beyond the cities and the plains and the fertile valleys, there was a phase of provincial life that was passed in the obscurity of the mountains. This region, extending beyond the limits of Tucuman into the provinces of Upper Peru, was a part of the high table-land which constitutes the northern boundary of the great Argentine plain. By reason of its broken surface, it offered few inducements to agriculture; but there were abundant opportunities for mining, and in the colonial period the Jesuits, in particular, made use of these opportunities. In some instances they constructed costly plants for exploiting the mines on a large scale. But with their expulsion in 1767, the mines they had worked were abandoned. The most thorough

collapse of mining in this region came, however, with the war of independence. Both the
owners and the laborers were called away; the
means of communication were destroyed; and
the works were plundered. After the events
which attended the fall of the colonial régime,
operations were continued at a few mines, but
the majority were closed, some doubtless because
of the failure of a profitable product, and others
because of the creole's inferiority to the Spaniard
as a miner.

It would be interesting to follow the fate of
this interior country which the indomitable energy
of the early Spanish colonists, in spite of almost
insurmountable difficulties, started on the way to
civilization. Such an attempt would show at the
outset that these vigorous pioneers have had no
successors. Moreover, the representatives of the
pure Spanish stock have disappeared completely.
They have either become crossed with the Indians
or mestizos, or have emigrated to the cities.

The Jesuits were not only successful miners,
they were also the first explorers to enter these
valleys of the Andean country. They brought the
Indian under their control, but they did not
teach him the habit of personal saving or the
rights of private property. They required him
to work, but neither the field which he cultivated
nor the house which he occupied was his. His
labor and all the property with which he had to

do was at the disposal of his Jesuit masters. The Indian neophyte under the Jesuits

"was a perpetual ward, restrained from the enjoyment of all civil liberties, without training for the transaction of business on his own account, even for maintaining social relations with his fellows. He was always a child and a semi-savage, so that when the Jesuits were expelled, and he found himself subject to the new government of violent corregidors and corrupt parish priests, he scorned the liberty that was offered to him and to which he was not accustomed, and returned to the wilds."[1]

The combination of the Indian stock with that of the arrogant, adventurous Spaniard produced the mestizo, who had some of the qualities of both races, but whatever of the Spaniard was reproduced was belittled and vulgarized. Neither the Indian nor the mestizo was capable of originating and carrying on great enterprises, and consequently on the withdrawal of the Europeans there came necessarily a social decline. In the last years of Spanish rule the inhabitants of the highlands included many families of respectable standing, that have disappeared leaving degenerate successors. In the colonial period there was a certain degree of progress, as also an improvement in the quality of the inhabitants through the immigration of Spaniards, who came as

[1] Paredes, *La Provincia de Inquisivi*, 75, 76.

priests,[1] public officials, and seekers of fortune. With the independence of the colonies, Spanish immigration ceased, and no other superior race has furnished a substitute.

[1] "Es un hecho digno de mencionarse, que en los cantones, es rara la familia acomodada ó blanca que no descienda de algún clérigo. El prestigio de acaudalado que gozaba el párroco, era tal en el coloniaje y durante los primeros tiempos de la republica, que mujeres de familias distinguidas, no tenian á menos pertenecerles, y estar en mancebia publica con clérigos; á eso se agrega, que los sacerdotes que iban á las provincias, eran gentes alegres y de vida licenciosa, que supieron aprovechar ventajosamente de la favorable predisposición que encontraron, dejando numerosa prole en las distintas localidades que les cabia permanecer."—Paredes, 80, note.

CHAPTER IV

THE COLONIAL CITY

THE circumstances of the establishment of the southern colonies furnished a certain basis for the separate existence of Argentina, Chile, Peru, and Paraguay, and for the later federal organization of Argentina. Chile, cut off from Peru by the desert of Atacama and receiving a governor or captain-general by the direct appointment of the king, was practically independent of the viceroyalty long before its independence was formally decreed by royal authority, in 1778. The provinces east of the Andes took their origin from three sources. Cuyo, embracing the cities of Mendoza, San Juan, and San Luis, was settled from Chile, and maintained its connection with that colony until the creation of the viceroyalty of Rio de la Plata; Tucuman, embracing the cities of Cordova, Salta, Rioja, Jujuy, Santiago del Estero, and Catamarca, was occupied by colonists from Peru; and the provinces in the valleys of the great rivers, Buenos Aires, Santa Fé, Corrientes, and Entre Rios, had a still different origin, deriving their inhabitants directly from Spain.

The separatist tendency was intensified by their commercial isolation and by the fact that Buenos Aires was a closed port, which made both Cuyo and Tucuman look to other sources for imported wares. But the removal of the trade restrictions on Buenos Aires, in 1778, tended to draw the several provinces together, to share the common advantages of the new commerce. Under the viceroy these three groups of provinces were drawn together politically, but their individuality continued to be recognized by the existence of the governors-intendants.[1]

Many of the forces that maintained the individuality of the colonies and the provinces operated to preserve the cities as distinct and self-sufficing centres. Asuncion, Buenos Aires, Potosi, and Cordova had to manage their local affairs without any reference to one another, and these were the most important affairs with which they were concerned. They were in a great measure autonomous, because what concerned one city did not involve the interests of the others. The governors, or *corregidors*, were accustomed to assume much power in the municipal governments of the cities where they resided. This was a direct interference with the autonomy of the cabildo, or ayuntamiento, or the local organization under whatever name it was formed.

The laws of the Indies, in keeping with their

[1] See Ramos Mejía, *El Federalismo Argentino*, cap. 11.

regard for details in general, prescribed the forms
to be observed in founding a town. In the English colonies of America the town grew up to meet
the the needs of the inhabitants of the country;
but in the Spanish colonies the population of
country grew to meet the needs of the towns.
The primary plan of the English colonist was to
live on the land, and to derive his support from
its cultivation. The primary plan of the Spanish
colonist was to live in the town, and to derive
his support from the labor of the Indians and of
such other persons as found themselves compelled
by unfavorable circumstances to turn to agriculture, or the work of the mines. The Spanish
colonial town was created consciously, in accordance with a plan of action predetermined. In
most cases the town had an individual founder who
went about his undertaking as one might proceed
to found a fortress or fix the site of a manufacturing establishment. The English colonial town
grew up where it was found, by the experience of
many persons, that commercial or other agencies,
gathered in a more or less compact community,
would be able to be of service to a large number
of persons or families. The Spanish founder
selected a site, and indicated the place for the
principal plaza. Here he erected a monument
as a sign of possession and royal jurisdiction. He
gave a name to the future city, marked out its
plan, distributed the lots, and determined the

limits of its jurisdiction. This having been done, all those persons present who were to become members of the municipality signed the act of organization, and took an oath to support it. The founder then appointed the *alcaldes* and *regidors*, or members of the municipal council, administered to them an oath, and when the ayuntamiento, or corporation, was thus installed, the founder himself took an oath before it. This body, when organized, exercised legislative and, through its *alcaldes*, judicial and executive powers. Having been created in the first instance by appointment, it was provided that subsequently the members should be elected; and the time for election, the term of service, and the limits of its authority were already fixed by a general law.

In some of the larger cities there were officers not found in the smaller organized towns. In Lima, besides the two *alcaldes* and the twelve councilmen, the law provided for a prosecuting attorney, a secretary, a sheriff, and a legal adviser; and among the officers appointed by the cabildo, there was a police magistrate and a *juez de aguas*. The last-named officer decided all questions relating to the water-works belonging to the city and the suburbs. The fact that a city was the capital of the viceroyalty led to certain unusual forms and practices in the city government. The viceroy was, for example, president of the cabildo, and the *alcaldes* took cognizance of cases that ordinarily were decided by the governors.

The ancient Spanish charters of municipal liberties established and guaranteed certain important privileges, or rights: 1. Equality before the law; 2. Inviolability of the domicile; 3. Justice administered by judges elected either by the people or by their council, except in certain special cases which fell under the royal jurisdiction; 4. Participation in public affairs, which was realized by the election of members of the council by the citizens; 5. Responsibility of public functionaries. The municipalities established in America did not possess all of these ancient guarantees. The members of the council were, however, elected every year, on the first of January. By royal decree of 1594, it was provided that the inhabitants of the city should elect their cabildos freely, the right to vote being exercised by resident householders of the city, provided they had not shops for the sale of merchandise, in which they were personally engaged. This phase of the constitution of the cabildo, or council, was from time to time modified by the interference of the superior authority. The first cabildo of Buenos Aires was organized by the founder, Garay, who affirmed his right to appoint the members, to indicate the beginning of the year, the end of their service, and also the time when other members should be elected to fill vacancies. The intervention of the governors in appointing municipal officials was in opposition to the will of the king, and the cabildo of Buenos Aires was led to send to him protests against the practice. The governor, moreover, under his right to confirm the result of the elections, sometimes assumed the right to nullify them and order a new election.

The original plan of constituting the cabildos was further violated by the practice of selling the places of members. This was in keeping with the earlier practice of selling offices and titles in Spain. In some instances the offices became liable to attachment for debt, like other property. The sale in Buenos Aires was by public auction held in the plaza near the entrance to the municipal building. This practice naturally took away from office-holding all idea of duty, patriotism, or sacrifice for the good of the community. The system of purchasing offices having been established, the purchasers made a business of politics, and were careful that their investments should not be unprofitable. They trampled the laws of the kingdom underfoot, if thereby they could gain a pecuniary advantage. They regarded their personal interest as the only good, and for this they were willing to sacrifice all other interests. "This policy," says an Argentine writer, "violated all notions of good order and administration. By selling offices, the government admitted implicitly that its affairs were exploitable, that they were articles of commerce. The evil which this tradition has wrought is incredible. It is the root of our political decadence." [1]

There were thus three ways by which one might attain the honor of membership in the cabildo: by appointment, by election, and by purchase at public auction. By whatever way they may have come to their positions, the members enjoyed certain privileges and advantages aside from the legitimate powers of their offices, but the superior authorities did not regard them or treat them with great consideration. The governor not infrequently traversed their will. He might call them to a meeting at an appointed time, direct their debates, or close the discussion when it pleased him. He sometimes sent them as prisoners to their houses or to the prison, when their conduct seemed to him to require punishment. The inhabitants of the city were practically affected only by the acts of these two authorities: the cabildo, or ayuntamiento, and the governor of the province or his deputy. Beginning as civilized camps in a savage wilderness, the question as to the amount of power which the law gave to these two authorities was of little importance. The needs of the common life of the city in its isolation and not the terms of a charter determined their action.

In no city should the number of *alcaldes* exceed two, but the number of *regidors*, or councilmen,

[1] García, *La Ciudad Indiana*, 169, 170.

6

might vary, with the size of the city, from six to twelve. In cases where they were elected, where the posts had not as yet been sold, persons with certain degrees of relationship with the candidates for these places were prohibited from voting for their kinsmen,[1] and the persons elected must be residents of the towns in which they were to serve. The election was held annually on the first of January, and in the presence of the governor. By this election, the members of the cabildo, or ayuntamiento, were selected, and the *alcaldes* were chosen by this body. The *alcaldes* exercised judicial power and were invested with this authority for only one year, in order that this honor might be shared by a greater number of the inhabitants, and it was recognized that appointments made for this short period would be less harmful in case the selection resulted in elevating to office an inefficient and unworthy person.[2]

The justice administered by the *alcaldes* in the city and the surrounding territory subject to its jurisdiction was patriarchial in character. The judge might or might not be able to read and write; this was not a matter of prime importance,

[1] "Mandamos à las justicias, cabildos y regimientos, que no consientan ni dèn lugar que en las elecciones de oficios se elijan ni nombren padres á hijos, ni hijos á padres, ni hermanos á hermanos, ni suegros á yernos, ni yernos á suegros, ni cuñados á cuñados, ni los casados con dos hermanas, que asi es nuestra voluntad."—*Leyes de Indias*, lib. 4, tit. 10, ley 5.

[2] *Libros Capitularis de Santiago del Estero*, i., vi.

but it was important that he should have the
sense to discern what decision would secure
essential justice in the usually simple cases that
were brought before him. The primitive form
of settling petty cases appears to have been
satisfactory; and there was strong opposition
to the introduction of a system that would involve the service of lawyers and the consequent
emphasizing of legal technicalities. The policy
of the king and the council of the Indies had
been to oppose the establishment of lawyers in
the colonies, and the colonists themselves entertained the same view. As early as 1613, the
cabildo of Buenos Aires had under consideration the advisibility of admitting three lawyers,
who had proposed to come to the city. The
opinions expressed in the discussion were decidedly
adverse to their coming. The treasurer affirmed,
"that lawyers are not needed in this country,
since those who have come to it have only served
to excite disturbances between the royal officials
and the governors and all the other inhabitants of
the town."

The ordinary *alcalde* acted as judge of first
instance. From his decision there were three
forms of appeal, depending upon the nature of
the questions involved. The first appeal was to
the cabildo, or municipal council, and might
be had when the amount involved did not exceed
6000 maravedis; the second was to the audiencia;

and the third, in Rio de la Plata, was to the
governor, from whom the *alcalde* had received
his commission.[1]   Here, as at many points in
the colonial government, there is observed a
mingling of judicial and general executive functions.

The municipal corporations administered the
limited funds that were left under their control;
cared for the repairing and cleaning of the streets;
regulated the price of grain; and inspected the pris-
ons and institutions of charity.[2]   They exercised,
in fact, general control over municipal affairs;
held whatever local autonomy was recognized as
existing under the colonial system; and disposed
of the regular revenues of the city.   The tribute,
however, which was due from persons who were
in most respects under the jurisdiction of the
city was paid to the *corregidor* or governor, and
the tax called the *alcavala* was also collected
by officers of the crown.[3]   In so far as the
cabildos acted independently, particularly in
managing the revenues, they generally acted
not only without foresight, but without ordinary discretion.   They were attentive to provide the luxuries, and left the necessities to be
secured if there should happen to be a surplus
of funds in the treasury.   They were wasteful

[1] Estrada, *Historia de la Republica Argentina*, i., 159.
[2] García, *La Ciudad Indiana*, 190.
[3] *Leyes de Indies*, lib. viii., tit. 10, ley 10; lib. viii., tit. 5.

and concerned more with outward appearances than with having the needful things well done. If it was a question between repairing a breach in a street that impeded traffic and paying for fireworks or a bull-fight, the street remained unrepaired and the celebration was held. But even in the narrow field marked out for the municipal corporations by law, they were not independent, whatever might be the position which the law seemed to accord to them. They were often practically subordinated, as already indicated, to the executive officer of the district called in different parts of the dominion governor, *corregidor*, or *alcalde mayor*, and the relation between the corporation and the governor was a subject of frequent disputes between the two authorities. The corporation, exercising power in civil and economical affairs, came into conflict almost inevitably with the military force that was in the hands of the governor. In some cases "every resolution of the cabildo provoked bitter debates between the military chief and the civil corporation, in which the military usually triumphed since it was supported by force; and by this it imposed silence."[1] The cabildo of the town where the governor resided usually suffered most from interference. This is noteworthy in the case of Montevideo as compared with the

[1] Bauza, *Historia de la Dominación Española en el Uruguay*, ii., 637.

three other cabildos of Soriano, Colonia, and Maldonado in Uruguay.

In December, 1749, José Joaquin de Viana became governor with his residence in Montevideo. According to his instructions, he was subordinated to the government and captaincy-general of Buenos Aires, especially with respect to all military affairs. In political and economical affairs, his government was like that of the other provinces of Rio de la Plata: the governor of Buenos Aires might intervene whenever he should decide that laws and regulations touching any point were not followed. He might also remove him from office, if, in his opinion, the good of the public service required such action. In the conflict between the governor and the cabildo, Vertiz, the governor of Buenos Aires, removed La Rosa, and appointed Viana to occupy temporarily the position of governor of Montevideo.[1] The new governor was required to visit the several towns of his province at least once during the term of five years for which he was appointed, but before leaving his capital he was required to notify the governor of Buenos Aires, and to await his reply, in order that the royal service might not be impaired by his absence.

In spite of the satisfaction which the people of Montevideo felt in having a person of rank at the head of their government, their political

[1] Bauza, ii., 205.

ideas as civilians were destined to clash with the
military ideas of their governor. While Viana
was preparing to enter upon the war of the Seven
Reductions, he appointed Pedro Leon de Romero
as his general deputy. In doing this he had
failed to observe some of the provisions of the
law which had created the office. Then followed
the ordinary civil-military controversy. The people were right, but the governor had the power.
The correspondence between the governor and
the cabildo was characterized by the incivilities
that seem to belong to such a debate; Romero,
however, supported by the governor, continued
to exercise his functions. Governor La Rosa
interfered in the affairs of the cabildo, attempting to control the votes of the members, and,
failing in this, apprehended them and ordered
them to prison. Pino banished them, and Feliú
used the armed force to secure the adoption of
resolutions. The struggle, however, did not
always turn out to the advantage of the governor.
In some instances he was defeated, and even
driven out of the city. These conflicts were in
many cases the means through which the towns
learned how to defend their autonomy, and acquired that experience which enabled them to
assume an attitude of independence in the later
general movement for emancipation.[1]

In 1530 Mexico was recognized by Charles

[1] Montes de Oca, *Cuestiones constitucionales*, 37.

V. as holding the first place among the cities of New Spain, "as the city of Burgos holds it in our kingdoms." [1]   This meant that as Burgos held the political primacy in Castile, a certain precedence in the Cortes over all the other cities, the same distinction was accorded to the city of Mexico, among the cities of New Spain.   The personality of the cities of Spain presented itself for recognition like the individual personality of all lands and times.   The king issued to cities patents of nobility, in essentially the same spirit as to individual persons.   After this they bore a coat of arms, and in all official matters they enjoyed a precedence over cities that had not been thus honored.   Through a subsequent law issued by Philip II. the city of Cuzco became the political primate "of all the cities and towns that are or may be in the whole province of New Castile." [2]

A city sometimes held a meeting that was called an open cabildo, which was a meeting of the official members with the people for the purpose of deliberating on public affairs.   In Montevideo, from its foundation, the inhabitants of the city regarded with great favor open meetings of the cabildo, and in them the imposition of taxes was always determined, and all important measures touching the general welfare were settled.   In

---

[1] *Leyes de Indies*, lib. iv., tit. 8, ley 2.

[2] *Ibid.*, ley 4.

such a meeting was decreed the political independence of Uruguay.[1]

"'To the cabildo is due," as affirmed by Bauza, "the
idea of the representative system and the first glimpse
of the division of power. From the time that they
took upon themselves the conduct of public affairs,
the people observed that not everything depended
upon the comprehensive authority of the military
chief, and, as a consequence, the rudiments of a
system of government more complex than the one-man
power began to permeate all minds. Soon the exercise of the right of petition before the cabildos became
customary, and from this they advanced to the
practice of petitioning the governors. The election
of members of the corporation, although carried out
in an imperfect way, succeeded in awakening an increasing interest among the citizens, who even if they
only contributed to the election as spectators, did not
by this fail to show their satisfaction in so far as the
act and its result agreed with their views. The conduct of the members of the cabildo will always be a
subject for applause, that although authorized during
many years by law to elect their successors, they
never nominated such as were traitors to the common
interests. Thus by means of these humble and per-
secuted corporations public spirit in Uruguay was born,
and among its inhabitants was formed the criterion
in accordance with which power should be exercised for
all in a regulated, equitable, and beneficent form." [2]

The nucleus of the city of Buenos Aires was

---

[1] Bauza, ii., 639.   [2] *Ibid.*, 639, 640.

the fort. It was constructed not only as a means of defence but also as a place of refuge for the inhabitants. It was flanked by monasteries, and surrounded by the straw and mud houses of the new town, "where lived the families protected by the soldiers of the presidio, while the men went out to their farms to work, as they might do every day without difficulty." Like the colonists of New England later, the settlers of Buenos Aires lived surrounded by Indians, and were therefore expected to keep arms, and now and then they were called out for review in the plaza.

In laying out the city, Juan de Garay provided that it should extend twenty-four squares from ·north to south, divided in the middle on the side towards the river by the plaza. It was made to extend back from the river eleven squares. Around this tract which was specially set apart for the buildings of the city, a certain amount of land was reserved as commons, a place for the recreation of the inhabitants. This was designed to be inalienable. Beyond this was the common pasture. The lands surrounding these tracts were early conveyed to private persons for cultivation. The municipal property was thus enclosed by a zone of private property, so that when the population had covered this interior portion, later settlers encountered the high prices demanded by the private owners of the surrounding territory. This led to the illegal occupancy of the lands that had been reserved for the commons. In its growth the city met an obstacle not only in the high price demanded by those who had a monopoly of the available land but also in the spirit of a dominant class of citizens. This class "was composed of a certain number of persons whose proverbial Spanish pride found in Buenos Aires an adequate and better field for development than in the mother country."[1] They held to the feudal idea, and regarded themselves as the lords and the Indians and creoles as the vassals. This was the fateful idea that very largely contributed to the unfortunate result of Spain's great colonial undertaking. It prevented the growth of a democratic society, without which it is impossible to maintain a democratic government.

At the beginning of Viceroy Vertiz's administration, the city of Buenos Aires showed the results of shameful neglect. Many of the streets were impassable the greater part of the year. The heavy rains carried off the loose material, leaving deep irregular gullies and stagnant pools. From the west a stream entered the city, which separated into two branches, formed deep water-courses that cut off almost completely different districts from one another. The inhabitants enjoyed few of the facilities which the size of the city and the wealth of the country entitled

[1] García, *La Ciudad Indiana*, 74.

them to expect. There was no hospital; no
public lighting; no police; and the streets were
unpaved. There was abundant wealth, but it
was largely in the hands of persons whose ignorance
or whose meanness prevented the public from
deriving any advantage from it. Even the idea
of placing a light in front of their houses at night
seems not to have occurred to the inhabitants
as desirable.

Vertiz undertook to remedy some of these
most evident defects. In spite of the lack of the
co-operation of the inhabitants, he began to
improve the streets; he founded a hospital,
established a home for foundlings, created an
orphan asylum, and took steps towards introducing a system of street-lighting. The foundling
asylum was supported in part by rents derived
from estates confiscated from the Jesuits; in
part from the proceeds of bull-fights; in part from
the income from the theatre; and in part from
the gains of the printing office. The municipal
lighting was supported by a door tax of two
reals on each street door. Recognizing that the
life of the city was barren and that there were
few social influences except those making for
degeneracy, he determined to establish a theatre
which might furnish a certain degree of inspiration through the heroic characters it would
present, and the cultivated language of the
plays. In carrying out this project he naturally

encountered the opposition of the clergy. A Franciscan friar, José Acosta, went so far as to censure, from the pulpit, these public amusements which the viceroy had patronized; "and declared in the name of the Holy Spirit that those who attended them would incur eternal damnation."[1] The viceroy, having learned of the attitude assumed by the friar, required him to be expelled from the monastery, and another preacher to repudiate his utterances.

The superiority of Buenos Aires over the other cities of the viceroyalty at this time lay solely in its geographical position. It was in no sense a centre of wealth or cultivation. It had an old fort, a town organization, and an old market. The suggestion that it would absorb the life of the other towns did not seem to point to a real danger. The cities of Cordova, Tucuman, and Salta seemed then so firmly established as not likely to be affected by the rivalry of the port. These cities were richer and more populous than Buenos Aires. Cordova had a university, while no such institution existed at Buenos Aires in the colonial period. Cordova, was, moreover, the residence of a bishop; and it was an important point on the line of trade between the eastern provinces and Chile, Cuyo, and Peru. In some respects Chuquisaca was even more important than Cordova. It was the seat of an audiencia,

[1] Lopez, *Historia de la Republica Argentina*, i., 372.

or supreme court, the residence of the archbishop
of La Plata, and the place of residence of many
persons of wealth.   In fact, the centres of wealth
and cultivation were not at the shore or in the
valley of the great rivers of the eastern part of the
continent, but in the mountains near the mines
of Upper Peru.   But Buenos Aires had one point
of advantage, that was destined to become appreciated when the significance of its agriculture
and foreign commerce with respect to progress
in civilization should become known.   The Spaniards were under the delusion that civilization could
be developed in isolation; that it was a matter of
precept, not a result of social contact and imitation.   In the last quarter of the eighteenth century, the society of the river country and that
of the mountain country were too different to
permit a great degree of sympathy to exist between
them; and Paraguay with the large Indian element in the population and its traditions of
theocratic government had also a character peculiar to itself.

Finding Buenos Aires without facilities for
printing and consequently without the desired
means for distributing information among the
people, Vertiz sought to supply this deficiency.
He fortunately discovered that the Jesuits, on
their expulsion, had left a full-equipped printing
office in the College of Nuestra Señora de Monserrat, in Cordova, the machinery and other

materials of which the viceroy caused to be brought to Buenos Aires. Here he met a new difficulty; he knew no one competent to set up the press and use it. He then sent inquiries to all the provinces for such a person, and was finally informed by the governor of Montevideo that there was in that city a young sergeant who had worked in a printing house in Cadiz. The viceroy called him to Buenos Aires to assume immediate charge of the new undertaking; he offered him for a wife any one of the inmates of the orphan asylum. The young man with marvellous modesty expressed his desire to accept the choice of his patron, which is reported to have been made with satisfactory discretion. Thus was founded a printing house, and at the same time an important family of the viceregal capital. The printing house continued to be known for many years under the designation of *Imprenta de los Niños Expositos*.

But around the colonial city was the colonial country, furnishing a varying background for the municipal life. Behind Potosi lay the rough and barren summits of the eastern Andes, with their rich mines of silver. On either side of the deep ravine in which lies the city of La Paz stretched the inhospitable plain of central Bolivia. Santiago flourished in the delightful valley of central Chile. Back of Buenos Aires were spread out the vast and fertile plains of Argentina, occupied by a few land-holders and the multitude of a homeless proletariat. In 1744, for 186 proprietors there were 5897 dependents. The latter were without some of the fundamental ideas of civilization. To them the plains and their herds appeared like the gift of God to the race. If they were hungry, there were the animals provided for man's support. If they needed shelter, there was the land on which they might erect their habitations. The new order of things under which the lands were claimed as private property, and the herds had individual owners, had been brought about by decrees of persons, who, from the view-point of the dweller on the plains, had no right to either. Why should the favoritism of a governor deprive them of their ancient privilege of wandering or settling at will? As the generations passed and the blood of the white man flowed in the veins of the proletariat of the plains, their views remained practically unchanged. The savages had not become civilized, but the descendants of the white man had moved towards the savage state. The cheapness of slave labor on the great estates drove the free men to the desert, or made them the unpaid dependents of the proprietors. If endowed with energy and daring, some of them moved beyond the limits of the territory that had been granted to private persons, and established themselves on the unappropriated lands, and made there little centres of cultivation. Their peace was not long; for a new grant brought a new proprietor to claim the results of their labor, or they were swept away by the nomadic savages.

The absence of a minute division of the land was in a large measure due to the persistence of the feudal ideal in the colonies. Such a division if it had been carried out might have furnished an independent possession to every man seeking a permanent home and property for himself and his descendants, and filled the country with a self-respecting population, democratic because of the essential equality of wealth, and fitted in good time to lay the foundation of a republic. Instead of this, the feudal notion of superior and inferior survived, making, when carried into practice, the great body of the people in the country either miserable dependents or free men who could find no place for a permanent home. This was the undemocratic state of society, on which it was later proposed to erect a democratic government.

The cities were undoubtedly weak and their administration often unwise, yet they contained a germ that might have been developed into a well-ordered government. Legally the people had a voice in the construction of the municipal corporations, and for this reason they might continue to act even if the power of the king were set aside and all the royal officers withdrawn. In the beginning of the period of emancipation they alone stood between the people and social chaos. The judgment of Sir Woodbine Parish concerning the rôle played by the municipal corporations in this period has been quoted with approval. The inquiries of nearly three quarters of a century have tended to confirm his views.

"But for the cabildos and municipal institutions," he wrote, "which still existed in most of the principal towns of the interior when the Spanish government was broken up, I believe every semblance of a legitimate authority would have ceased. They retained to a certain extent powers not only for the preservation of the public peace, but for the administration of justice; and although, perhaps, under the circumstances, they afforded facilities for confirming the establishment of the federal system in opposition to a more centralized form of government, there is no doubt they saved the isolated towns in the interior from worse consequences.

" Those institutions were by far the best part of the colonial system planted by the mother country, and they were framed upon principles of liberality and independence which formed a singular exception to her general colonial policy. I doubt whether those which in most cases have been substituted for them have been so wisely cast, or are so suitable to the state of society in those countries. The people at large were habituated and attached to them, and had they been retained, with some reforms adapting them to the new order of things, they might have been made the very best foundations for the new republican institutions of the country. But the truth was, they were essentially too democratic for the military power which arose out of the change; they succumbed to that, and the people having no real voice in their new governments, made no struggle to preserve them." [1]

[1] Parish, *Buenos Aires*, 320.

CHAPTER V

THE SOCIAL CLASSES

THE characteristic feature of society in the Spanish colonies at the close of the eighteenth century was its lack of homogeneity. The Europeans, the Indians, and the negroes represented three distinct races. Besides the representatives of these races, there were various classes with mixed blood. The most important of the mongrel classes were the mestizos, the offspring of the union of Europeans and Indians; the mulattoes, the offspring of the Europeans and negroes; and the sambos, the offspring of the union of Indians and negroes. The legal and other obstacles that were opposed to the emigration of unmarried Spanish women to America and the lack of any sentiment hostile to the union of the Spanish and the Indians led to the development of a large class of mestizos, greatly exceeding in numbers any other mixed class. The same freedom, however, did not exist with respect to the union of the Indians and the Africans. In fact, the government sought to prevent the amalgamation of these races, and prohibited their union by cruel and unusual penalties.

Sambo's contemporaries appear not to have thought very much of him, particularly of his moral qualities. Depons, writing at the end of the eighteenth century, says he

"is well formed, muscular, and able to endure fatigue; but all his tastes, all his inclinations, all his faculties, are turned to vice. The mere name of Sambo signifies in the country a good-for-nothing idler, drunkard, cheat, thief, and even an assassin. Of ten crimes that are committed eight always appertain to this cursed class of Sambos. Immorality is their characteristic. It is not perceived in the same degree, either in negroes, mulattoes, **or any** other race pure or mixed."[1]

Through the arrogance of the Spaniards, the creoles, persons of pure European blood born in America, came to be regarded as a class by themselves. The character of the creole was developed under very unfavorable conditions. As a child he was turned over to the care of a confidential negro slave, and he remained under this barbarian tutelage for five or six years. Then he passed into the hands of a mulatto instructor, "with whom he neither saw nor heard anything worthy of imitation." He acquired a slave's notion of duty, which recognized little or no spontaneous effort for others, but whose rule of action is the command of the master enforced

[1] *Travels*, ii., 249.

by the lash. From his teachers he acquired
notions of religion that were full of paganism,
without the grace and poetry of pagan worship.
Outwardly he adapted himself to the forms of
civilized life but his mind was full of the superstitions acquired from the barbarous companions
of his childhood.[1]   The Spaniards, who had been
born and educated under more favorable conditions, had little sympathy with the creole, and
apparently concluded that no worthy characters
could rise out of his unfortunate circumstances.
They regarded him as essentially inferior to
themselves, and nothing more was wanting but
the ambition of the creole to give rise to a bitter
antagonism between these two classes.   Through
this antagonism the creoles were ultimately driven
into an attitude not only of social, but also of
political, hostility to the Europeans.   The practical expression of Spanish hatred which the
creole resented most vigorously was his exclusion
from the higher offices of the colony in which he
lived.   Of the 166 viceroys and 588 captains-
general, governors, and presidents who had held
office in the colonies, in all 754, only 18 were
creoles.   There was, however, no lack of men
of this class fitted to perform the duties of these
offices; for many had been educated in Europe,
and even those who had resorted to the colonial
colleges were sufficiently well trained to admin-

[1] García, *La Ciudad Indiana*, 84.

ister successfully the local affairs of the colonies. But they lacked the influence necessary to obtain these positions. The gravest evil resulting from this exclusion of Americans was not merely that the native inhabitants of European descent were deprived of the privilege of having a part in governing themselves, but "the moral degradation consequent upon the absence of all motive to generous exertion, and the utter hopelessness that any merit could lead to useful distinction." [1]

But there were some persons who saw clearly that even the despised creole, using all available opportunities to improve his standing, would ultimately turn and demand recognition. In a memorial addressed to Philip V., Don Malchor Macanaz pointed out the effect of this exclusion. He called the king's attention not only to the injustice of the policy of exclusion but also to its evil political consequences.

"As the natives of those, your Majesty's dominions, are equally deserving of filling the principal offices of their own country, it appears reasonable, that they should not be divested of all management in their own homes. I am fully persuaded, that in those countries there are many discontented persons, not because they are under the control of Spain; but because they are cast down, and tyrannized by the very persons, who are sent over to exercise the duties of the judicature. Let your Majesty give these

[1] Basil Hall, *Journey*, ii., 237.

offices to subjects of that country, and by this means disturbances will be avoided." [1]

In the course of time hostility between the creoles and the Europeans became a noteworthy feature of life in the colonies. The creoles resented the neglect they experienced under the Spanish government, and made common cause with the mestizos and all the subject classes. In this manner a line separating one party from another was drawn, leaving the majority on the side of the creole. This was the breach leading to the struggle which ended in independence.

The Europeans, the Indians, and the negroes, representatives of distinct races, had different antecedents, and consequently different social aims. The attitude of the Spaniards towards the Indians and the negroes, as well as their attitude towards the creoles, did not indicate that the prejudice of race was to be laid aside. In spite of the rise of the creole, and the increase of the mixed races, the Europeans were determined to maintain their position as the dominant element in the population. They

"were the lords of the soil, the owners of the mines and the factories, the great political, ecclesiastical, and military functionaries; they monopolized the riches and the honors. The Indians were the Pariahs of the colonial régime; they were overworked in every

[1] See Walton's *Exposé*, 48.

kind of labor, without ever profiting by the fruit of their toil. The negroes, in the lamentable condition of slaves, were removed from the protection of the law."[1]

As early as 1501 the Spaniards were permitted to take negroes to America, but the decree granting this privilege provided that only such negroes should be taken as had been born under the power of Christian masters. After the introduction of sugar-cane into Cuba in 1506, and the determination of a number of persons to take advantage of the very favorable climatic conditions for its cultivation, negroes were introduced in such great numbers that the colonists feared an uprising. Later in this year further importation of negroes was prohibited; at the same time permission to marry was extended to those already in the colonies. This prohibition to take negroes to America was subsequently removed, and in 1517 it was required that one third of those imported should be women. With the increase in numbers the fears that had been entertained of an uprising were seen to be well founded. From the beginning the negroes were the cause of serious social disturbances, and in 1550 they committed great atrocities, and burned the city of Santa Marta. Five years later a negro calling himself king headed an insurrection, which was

[1] Oliveira, *La Política Económica de la Metrópoli*, 5, 6.

marked by all sorts of crime, and was put down only after strenuous exertions on the part of the authorities. These and similar disturbances led the king again to prohibit taking negroes to the Indies. At this point Las Casas appeared on the scene with his petition that the importation of negroes should be permitted to relieve the Indians; and as a consequence of his advocacy four thousand negroes were admitted to Cuba, Porto Rico, Jamaica, and San Domingo, on the payment of an import duty, which was devoted to the construction of the palaces at Madrid and Toledo. This action established the policy which was later carried out through contracts with various companies for introducing negro slaves into the Spanish colonies of America.

It is probable that the brutality of the negro as displayed on many occasions had much to do in determining the manner in which he was treated. "No difference was made between a negro and any animal whatsoever. He was a beast of burden that the master disposed of at any moment in the same manner as a mule."[1] The following advertisements appeared in the *Diario de Lima*, May 16, 1792:

"*Venta.*—Quien quisiere comprar una criada preñada en dias de parir, bozal, reformada, ocurra, á la calle de Bodegones la primera casa, donde fué café.

[1] Romero, C. A., *Negros y Caballos*, 11.

Arriba en los altos vive su ama en la segunda
mampara."

"*Venta.*—Quien quisiere comprar una pareja de
mulas de coche de siete cuartas, bien altas y
nuevas, que acaban de llegar de Piura, ocurra á la
barbería de la plazuela vieja de San Juan de Dios
donde darán razon de su dueño, con quien se tratará
del precio en que se venden."

The following advertisements of slaves for sale
are taken from the papers of Buenos Aires:

"Se vende, una criada sana y sin vicios, en cantidad
de 300 pesos.   En esta oficina darán razon."
"Se vende, una mulatilla sana, sin vicios, primeriza,
con leche de cuatro meses.   En la casa de Espósitos
darán razon."

In 1536 negroes were prohibited from appearing
on the streets of Lima at night, except when
accompanying their masters. The penalty for
violating this ordinance was a hundred lashes for
the first offence, and brutal mutilation for the
second offence. A Spaniard meeting a negro at
night in the street might take away his arms;
and if the negro dared to defend himself, the
Spaniard might kill him. The negro who ran
away from his master for a period of six days
might be mutilated, and if he was absent for
a longer time might be killed. For even the
minor offence of stealing corn, negroes were
punished with one hundred lashes for the first

offence and mutilation for the second.[1] The severest regulations were established to prevent members of the Indian and negro races from living together.[2] The severity of these penalties was not lessened when Pedro de la Gasca assumed full authority over Peru. The disposition of some of the negroes to resume the practices of savagery induced the authorities to offer a reward of from five to twenty-five dollars for hunting down the unruly negroes. If they could not be taken they might be killed; and in order to get the reward it was only necessary to present the head of the negro at the cabildo, or city council.[3] The negroes might not wear fine clothing, silk, or jewels; it was forbidden to sell them wine or *chicha;* they might not ride on horseback; and when they died, whether free or slave, their remains might not be carried away in a coffin.

At the end of the century, the king undertook to improve the relations then existing between the Spaniards and the negroes, and on the 31st of May, 1789, he issued an order relating to the education, treatment, and occupations of the slaves in all the Spanish dominions of the Indies.

---

[1] Romero, *Negros y Caballos*, 12; for the ordinances covering these cases, see *Revista de Archivos y Bibliotecas*, v.

[2] "No podían los negros tener tratos ni contratos con los indios, y el que tuviese manceba india habia de ser castrado, y á la negra que accediese á los requilorios de algun indio, habíanle de cortar las orejas."—Romero, *Negros y Caballos*, 13.

[3] Romero, 14.

Under this order every owner of slaves was required to instruct them in the principles of the Catholic religion, that they might be baptized; and to this end he should explain to them the Christian doctrine on certain feast days, on which neither the slaves nor their owners should work. All the owners of slaves were required to comply strictly with their obligation to feed and clothe the slaves, as also their wives and children, although these might be free. All the slaves of both sexes, between the ages of seventeen and sixty, should be assigned tasks suited to their age, sex, and strength, and they should be required to work from sunrise to sunset, with the exception of two hours each day which might be employed in occupations for their own personal advantage. On the feast days, after the mass and the Christian instruction, the slaves might have simple amusements, in which the sexes should be kept apart; and they should be had, moreover, in the presence of the owner or overseer; and they were required to avoid the excesses of eating and drinking, and to conclude their amusements before nightfall. The owners were required to furnish distinct apartments for the two sexes except in the cases where they were married, and also the necessary beds and clothing; and the sick should be supported by the owner, or sent to the hospital at his expense, and in case of death the owner should bear the expense of burial.

The owners were, moreover, required to support the old slaves and the children of both sexes, and they might not set them at liberty without at the same time assigning them perpetual support, to the satisfaction of the prosecuting attorney. The owners might not prevent the slaves from marrying, whether with a slave of the estate to which he belonged or with a slave from another estate. In the latter case the wife should follow the husband, and the owner of the husband was required to purchase the wife. In view of the fact that the owner held a paternal relation to the slave, if the slave failed to fulfil his filial obligation, he might and ought to be given reformatory punishment either by the owner or the overseer; only, however, with imprisonment, fetters, chains, a club, stocks, or lashes, and the lashes might not exceed twenty-five. In case the slave committed a crime against his master, the master's wife or children, or any other person, he should be turned over to the civil judiciary and be subjected to the same trial as a free person. If an owner or overseer should violate any of these provisions, he would be liable to a fine of fifty dollars for the first offence, one hundred dollars for the second offence, and two hundred dollars for the third offence; and if a more severe punishment should be inflicted than that designed by the royal order the prosecuting attorney should proceed against the owner or overseer who had given the punishment. If the owner or overseer should injure, wound, or kill a slave, he should be subjected to the same penalty as if the violation affected a free person. Each owner was required to make an annual sworn statement as to the number, sex, and ages of the slaves on his estate.

This law, like many others proceeding from the king and council of the Indies, encountered practices too thoroughly established to be reformed by a decree from Spain. It, moreover, came too late to be of great historical significance. The traditions that had been created by centuries of misrule were destined to continue without important abatement until the end. The slave had become a part of the social organism, and convenience or the will of the dominant social factor had determined his place, his treatment, and his uses. In the face of established custom no sudden change was possible. Slaves had often been held for ostentation, and this practice and the desire underlying it could not be abolished with a single stroke. Ladies of distinction wished to be attended by slaves while going to church, and they naturally sought to rival one another in the number of their attendants. They used them as a means of indicating their social standing. But slaves were also employed as a source of profit. The house was a kind of workshop, in which the slaves produced various articles for the market. One hundred or two hundred dollars invested in a slave returned through his labor eight or ten dollars a month. Thus, a gain of from forty-eight to one hundred and twenty per cent. a year was a sufficient profit to maintain the institution in favor. But the impression which the system of slave labor made, as carried out here, whether in the house or in the fields, was essentially the same as that observed where-ever in an industrial community slavery has existed. Children growing to maturity in the presence of its practice came to despise work as they despised the position of the only workers they had seen. Add to this the other forms of corruption that were fostered by the association of the youth and the slaves, and it becomes evident that the dominant element in the population acquired a character that unfitted it to lay successfully the foundation of a new society, a character many of the features of which are clearly seen in this latest generation.

Besides the families that were able to maintain slaves and the slaves who served them, there was another element that constituted a ragged fringe of the society, an element that had ceased to entertain expectations of improvement in its state. It embraced those who were personally free; but their material condition was not better than that of the slaves. They lived wherever they could find shelter, in huts erected on the unoccupied lands, or wherever there were vacant quarters which they could appropriate. The exploitation by slave labor of all of the sources of profit that had been opened left them no field of enterprise, and their hopeless misery had deprived them of the power to initiate undertakings of their own. Their fate was that of the free poor usually in the presence of a system of slavery.

The antagonism between the Europeans and the creoles was hardly less severe than that which existed between groups of different races. The fact that the creoles were of the same blood or of the same family as the Europeans did not seem to abate the hostility. The differences were class differences, and were naturally stronger in the isolated centres of population, than in those towns frequented by foreigners. Among the influences tending to maintain the breach between the Europeans and the creoles, Ulloa found two that were more powerful than the rest:

"The excessive vanity and overbearing manners of the creoles, and the forlorn and penniless condition of the Europeans who emigrate to that country. The latter accumulate a fortune with the aid of relatives and friends, as well as by dint of labor and industry, so that within a few years they are enabled to form an alliance with ladies of distinction; but the low condition in which the creoles first knew them is not wholly effaced from remembrance; and on the first occasion of misunderstanding between the European and his relatives, the latter expose, without

8

the least reflection, the mean origin and profession of the former, and kindle the flames of discord in all hearts. The Europeans espouse the cause of their injured countrymen, and the creoles that of the native women, and thus the seeds of dissension spring up, which had been sown in the mind from the remote period of the conquest." [1]

The pretensions of the creoles were stimulated by the policy that had been carried out "of granting patents of nobility to all Spaniards who would go and take up their residence in America." [2] The descendants of these spent much time in

"discussing the order and line of their descent; so that it would appear, as it respects nobility and antiquity, they have nothing to envy in the most illustrious families of Spain; and, treating the subject with the ardor of enthusiasm, they make it the first topic of conversation with the newly-arrived Europeans, in order to acquaint them with their noble origin; but when this is investigated impartially, we are met at the first step we take, with so many difficulties, that a family can rarely be found that has no mixed blood, not to mention objections of minor importance. In such cases it is amusing to observe how they become mutually the heralds of one another's low birth, so that it is needless to investigate the subject for one's self." [3]

[1] *Noticias Secretas*, 417.   [2] *Ibid*, 423.   [3] *Ibid.*, 417.

The vanity of the creoles, moreover, led them to avoid labor and to refuse to engage in trade.   This left them to a life of inaction and, in many cases, to a life of vice.

"Hence it is they soon see the end of all that which their parents have left them, by wasting their money, and neglecting the cultivation of their estates; and the Europeans, availing themselves of the advantages which the neglect of the creoles affords them, turn them to account, and amass an estate; for by engaging in trade they soon succeed in getting upon a good footing, enjoy credit, accumulate money, and are solicited for marriage by noble families; for the creole women themselves, aware of the wasteful and indolent habits of their countrymen, hold Europeans in high esteem, and prefer to be allied with them."[1]

Through the antagonism of the Europeans and creoles arising from these and other circumstances, the social life of the cities of Peru was marked by tumults and bitterness of spirit. Under conditions "where they might pass the most agreeable and tranquil life that could be desired,"[2] they led a wretched existence, kept in a state of perpetual commotion by uncontrolled passions.

Another element of importance in the social life of the southern colonies was the clergy. In the eighteenth century they had ceased to be

---

[1] *Noticias Secretas*, 418, 419.   [2] *Ibid.*, 422.

a force making for righteousness, if we may accept Ulloa's observations; for in his report concerning them he found it necessary to emphasize their vices and not their virtues.

"The persons," he wrote, "who compose the two orders of the clergy are guilty of such licentiousness, that, making due allowance for the frailties to which human nature is liable, and the weaknesses to which men of every class are subject, it would appear that those ecclesiastics regard it as their peculiar privilege to go before all others in the career of vice; for while they are under the most sacred obligations not only to practise virtue, but to correct the errors incident to frail nature, it is they who, by their pernicious example, sanction the practice of iniquity, and in a measure divest it of its heinous nature.

"The parish priests are extremely vicious in their habits; but, whether it happen that an error or crime in them attracts less notice, or whether they are more careful to conceal it, or for both reasons, which is the more probable, disgraceful as the consequences are known to be, they never reach such a degree of scandal as do those of the monks; for the latter, from the first step they take, and even without leaving the monasteries, pursue a course of conduct so notorious and shameful that it becomes offensive in the extreme, and fills the mind with horror.

"Concubinage is so general that the practice of it is esteemed a point of honor; and when a stranger arrives and continues his residence there for some

time without having adopted the customs of the
country, his continence is attributed not to a principle
of virtue, but to the passion of avarice, as it is generally supposed that he lives so in order to save
money.

"In large cities, the greater part of the monks live
in private houses, for the convents furnish an asylum
to those only who cannot keep house, or to the
choristers, novitiates, and such like, who live there
from choice. The same is true of the small cities,
villages, and hamlets. The doors of the monasteries
are kept open, and the monks live in their cells,
accompanied by their women, and lead in every respect the life of married persons." [1]

"The fandangoes or balls are usually devised by
the members of the religious orders, or more properly
by those who call themselves religious, although, in
fact, they are far from being so; for it is they who
pay the expense, who attend in company with their
concubines, and who get up the fray in their own
houses. Simultaneously with the dance, the immoderate use of ardent spirits begins, and the entertainment is gradually converted into acts of
impropriety so unseemly and lewd, that it would be
presumption even to speak of them, and a want
of delicacy to stain the narrative with such a record of
obscenities; and, letting them lie hid in the region
of silence, we shall only remark, that whatever the
spirit of malice could invent in respect to this subject,
great as it might be, it could never fathom that
abyss into which those corrupt minds are plunged,

[1] *Noticias Secretas*, 490, 491, 492.

nor give any adequate idea of the degree of excess
to which debauchery and crime are carried." [1]

Noticias Secretas, 497; an elaborate presentation of this
phase of Peruvian society as it appeared in the eighteenth
century may be found in Juan and Ulloa, *Noticias Secretas*,
Pt. II, chapter viii.

CHAPTER VI

THE CHURCH AND ITS RELATION TO THE CIVIL POWER

THE peculiar relation of the Church to the King of Spain and to the Spanish colonial government in America was due, in a great measure, to the fact that independently the pope was unable to occupy the great missionary field that was opened to the Church by the discovery of America. He "could do nothing by himself in this immense territory; he had not the means of establishing in it the institutions necessary for the propagation of religion, nor was it even possible for an order by him to reach that region unless carried by a costly expedition." Whatever ecclesiastics or other persons went thither had to follow the direction of the Spanish court, or the captain to whom they were subordinated.[1] It was impossible for the Holy See to proceed in Christianizing the inhabitants of the New World without abiding by the rules, and soliciting the aid, of the civil power. The pope had subjects

[1] Sarsfield, *Derecho Publico Eclesiastico*, Buenos Aires, 1889, 18.

who were not Spaniards, whom he might wish
to employ in the work of converting the Indians,
but the execution of such a plan was prevented
by the order of the king limiting the emigration
to the colonies to Spanish subjects.   Whatever
power over America the pope may have claimed,
whether with or without valid ground, had been
transferred to the crown of Spain by the bull of
Alexander VI. in 1493.   This transfer with respect
to the territories in question was absolute and
entire: "We give, concede, and assign them in
perpetuity to you and the Kings of Castile and of
Leon, your heirs and successors: and we make,
constitute, and depute you and your heirs and
successors, the aforesaid, lords of these lands,
with free, full, and absolute power, authority,
and jurisdiction." [1]   The subsequent recognition
of this cession became a necessary part of the
papal policy.   The position assumed by the crown
under this cession set aside the grounds of the
medieval debate between the Church and State.
With respect to Spain's dominions in America,
papal action was subject to criticism and veto by
royal authority.   That this power was not used
to hinder the work of the Church may be inferred
from the fact that, as new settlements were made
the field of practical activity of the Church was
expanded.   The conversion of the Indians everywhere attended the conquests of the civil power;

[1] See Montes de Oca, *Cuestiones Constitucionales*, 4

the Church even encountered no opposition in
erecting its peculiar tribunals of the inquisition.
The king was dominant, but he was in sympathy
with the purposes and methods of the Church;
and it was this sympathy which made peaceful
co-operation possible where the relations of the
Church with the sovereign had "no precedents
either in law or in ecclesiastical usages or customs."[1] In this phase of American history we
have to do not with the ecclesiastical law
of Europe transplanted, but with laws and pontifical briefs and bulls framed for America and
a new body of civil legislation which comprehends the administration and government of the
Church of the New World.[2]

At the beginning of the conquest the plan for
converting the Indians was only partially formed.
Any ecclesiastics available were employed, and
these served as priests for the Spaniards and
Indians without obtaining or even asking a
license from the bishop; in fact, there were at the
time no bishops whose jurisdiction embraced
any part of America. "The whole region was
governed by the king, and was subject to his
direction, administration, or nomination, or to
those who acted in his stead in virtue of the
commission and delegation which they held for
this purpose from the Apostolic See."[3] The

---

[1] Sarsfield, 22. [2] *Ibid.*, 23.
[3] Solórzano, *Politica Indiana*, ii., 122.

same complete authority was exercised by the king with respect to the territorial limits of the jurisdiction of the different grades of ecclesiastics. He, for example, fixed the boundaries of the bishoprics, and issued orders which ecclesiastical assemblies obeyed. "All causes between the bishops, the parish priests, the canons, and the dignitaries concerning their benefices, or concerning the canonical capacity to obtain them, were decided alone by the sovereign of the Indies, although it might be regarded as a spiritual matter, and be between persons under ecclesiastical jurisdiction."[1] And whatever powers the ecclesiastical prelates exercised in the spiritual government of the Church of America were conferred by the king. Similar extensive powers had already been granted to the king of Portugal with reference to his possessions in the East, and this fact is recalled in the bull of 1493, in which Alexander VI. "concedes to the kings of Spain in the New World all the favors, privileges, exceptions, faculties, liberties, and immunities conceded to the crown of Portugal."[3] Some of the earlier writers, members of the council of the Indies, and among others, Solórzano, refer to the king as holding not merely the rights of patronage but also the office of papal delegate.[3]

---

[1] Sarsfield, 27. [2] *Ibid.*, 29.

[3] "De lo cual se colige que Vuestra Magestad goza en las Indias de mayor derecho, que el derecho de patronato concede al patron, porque goza de oficio de delegado del Papa para el

It was, however, through the right of patronage that the kings of Spain made practical their great power in ecclesiastical affairs; and they claimed and exercised this right even before any formal cession of it was made by the pope. It was formally granted by the bull of July 28, 1508. Sixty-six years later the right of patronage of the Church in America was established by a civil decree, dated July 10, 1574. This decree sets forth with sufficient clearness the position of the king, in the following form:

"The king.—Our viceroy of the provinces of Peru, or the person or persons who for the time being may hold the government of the country. As you know, the right of ecclesiastical patronage belongs to us, in the whole state of the Indies, for having discovered and acquired that part of the world, and built and endowed churches and monasteries in it at our expense, and at the expense of the catholic kings, our ancestors; also for its having been conceded to us by bulls of the supreme pontiffs, given voluntarily; and in order to preserve it and the justice by which

dicho fin de la conversion de los Indios, y así aprieta más esta obligacion á los Reyes de España, pues si vé claro haber Su Santidad descargado en este particular su conciencia y obligacion, y puestola en la diligencia y cuidado de esta corona" (Padre Juan de Silva, *Advertencia para et Gobierno de las Indias*, 67). Dr. Araciel, of the council of the Indies, says: "Particularmente que V. M. se considera en las Indias mas que patrono, y como delegado de la Sede Apostólica y á quien estan concedidas las veces de Su Santidad en todo lo eclesiástico, así por Bulas como por costumbre."— Quoted by Sarsfield, 31.

we hold it, we order and command that said right of patronage, one and undivided in all the state of the Indies, may be always reserved to us and to our royal crown, without the possibility of losing it wholly or in part, and that we may not be seen to concede the right of patronage by grace or mercy, or by statute, or by any other disposition which we or the kings, our successors, shall make.

"And, moreover, that neither by custom, nor by prescription nor by any other title, shall any person or persons, or ecclesiastical or secular communities, churches, or monasteries, be able to use the right of patronage, except the person who in our name and with our authority and power shall exercise it; and that no person either secular or ecclesiastical, order, convent, religion, community of whatever state, condition, quality, and pre-eminence it may be, judicially or extrajudicially, on whatever occasion, or by whatever reason, may dare to intermeddle in any affair that may concern our royal patronage, neither to prejudice us respecting it, nor to appoint to any church or benefice, or ecclesiastical office, nor to receive such appointment that may be made in any part of the state of the Indies, without our nomination or the nomination of the person whom we by law or by patent shall have authorized; and he who shall act contrary to this, being a secular person, shall incur a loss of the favors which he shall hold from us in the whole of the state of the Indies, and he shall be incompetent to hold others, and shall be forever banished from all our kingdoms and dominions, and, if he should be an ecclesiastical officer, he shall be regarded as a stranger and an alien in all our kingdoms and dominions, and shall not be able to hold any benefice or ecclesiastical office in them, and shall, moreover, incur the other penalties established against such acts by the laws of these kingdoms; and our viceroys, audiencias, and royal justices shall proceed with all rigor against those who shall be or act in opposition to our right of patronage, proceeding on the charge or petition of our fiscals, or of any party whatsoever who may request it; and great care shall be had in the conduct of the case. We wish and command that there shall not be created, instituted, founded, or constituted any cathedral or parochial church, monastery, hospital, votive church, or any other pious or religious place without our express consent, or that of the person who shall have our authority and commission for this purpose. And again, that there shall not be instituted or established any archbishopric, dignity, canonry, prebend, beneficed curacy, or any other benefice, or ecclesiastical or religious office, without our consent or presentation, or that of the person who shall have our commission, and that such presentation or consent shall be written in the usual form."

Under the order of things thus established, any persons appointed to an ecclesiastical position in the Indies was required to give notice to the viceroy, president, audiencia, or to whatever person might be at the head of the government of the province in question, and show him his certificate of appointment, in order that he might receive whatever favor or assistance might be

necessary to enable him to perform the functions of
his office. The right of patronage held by the king
excluded the existence of a similar right in any
other person. Every ecclesiastical office in America was, therefore, filled by the king's nomination.
By law, however, as in the Ordinance of Intendants, in Buenos Aires, the right of patronage might
be vested in a vice-patron. In this case the right
of patronage in the viceroyalty of Buenos Aires
was made to reside in vice-patrons, and these
were the viceroy in the metropolis and the governor-intendants in the provinces.

In maintaining practically the right of patronage, the courts of the civil government and not
the ecclesiastical authorities considered all cases
of violation of the rules involved. They considered all questions involving the limits of bishoprics, the rights and prerogatives of the holders
of benefices, controversies between ecclesiastical
councils and their bishops or archbishops concerning the administration of the Church, all
disputes between parish priests and their parishes,
in a word, all cases that in any manner touched
the royal patronage. Even matters spiritual
and cases between persons of a privileged tribunal
were not excepted from the civil jurisdiction;
but certain cases might be brought before the
viceroy, and, if desired, an appeal might be taken
from the viceroy's decision to the audiencia.[1]

[1] Sarsfield, 51, 52.

There was, however, in each bishopric an ecclesiastical court. Although the bishop, the fiscal proctor, and the provisor were the members of the court, all ordinary cases were tried by the provisor, and the decisions were rendered by him. The more important cases were decided by the bishop. An appeal from any of the decisions might be taken to the archbishop. In case the appellant won, the defeated party might make a final appeal to the nearest bishop, and the decision on this appeal was executed. In case the appellant lost, no further appeal was permitted. Cases that might be brought before the ecclesiastical courts were such as concerned benefices, patronages, tithes, marriages, legitimation, funerals, donations to churches and to other pious uses, legacies to churches by will or contract, and all those matters which fall within the scope of pious works. If a civil, or temporal, case arose between priests, or a case arose in which a layman brought action against a priest, these were tried before an ecclesiastical court; but if a priest brought action against a layman in a civil, or temporal, suit, the case was tried before a secular tribunal. In the ecclesiastical courts essentially the same form of procedure prevailed as in the secular tribunals.

In the general organization, the Church had not only a hierarchy of officers, but also several grades of assemblies. The highest of these was the

general council. It was composed of the archbishops, who, as judges of the faith, were called
to constitute this great assembly, but other members were called sometimes, cardinals and generals
of the regular orders, by reason of their high
position, to participate in these meetings. The
bishops were admitted as *procuradores*. The
conclusions of a general council were not applicable
solely to the countries from which there were
representatives present. In the council of Trent
there was no bishop or archbishop from America,
yet the pope held that "the state of the Indies"
was comprehended under the decisions. Such
councils were under the presidency of the pope,
who was generally expected to present the subjects
for deliberation. The conclusions were ordinarily
reached by the members voting as individuals,
but sometimes the vote was taken by nations.
Having been adopted by the council, these conclusions were passed to the pope, who held the
power to veto them. If they were confirmed by
him, they might still be rejected by the Church
of any given nation. Spain, for instance, did not
accept the decisions of the Lateran council held
under Alexander III., and France refused to
carry out certain resolutions of the council of
Trent. Although the general council was a council
of the Church as a whole, it is noteworthy that the
individuality of nations was recognized in it, as when
on certain occasions the vote was taken by nations.

In the general administration of ecclesiastical affairs, the individuality of the nations was furthermore recognized by the Church in holding national councils, that is to say, councils of the Church, all the members of which were drawn from within the limits of the nation. Such a council was composed of all the bishops and archbishops of the Church whose jurisdictions were embraced within the national boundaries. Such a council was held under the presidency of the patriarch [1] or primate; for instance, in Spain a national council was held under the presidency of the archbishop of Toledo, the primate of Spain. But this title of primate, although sometimes applied to the archbishop of San Domingo and to the archbishop of Lima, never existed by authority in America.

A provincial council in the Church is a meeting of the bishops of an ecclesiastical province under the presidency of the metropolitan archbishop. Such a province is formed by a union of several dioceses and at the head of it stands an archbishop. It appears to have been the design of the Church to have the ecclesiastical divisions correspond with the civil divisions of the territory

[1] The title of Patriarch of the Indies which we encounter in accounts of Spanish affairs was merely a title of honor held by the first chaplain of the king, "to whom was given the general vicariate of the Spanish army and navy; but this vicariate was not extended to the troops and armies of America."—Sarsfield, 60.

of the state, thus making the political capitals
the seats of the metropolitan archbishops. The
organization in Spanish America has not always
followed this plan. After the bishopric of La
Plata, or Chuquisaca, was made an archbishopric,
the province under the archbishop embraced the
bishoprics of Upper Peru, Salta, Cordova, Paraguay, and Buenos Aires. This province, although
there was in it a subordinate court or audiencia,
was nevertheless subject to the viceroy of Peru.
The viceroyalty of Rio de la Plata was created
in 1776, and Buenos Aires became the capital, but
the archbishop of Chuquisaca continued to be
the metropolitan and the bishop of Buenos Aires
a suffragan. The captaincy-general of Chile
became independent of the viceroyalty of Peru,
except in matters of war, yet the bishop of Santiago, the capital of Chile, remained a suffragan
of the archbishop of Lima. In the beginning it
was not permitted to hold a provincial council
in the Indies without first notifying the king and
receiving his consent. Later the holding of such
a council might be authorized by a viceroy or a
captain-general. These councils might be held
regularly every twelve years. If it was desirable
that there should be a meeting in the intervening
period, it might be had, if specially ordered by the
pope and approved by the proper civil authority.
The call for a provincial council proceeds from
the metropolitan; but if the metropolitan church

is vacant, the call may be issued by the senior bishop of the ecclesiastical province. Not only the bishops but also the canons and the dignitaries are invited, and the viceroy is present representing the king; but the bishops alone have an authoritative vote, which is taken by the bishops present voting individually. The conclusions of the provincial councils of America under the rule of Spain were remitted to the council of the Indies, and if the council of the Indies approved them for publication, it sent them to the pope. These conclusions of the provincial councils when properly confirmed were authoritative only within the limits of the ecclesiastical province where the council was held.

The Church in America recognized the provision of the council of Trent which required the bishop to hold every year a synod of the prelates and clergy of his diocese. The bishop, who was in the full exercise of his episcopal powers, issued the call for such a meeting. The resolutions of the synod, having been approved by the bishop, were sent to the viceroy and the governor of the district, who finding nothing in them controverting the rights of the sovereign, or likely to produce any inconvenience, ordered their execution, and the bishop then caused them to be published. But if they did not meet the viceroy's approval, they were overruled, and sent to the council of the Indies for such action as that body might see fit

to take concerning them. Thus at every step in
the administration of ecclesiastical affairs in
America the presence and dominance of the civil
power were recognized.

This general control of ecclesiastical affairs by
the king and his council of the Indies is made
evident and emphasized by the law which required all bulls, briefs, rescripts, and despatches
of the Roman Curia which contained laws,
rules, or general statements to be presented to
the council of the Indies before their publication,
in order that their execution might be sanctioned
in so far as they were not in opposition to the
regalias, concordats, customs, laws, or decrees of
the nation; or did not stand in the way of the
nation's achieving its proper purposes.[1]

In case the king refused to allow a bull to pass
and be published in America, he made no report
to the pope of the grounds of his objection, nor
did he suggest any course of papal action that
would be acceptable to him.   The attorney who
had examined the bull for the king simply begged
his Holiness to retain the document.   But in
practice this formal petition of the attorney
never reached the pope; it was retained by the
council of Spain, and the government conveyed

[1] Sarsfield, 77, 78; when these documents were brought
before the council, they were copied in the record books of
the secretaries and the originals were placed in the archives
of the council or in the archives of Simancas, authorized
copies being made for convenient use.

the information it contained at such time and under such circumstances as appeared to it opportune; usually by an oral statement to a diplomatic officer.[1]

The monks who came to America required the consent of the viceroy or governor, together with that of the prelate of the diocese, before they were able to construct a monastery; in fact, these officers determined the towns in which the monasteries should be established. The several orders distributed their members into different provinces, but the permission of the governor of the state was needed to form these provinces. From time to time the *padres* of a province assembled to elect their provincials, guardians, and friars of the monasteries; and these early applications of political methods were sometimes attended by serious conflicts. They furnished an instance of democratic procedure without the laws democracy has found it necessary to establish to preserve order at the polls. In view of this state of things, the law finally provided that the viceroy should be present at these meetings to preserve the peace and cause the constitutions of the order to be respected; but if the viceroy was absent from the place of holding the meeting and unable to attend, he was required to write to the monks admonishing them and charging them to abide by and preserve their

[1] Sarsfield, 86.

institutions. In case of disturbance, he might even cause them to be arrested, and taken out of the province; and when the election had been held, the bishop or archbishop might exercise the power of veto, if in his opinion the person elected was not fitted to fill the office for which he had been selected.[1]

The consent of the civil authority was also required for the erection of cathedral or parochial churches, temples, monasteries, and other places for religious exercises.[2]

" And if in fact or by dissimulation any person shall make or begin to make any of these edifices, without this prerequisite, the viceroys, audiencias, or governors shall cause them to be demolished, and everything reduced to its previous state, without excuse or delay."[3]

And the substance of this injunction was always contained in the general instructions given to the viceroys of Mexico and Peru.[4]

The expenses of erecting the cathedral churches were in three parts; the first part was contributed by the royal treasury, the second part by the Indians of the bishopric or archbishopric, and the third part by the *encomenderos* of the diocese. These three parties were, moreover,

---

[1] *Leyes de Indias*, lib. 1, tit. 13, ley 2; lib. 1, tit. 14, leyes 60, 61.

[2] *Ibid.*, tit. 6, ley 1.   [3] *Ibid.*, tit. 3, ley 1.

[4] Solórzano, lib. 4, cap. 23.

the contributors to the funds by which the parochial churches were built, but it was understood that the contribution from the royal treasury was simply for the first construction of the church, not for later enlargements or modifications. The archbishops, bishops, and abbots were required to report to the king the number of churches that had been erected; and when the building of churches had been undertaken, the viceroys and prelates were to take care to have them completed as soon as possible.

The license for building a church or monastery having been issued to one of the regular orders, the viceroy, president, or governor, each in his district, was required to prohibit more space being taken for the building than was necessary for the convenient accommodation of the occupants. A term, moreover, was set for the completion of the establishment, and if it was not completed within this term, the viceroy might transfer it to another order.

In the first century of the colonial period, the archbishop of Lima was the metropolitan for all the territory of South America that was under Spanish rule. His jurisdiction was thus coextensive with that of the earlier viceroys. In 1609 the bishop of La Plata, or Chuquisaca, was made an archbishop, and within his province were included the bishops of Upper Peru, Salta, Cordova, Paraguay, and Buenos Aires. In Europe the pope

sometimes created archbishops, under whom
there were no bishops, archbishops who were
given their titles not because there was work for
them to do as archbishops, but because it was
desired to accord honorable distinction to certain
persons. In America this form of ecclesiastical
favoritism did not appear. There were various
reasons for its absence. In the first place, almost
all the bishops and archbishops were Europeans;
in the second place, there were not many towns
in South America, in the early period, which a
European would select because of the opportunities
it afforded for luxurious living; and in the third
place, the king was anxious that no more of
his revenues than was necessary should go for
salaries of archbishops. If, therefore, one was
to be an archbishop without a province, he would
doubtless find it more agreeable to be archbishop
of Lucca or Ferrara, than archbishop of Oruro or
Riobamba, and he would not have the objections
of the king to overcome.

Besides the bishops and the chapters, the
curates were especially important in determining
the character of the religious work in the colonies.
In some of the parishes Spaniards constituted
a predominant part of the population. The curates
who officiated in these parishes were called
rectoral curates. There were other parishes composed almost entirely of Indian villages, and the
religious teachers who officiated in them were

known as doctrinal curates. The differences
of function between these two classes were
chiefly only such as were made inevitable by the
differences of the communities concerned. There
was a third class of religious teachers who were
appointed to instruct the Indians in the catechism
and in the manners and customs of civilized
life. These were the missionaries who led the
advance against paganism and savage customs.
When the Indians had adopted the essential
features of civilization, they were transferred to
the parish of a doctrinal curate, and the missionaries moved their posts farther into the wilderness, and renewed their crusade against ignorance
and unbelief. Enlistment in the ranks of the
missionaries was without any compulsion whatsoever; those who entered upon the great undertaking, in the early decades, appear to have
been moved by a desire to propagate the faith,
and thereby to redeem the race. Later, enthusiasm
gave way to indifference and members of the
religious orders, leaving Spain full of zeal for
the spiritual conquest of the Indians, found "the
lives of their brethren rather fashioned according
to the spirit of man than the spirit of God," and
under the influence of those already in the field,
they came to regard a life of indolence more
attractive than a death of glory.[1] In the later
years of Spanish rule, the missionaries on the

[1] Depons, *Travels*, i., 352.

frontier made few conversions, and advanced, among the Indians, but little a knowledge of the ways of civilization; and on the basis of the facts observed, Depons concluded that neither the cause of religion nor national sovereignty derived any material advantages from their labors.[1]

The curate of a parish inhabited chiefly by Spaniards was not entirely dependent for his support on his salary. There were numerous fees and perquisites to supplement the compensation which he received from the king. The missionaries, on the other hand, who ministered solely to the Indians were generally obliged to maintain themselves with the royal stipend, since the services of the Church in these cases were gratuitous. Sometimes, however, they violated the spirit while they observed the letter of the law. They sold the Indians various articles, such as rosaries and little images of the Virgin, at a thousand per cent. profit; and persuaded them to work without compensation.

In America the monks were given a somewhat unusual position. According to the canon law they were not able to hold beneficed curacies, but the extent of the American field, and the limited number of the clergy available to occupy it, induced Leo X., Adrian VI., Paul III., Clement VIII., and Pius V. to permit them to become parish priests. Under this order a very large

[1] Depons, i., 354.

number of the parishes in America in the first century were occupied by friars. But in the middle of the eighteenth century, this privilege was withdrawn, leaving them only two parishes in a conventual province.

Wherever the Spaniards established themselves in America, with their Indian serfs and their negro slaves, labor soon came to be regarded as the proper occupation of the inferior races. Through this fact it very naturally became despised by the Spaniard and the creole, and yet other openings for their profitable employment were not numerous. The door of the monastery was, however, always open. There one might lead a tranquil life. If he had sufficient intellectual cultivation to enable him to engage in some narrow field of inquiry, there was his opportunity. If he found delight in vague contemplation and mystical day-dreaming, the atmosphere of the monastery favored his desires. There his support was assured; there behind the walls that enclosed him and his brethren he might have a hand in directing the other social classes; and, in his theoretical poverty, he might enjoy more of the things of this world than fell to the ordinary lot of man.

Yet at the end of the eighteenth century there was observed a diminution in the number of ecclesiastics. This was true both of the monks and of the secular priests. Several causes have been pointed out as contributing to this result. One has been found in the greater prominence given to the organized militia, in which there was an opportunity for honorable maintenance without a form of labor humiliating to Spanish pride. Another was found in the multiplication of posts in the civil service, which furnished attractive livings to persons who might otherwise have accepted places in the Church. In the beginning, turning from the wars against the Moors, the Spaniards were strongly moved by a desire for ecclesiastical conquest; but in the course of time the spread of stories of the fabulous wealth of Peru and the possible spoils of other chiefs naturally attracted to the colonies a large number of persons who were more interested in the attainment of wealth than in the conversion of the Indians. There was observed, however, no diminution of zeal on the part of the ecclesiastical organizations to accumulate property; and men of wealth recognized that donations to churches and monasteries furnished the surest means of securing for their names a fragrant memory. Facing the end of life, many persons did not hesitate to purchase the favor and service of the Church in their own behalf, even to depriving their families of their expected inheritances. The government recognized this evil, and sought to offer a remedy by issuing a law forbidding any notary to pass an act or an instrument of donation by which a sick person, or a person on a bed of death, proposed to convey his property to his confessor or to an ecclesiastical organization for pious uses. This law, however, found no adequate support in public opinion, yet on the initiative of the Spanish government it was revived in Caracas in 1802.

The monotonous routine of the monastery in Spain must have often been irksome to many of the more active and venturesome members of the orders. It was inevitable that some men should find themselves in the religious houses who were better fitted by nature for the practical work of pioneers than for contemplation and a continuous round of religious exercises. To such men the opportunities for a more adventurous life in America appeared attractive, and made them willing to respond to the call for missionaries. Fretting under a rigid discipline, they looked to the colonies for a larger measure of freedom. This expectation of freedom was usually realized when charged in America with the duties of a parish priest. While performing the functions of this office they were removed from the immediate supervision of their monastic superiors, and the results of this independence with respect to their conduct were such as to indicate that their training had not been of a character to enable them to withstand their inevitable temptations and meet properly their responsibilities. The scandalous lives of some of the regular clergy while in charge of parishes called forth strong protests from many of the most zealous members of the Church. The secular clergy regarded the assignment of monks to parishes as an encroachment on their peculiar functions. This view became widely accepted, and in 1757 King Ferdinand VI. issued an edict, prohibiting monks from taking charge of parishes, and providing that, as regulars holding these positions died, only members of the secular clergy would be appointed to the vacancies thus created. This edict made complete the change that had been initiated a few years earlier.

CHAPTER VII

A COLONIAL UNIVERSITY

THE survival of medievalism in the society of the Spanish colonies is very well illustrated by the history and character of the University of Cordova. In point of age this University holds the third place in America. It was preceded by the University of San Marcos in Lima, and by the University of Mexico. It was founded by Friar Fernando de Trejo i Sanabria, bishop of Tucuman. Bishop Trejo was one of the few creoles who, under the Spanish régime, attained to the episcopal dignity. He was born in Asuncion in 1554, sixteen years after the foundation of the city. He studied in Lima, and here became a member of the Franciscan order. He had been provincial of the Franciscan province of the Twelve Apostles of Peru, and was guardian of the principal monastery of Lima, when Philip II. appointed him bishop of Tucuman.[1] He was consecrated in Quito by Bishop Luis de Solis, and assumed the duties of his diocese in 1595.

[1] Tucuman in the seventeenth century embraced the present districts of Cordova, Tucuman, Salta, Jujuy, La Rioja, Catamarca, Santiago del Estero, and a part of Chaco.

Trejo held the office of bishop of Tucuman
for nineteen years, and during this period he made
his influence felt as the protector of the generally
despised Indians and negroes. He caused them
to be organized in brotherhoods in connection
with the churches in all the reductions and towns
within his jurisdiction. But his supreme claim
to the grateful memory of his countrymen
rests on his zeal in behalf of the education of
youth, at a time when it was difficult to pene-
trate the dense ignorance that overshadowed
them. In the heart of the continent, with long
stretches of the wilderness on all sides, with
no schools, no books, and no associations except
such as made for barbarism, it required more
than ordinary hope and courage to undertake
the task of educating that depraved generation.
In Santiago del Estero, Bishop Trejo established,
in 1609, a school under the name of *Colegio de
Santa Catalina;* and a few years later he carried
out his desire to found a university, in which
"Latin, the arts, and theology" would be taught.
By a formal document, dated June 19, 1613,
he agreed to give within three years to the proposed University forty thousand dollars. In the
meantime he would give fifteen hundred dollars
a year for the support of the instructors and the
building. And as there might be needed more
than the two thousand dollars which it was
supposed the forty thousand dollars would yield,

he agreed to make to the University a donation "pure, perfect, and irrevocable, which the law calls *inter vivos*, of all my property real and personal, which I have or may have, money, wrought silver, books, slaves, and inheritances, and in particular that which I have called Quimillpa, within the jurisdiction of the City of San Miguel, with all the lands, mills, goats, asses,"

and all the other property.

The bishop did not live long after making this gift. Finding his health failing while in Cordova in 1614, he acted on the advice of his physician and set out to return to Santiago del Estero. The Jesuits, to whom this donation was made and with whom he was living in Cordova, opposed his going; but he persisted, and on the second day of the journey he was obliged to halt. Knowing his end was near, he sent Padre Vasquez Trujillo on to Santiago to take possession of his property, which he had donated for the establishment of the University. He died on the 24th of December, 1614, and his body, in accordance with his request, was taken back to Cordova and buried in the church of the Jesuits. Before his death, however, he issued a second document confirming the gift of 1613.[1]

In February, 1614, the institution founded by Trejo, under the title of *Colegio Maximo*, opened

[1] Garro, *Bosquejo Historico de la Universidad de Cordova,* 29.

10

at Cordova with fifty students, but it was not until eight years later, 1622, that it was formally authorized by Pope Gregory XV.[1]   At this time it assumed the name and character of a university as then conceived.   Like all other documents issued by the pope relating to American affairs, this bull of authorization was submitted to the council of the Indies.   After it had been approved by that body, the king ordered his officers and subjects in the Indies to comply with its terms and assist in its execution.

The death of Bishop Trejo before his foundation had been approved left the institution without a certain important force it would have had in case his life had been prolonged.   In fact, the forty thousand dollars which he had agreed to convey was never actually turned over to the Jesuits. They, however, inherited at his death all, or the greater part, of the articles of property which formed his patrimony; yet these did not amount to the sum specified in the instrument of his gift.[2]

By the approval of the pope, confirmed by the king, the Colegio Maximo assumed the rank and dignity of a university in 1622, and in the following year it awarded its first degrees under its new title.   In the early period of the University the degrees were conferred by the bishop of the

---

[1] This document is printed in Garro, *Bosquejo Historico de la Universidad de Cordova*, 42–44.

[2] Garro, 32.

diocese, whose seat was not Cordova but Santiago del Estero. The students who were prepared to receive their degrees were, therefore, either obliged to wait until the bishop might come to Cordova, or to make a journey to the place where he might then be. Both courses involved inconvenience and expense. This system, moreover, provided ample opportunity for fraud. It was sometimes easy for a person wishing a degree, although he had not made the requisite studies at the University, to deceive the bishop. There were serious abuses growing out of the power of the bishop to confer the degrees of the University wherever he might happen to be when the applicant presented himself; and knowledge of these abuses came to the king, as may be seen from the decree issued by Philip IV. in 1664. In the introduction to this decree the king affirmed that the bishop had given the degrees "sometimes to those who had not studied at the University, nor attended the examinations."[1] As a remedy he ordered that whenever the bishop was absent from Cordova the "*maestre-escuela*" might give the degrees. Somewhat later other steps were taken to set aside this difficulty. In 1680, the king authorized the rector of the University to confer degrees in the absence of the bishop and the "*maestre-escuela*." Then, in 1700, Cordova became the seat of the bishop.

[1] This decree is printed in Garro, 49, 50.

In the fifty years immediately subsequent to
its foundation the University passed through a
preliminary stage of imperfect and unstable
organization. But in 1664 it adopted a fundamental law that determined its form and usages
for about one hundred and fifty years, or until
its reorganization in the beginning of the nineteenth century. This law is an important source
of information respecting the character of the
University during the colonial period. It recognized Ignatius Loyola as the patron saint of the
University, and required that his statue or picture
should be assigned a conspicuous place, and that
the anniversary of the saint's day should be
solemnly celebrated, and the celebration be attended by all the doctors and masters.

The University should keep as its archives all
papers, such as papal bulls, royal decrees, and
other provisions, relating to it, as well as all books
of record. It should have a chest in which to
keep all of its funds and all funds entrusted to it,
such as the *propinas*, or fees to be distributed
on behalf of the candidates for degrees. The
chest should have two keys, one held by the
rector, and the other by the dean or the doctors
residing in the city, or by the treasurer; and it
should not be opened except in the presence of
the holders of both keys and of the secretary. The
secretary was required to make a record of the
amounts put into the chest, and the amounts taken

out, as well as the purpose for which they were withdrawn; and the book containing this record should be kept in the chest.

The two most important officers of the University were the rector and the treasurer. They administered the affairs of the institution. The subordinate officers were the beadles and the secretary, who were appointed by the rector. The functions of the beadle were a combination of those of a chief janitor and master of ceremonies. On the secretary devolved the duty of keeping all the ordinary records of the University, and of acting as secretary of the meeting known as the *claustro*. This was a meeting called by the rector, and was composed of all the doctors and masters who were in the city or who might wish to attend though residing elsewhere, together with the professors and the treasurer; or, in the terms of a modern university, a meeting of the members of the faculties and all the alumni residing in the neighborhood of the institution, or who might wish to attend wherever residing, together with the principal officer of the financial administration. The *claustro* discussed general questions of university policy, and took action on them, which became effective as amendments to the fundamental law. It guarded attentively the observance of this law, insisted on the maintenance of discipline, and kept the government consistent with its traditions. It constituted a broad basis of

university government, under circumstances where
both the church and civil affairs were subject
to a system of absolute rule. The first *claustro*
was held in December, 1664, and afterwards it
was called annually.

The students were required to matriculate annually, and for this they were allowed forty days
from the beginning of the instruction. Applicants,
after this period, could not enter upon the courses
without the permission of the rector, and all were
required to take an oath of obedience to him.[1]

The annual courses of instruction lasted six
months and a day at first, but later they were
made to continue seven months; and, except in
the case of the students of Latin, no examination
was required in passing from one course to another.
Certain evidence of attendence had, however,
to be presented. In some courses the student
had to show, as a minimum, that he had heard
two lectures, but in other courses a more extensive attendance was required.

[1] "Ego N. juro per Sancta Dei Evangelia corporaliter
per me gratis tacta, quod vobis Domino Rectori meo, et pro
tempore futuro rectoriam exercentibus, et omnibus, et singulis
mandatis vestris in licitis, et honestis obedientiam, et in ne-
gotiis Universitatis, et factis consilium, auxilium et favorem
fideliter præstabo; nec prædicta contra ipsam Universitatem,
seu ejus bonum alteri dabo; et ad vocationem vestram veniam,
toties, quoties fuere requisitus, sic me Deus adjuvet, et hæc
Sancta Dei Evangelia; neque ero in consilio acversus con-
stitutiones, et statuta prædictæ Universitatis."—See Garro,
443.

Like most medieval universities, the University of Cordova was primarily a school of theology. It embraced two faculties, a faculty of arts and a faculty of theology; but the studies of the first— logic, physics, and Aristotelian metaphysics— constituted a preparation for those of the second. A knowledge of Latin was prerequisite for the study of philosophy. Of the study of Latin, here, Dean Funes, later rector of the University, said it was carried on "without that accumulation of trifles which makes the memory groan." It was conducted with great efficiency and profit by excellent instructors. The students acquired familiarity with the best Latin authors, whose writings became their models for compositions both in prose and verse. Having shown their proficiency in this subject by a public examination, they were admitted to the study of philosophy with the faculty of arts. The studies with this faculty were continued for three years. The first year was devoted to the study of logic, the second to physics, and the third to metaphysics. There were two lectures daily of one hour each. The lecturer devoted a quarter of an hour after each lecture to answering questions and solving the difficulties that had arisen in the minds of the students. In the course of time the discipline became more strict, and the attendance of the students was rigidly required. The course of instruction was then concluded with an examination before "five incorruptible judges," and still later, examinations of greater length were held.[1]

After three years of philosophy, the student passed to the study of theology, which was continued at first four years, and later five years and a half. Of this longer period, the student was required to be in residence only three and a half years. At the conclusion of two and a half years of theology, he might receive the degree of master of arts; and at the end of the whole course, the degrees of licentiate and doctor.

Writing of the quality of this instruction, Dr. Funes said that these studies were corrupted with all the vices of their century. Logic suffered notable defects. The ideas of Aristotle obscured by the barbarous comments of the Arabs could not enlighten the reason. Dialectics was a science of vague notions and insignificant terms, better adapted to forming sophisms than to discoursing with effect. Metaphysics presented phantasms which passed for true entities. Physics, full of formalities, quiddities, forms, and secret qualities, explained by these means the most mysterious phenomena of nature.

"Theology was in no better state. Like philosophy it was also corrupted. The philosophy of Aristotle applied to theology, formed a mixture of things

[1] Funes, *Ensayo Historico*, lib. ii, chap. 16; *Primeras Constituciones de la Universidad*; see Garro, Appendix III.

sacred and profane. Theology had abandoned the
study of the Fathers to devote itself to frivolous
and irrelevant questions. Purely human reasoning,
subtleties, deceptive sophism, this was what had
come to form the dominant taste of these schools."[1]

In each of the faculties there were three degrees.
Those of the faculty of arts were bachelor, licentiate, and master. Those of the faculty of theology
were bachelor, licentiate, and doctor, the doctor-
ate of theology being the highest degree conferred
by the University. In order to attain it, it was
necessary, among other things, to pass five "rigor-
ous" examinations. The first of these covered the
first part of the *Summa* of Thomas Aquinas, and
dealt with the subjects, God, predestination, the
trinity, and angels; the second, beatitude, good
and evil, laws, sin, and grace; the third, faith,
hope, and charity, contracts and restitution;
the fourth, incarnation, sacraments, penitence,
and the eucharist, the third part of the *Summa;*
the fifth was called the *ignaciana,* in recognition
of the patron saint, and lasted five hours, divided
between the morning and afternoon.

The student having completed the courses of
study required for the degree which he sought,
there remained only the ceremony of his promotion. If he was to be a doctor, this ceremony
began with a public procession, in which all the
doctors, masters, and invited guests appeared

[1] Funes, i., lib. 2, chap. 16.

mounted, with all the insignia pertaining to their rank. In the afternoon of the day preceding the final ceremony, the procession passed to the house of the candidate, in whose doorway was placed, under a canopy, the standard of the University, showing not only the arms of the University but also the arms of the student to be promoted. A shield also bearing his arms was placed near the standard. At the hour designated, the procession moved. It was led by the musicians and the beadle carrying the burnished mace, followed by the standard-bearers and the masters, among whom was the secretary; then the doctors in their gowns and hoods, the city council, the principal citizens of the city; and, at the end of the procession, the candidate in a white gown, but without a cap, between the eldest doctor and the *padrino*. Formed in this order, the procession passed through the principal streets of the city, following an itinerary determined beforehand, and returned to the starting-point, leaving the candidate at his house, "where," the record says, "he awaited with infinite anxieties the emotions of the following day."

On this day the candidate was conducted by the same procession to the place where he was to receive his degree, usually the church of the Jesuits adjoining the University where a tribune had been erected for the doctors, masters, and

other graduates. In front of this tribune, under
a canopy, were placed the royal arms; at the
right of them the arms of the bishop or of the
person who might confer the degree in his name;
on the left the arms of the University, and, a
little lower, those of the candidate. On a table
also in front of the tribune were placed the insignia of the doctor, the bible, and the *propinas*,
which were required in case of granting the degree
in question. "Considering the rich hangings, the
luxurious carpets, the splendid chairs, the flowers,
and the perfumes, one will have an approximate
idea of the improvised temple of Minerva."

When the members of the company had taken
their seats in the order of their ages, the *padrino*
went up to the speaker's stand and proposed a
question for the candidate to discuss. At the conclusion of the candidate's discourse the beadles
accompanied the *padrino* to his seat. The master
or doctor who had to reply took the speaker's
place and made his criticism, which lasted about
half an hour. This address was not an extempora-
neous criticism, but it had been prepared beforehand by the rector or by some person appointed
by him, and committed to memory by the speaker.
At the close of this reply, the beadles conducted
the *padrino* from his seat to the table, where he
presented the candidate to the bishop or the person
who was to confer the degree, who now made a
brief address, to which the candidate or one of

the doctors replied. The candidate then knelt before the bishop and took the oath that was required as a part of the ceremony of granting the doctor's degree. He afterwards made the confession of faith, the form of which was a part of the fundamental law of the University. The degree was conferred by placing on the candidate's head the cap with the tassel, and the bishop or the person conferring the degree made use of the appropriate formula established by law.[1]

The *padrino* performed the rest of the ceremony. He first bestowed the kiss of peace on the candidate's cheek, with the formula, *accipe osculum pacis in signum fraternitatis et amicitiæ*. Then he placed a ring on his finger saying: *accipe annulum aureum in signum conjugii inter te et sapientiam tamquam sponsam clarissimam*. Finally he handed to him the *Maestro de las Sentencias*, saying: *accipe librum sapientiæ, ut possis libere et publice alios docere*.

The final scene of this ceremony may be presented in the language of the law:

" The degree having been conferred, the *padrino* shall come with the new doctor, who will be embraced by the rector, or the person who confers the degree; then by the doctors and masters in their order; first those on the right, then those on the left, and finally by the *padrino*. Afterwards they shall take their seats, the *padrino* on the

[1] See Garro, 438.

left of the rector, and the new doctor on the right, while the *propinas* and the gloves are distributed. This last act concluded, the procession will return and leave the new doctor at his house."[1]

The *propinas*, it may be said in explanation of the use of the term here, are the fees paid to certain persons who participate in the procession and other parts of the ceremony. The payment of these fees is imposed as an obligation on the candidate for graduation. They were established under the supposed necessity of furnishing compensation for the loss of time and the expenses incurred by the graduates and officers of the University who took part in the ceremony. They varied with the degrees conferred. For the doctor of theology they were more than for the lower degrees. The new doctor was, moreover, required to pay most of the expenses of his graduation, even the cost of arranging and decorating the places of meeting.

There were other expenses that fell to the graduate, particularly for clerical work for which the secretary received payment. But a reference to the fees required is sufficient to indicate that graduation involved an expenditure which many students would find it difficult, if not impossible, to meet. This fact was recognized, and an effort

[1] *Primeras Constituciones de la Universidad, Constitucion* 52; see Garro, 421.

was made to establish such provisions as would secure to every student, however poor, an opportunity to acquire a degree. This was found to be difficult without making the student's poverty the object of public attention.

In the university community, on the occasion of any public exercise, great care was taken to have a definite and well-established order of precedence observed. The licentiates and doctors in theology preceded the masters in arts, who in their turn preceded the bachelors in arts. The minor distinctions in dress made observable any departure from this rule of precedence. After beginning the studies in arts or philosophy all students were required to wear the clerical dress, and without complying with this requirement no one would be approved for any degree in theology. Any one who would have a doctor's degree from the University, whether intending to be a priest or not, was obliged to wear the clerical dress, and this was, in fact, since the instructors were Jesuits, the only dress that was worn in the University.

At first when there were no strictly enforced requirements concerning attendance and examinations, the results of the instruction were unsatisfactory. The students gave little or no attention to any subjects except those on which they were to be examined for their degrees. They passed from one course to another with a very imperfect knowledge of the subjects supposed to constitute a necessary introduction to the course before them. When they found themselves near the final examination, a few undertook to repair their deficiencies by assiduous effort, but the majority found that the career of a scholar had not the attractions they fancied, and turned away to other pursuits. The evil of this state of things clearly demanded correction, and this was attempted, in 1680, by lengthening the course to ten months, and insisting on attendance. Annual examinations were established three years later, and it became necessary to pass them with approval in order to be advanced to the succeeding courses. This tightening of the lines of discipline led to acts of insubordination on the part of the students. That in an institution of learning they should be required to listen to lectures and pass examinations seemed to them an interference with their rights as students, and they instituted a rebellion. The *claustro*, however, firmly supported the other authorities, and the two leaders of the rebellion were expelled, and order restored.

In the course of the eighteenth century, the number of students was greatly increased. They came not only from Tucuman, but also from Rio de la Plata, Paraguay, and even from Chile and Peru. When, in the course of time, they had acquired their degrees and, in considerable numbers, attended the ceremonies of graduation, the *propinas*, or fees, which the candidates had to pay, became a greatly increased burden. In order to avoid the payment of these fees many students took their certificates of record and applied for degrees at other universities, in Chili, Chuquisaca, and Cuzco. But others, who wished neither to bear the expense nor to undertake the long and difficult journey over the mountains, retired from the University without taking a degree. To set aside the inconvenience of the burdensome fees, it was provided that they should be reduced by one third of their several amounts. Even this reduction left them so great as to make the degree quite beyond the reach of the majority of the students; and more and more of them took advantage of the special provisions that had been made for the poor. This was regarded as an abuse of a privilege, and steps were taken to limit the number to three annually in each course who might be graduated under these provisions. Somewhat later greater liberality was shown to candidates coming from Buenos Aires and Paraguay.

The primary purpose of the University in the mind of the founder, a Franciscan friar, was instruction in theology, to prepare young men for service in the Church. In keeping with this design, the fundamental law of 1664 provided that the taking of holy orders was a prerequisite for receiving the degree of doctor. One hundred years later, in 1764, seven candidates were absolved from this requirement, and were given their degrees, but under certain other restrictions. This was the beginning of a liberal policy with respect to graduates, and it was made more liberal after the Franciscans came into control of the University on the expulsion of the Jesuits. By the end of the eighteenth century all restrictions of this kind with respect to graduation had been swept away. In the meantime, another restriction had come into force. The early law did not raise the question of the legitimacy or illegitimacy of the candidate. When, therefore, in 1710, a person of illegitimate birth applied for a degree, it was conferred upon him, since there was no special prohibition touching the subject. It was, however, later definitely provided by the *claustro* that no degree should be given by the University to any person who was not of legitimate birth and whose legitimacy had not been established.

The expulsion of the Jesuits effected important changes in the affairs of the University. The *Instructions* of March 1, 1767, framed by the Count of Aranda, required that, in the towns which might have houses or seminaries of education, secular priests should be substituted for the Jesuit directors and masters, that the schools and seminaries should be continued by these

11

substitutes, and that the instructors who were not priests should remain and continue their instruction. The provisions of Aranda's instructions were, however, not carried out, and the places of the Jesuits were filled by Franciscans, apparently in direct violation of the royal will. After the departure of the Jesuits, the independence which the University had enjoyed under their administration was in a large measure lost. The superior authority in its affairs became vested in the governor of Buenos Aires, and afterwards in the viceroy. By virtue of his powers as vice-patron, he appointed the rector and the professors and almost immediately the institution began to experience the baneful effects of its political dependence. The first evidence of political scheming was the project to have the University transferred from Cordova to Buenos Aires. Aranda opposed this project, and begged the king to allow the University to remain in Cordova; and when the arguments for and against removal had been considered by the council of the Indies, the conclusion was that it should remain in Cordova, as being there in the most central position. At the same time the king and his council decided that the peculiar doctrines of Jesuits and their books should be excluded from the instruction. In another respect, the University suffered from its political connection. The viceroy interfered in the internal affairs, and sought to set aside in certain cases the established prerequisites for graduation. In the presence of these attempts at political aggression, the *claustro* stood stoutly for the rights of the University, although the rector affirmed that he was compelled to act in accordance with the will of his superior. As a political appointee the ancient virtue of independence had gone out of him.

The question as to the fees to be paid by the graduate continued to engage the attention of the university community. In spite of all previous reforms, they still remained, in 1780, sufficiently burdensome to prevent many persons from receiving degrees. Finally it was decreed that there should be certain fixed sums for the several degrees, and the sum pertaining to any given degree had to be paid into the treasury of the University before the degree sought would be granted. The parts due individual persons under the regulations were then distributed, and the balance remained in the treasury. The amount to be paid by the doctor was two hundred and fifty dollars.[1] These regulations continued in force with unimportant modifications until the final abolition of the system of fees.

For nearly two hundred years, through all the petty discussions as to forms and fees, the intellectual horizon of the University remained unchanged. Latin, Philosophy, Theology, these

[1] See Garro, 153-156.

constituted the whole world of thought which the student was invited to survey; not the philosophy or theology of an enlightened age, but the semi-barbarous discussions that went under the name of Aristotle, and theology as set forth by Thomas Aquinas. There was no library to which the students might be directed to pursue free inquiries; on the contrary, they were practically confined to their notes written as dictated by the lecturer.

The first important step out of the depths of medievalism was the introduction of the study of jurisprudence, in 1791. A practical beginning was made by establishing a professorship of the *Institutes*. With this the University ceased to be purely theological; yet it was the last of the universities in Spanish America to depart from its primary plan. Gradually other chairs in law were established and the University acquired the right to confer the degrees of bachelor, licentiate, and doctor of civil law. The first degree of doctor of civil law was conferred in 1797.

A contest between the Franciscans and the secular clergy for the control of the University marked the last forty years of its history under the old régime. As clearly indicated, the *Instructions* of the Count of Aranda, of March 1, 1767, ordered that the Jesuits should be replaced by members of the secular clergy. In spite of this expression of the royal will, Bucareli, the governor of Rio

de la Plata, handed over the government of the
University and of the affiliated college of Montserrat to the Franciscans. By this the expectations and aspirations of the secular clergy were
defeated. They, therefore, began a struggle to
acquire the authority which their rivals had
usurped. This little war brought into the dull
and monotonous life of Cordova a subject that
interested everybody; but, in spite of the arguments and appeals to the law, the Franciscans
held their position. The governor favored them,
and his support was more immediately effective
than the will of the king in opposition. In 1800,
the subject was finally before the council of the
Indies, and that body rendered a decision justi-
fying the claims of the secular clergy. The
decree was issued on the first of December of that
year. It had the form of a new act of foundation.
The sovereign resolved that there should be
founded and erected anew in the city of Cordova,
in the edifice which belonged to the *Colegio
Maximo* of the Jesuits, "a greater university with
the privileges and prerogatives which are enjoyed
by institutions of this class in Spain and the Indies
with the title of Royal University of San Carlos
and of Our Lady of Montserrat." The decree
also provided that "the Franciscans should be
separated from the government and direction
of the new university, as had been established
by the royal resolution of 1778." The rector,

vice-rector, and treasurer, and the other officials were to be appointed by the *claustro*. This action appeared to involve the immediate overthrow of the friars, but the political authorities of Buenos Aires again came to their rescue, and succeded in burying the decree in the archives of the viceroyalty. Its resurrection was, however, effected seven years later by Liniers, who, on November 29, 1807, ordered that it should be carried into effect immediately. The reorganization introduced by the decree of 1800 made the beginning of a new period in the history of the University. Henceforth the University of Cordova was to be regarded as having the same standing as the renowned universities of Salamanca and Alcala de Henares, in Spain, and the universities of Mexico and Lima in America. But before it had fully entered upon this later period of its career, Spain's domination had ceased, and the inhabitants of Rio de la Plata had undertaken to form an independent republic.

CHAPTER VIII

AN OFFICIAL REPORT ON THE INDIANS

THE foundations of the viceroyalty of Buenos Aires were scarcely laid before the southern part of the continent was startled by a great popular uprising. The Indians of Upper Peru had at last turned upon their aggressors, and sought relief under arms. With the results of the rebellion before us, we are able to see clearly what the Indians themselves dimly discerned, that the resort to force carried little hope of success, but it was the only hope the Indians had of attaining the conditions of even a tolerable existence. What their actual state was, which furnished the motive and reason of revolt, has almost entirely passed out of the mind of this generation; and if a writer of the twentieth century, not greatly influenced by Spain's ancient political or ecclesiastical ideals, should tell plainly the story of the Indians under the colonial administration, he would hardly be believed. He would run the risk of having his statements attributed to ignorance or prejudice. If, however, loyal Spaniards and devoted churchmen speak of what they saw and what their personal investigations revealed, their report ought to be accepted. Fortunately we are able to listen to the testimony of two Spanish witnesses whose distinguished scholarly and scientific attainments, and whose attachment to the interests of the Church and the government have not been questioned. They are George Juan and Antonio Ulloa, and under the king's orders they wrote of their observations and investigations during their residence in Ecuador and Peru just before the middle of the eighteenth century. During the whole of the last half of the century, the king and his council of the Indies had before them this report, which was finally published in London about a hundred years after it was written. It is the famous *Noticias Secretas de America*. Although it brought to the king unimpeachable evidence of the oppression and misery the Indians were suffering at the hands of the officials and the clergy, he refused to spread abroad the information contained in the report, or to make it the basis of the needed reforms. This refusal was not, however, an indication of sympathy with the abuses practised in America; on the contrary, it was simply the result of weakness, of lack of courage, of helplessness in the presence of the impending fall of a great governmental structure that had been wrecked by the avarice and incapacity of those immediately in charge of it.

The writers of this report maintain that the oppression under which the Indians were living arose from an inordinate desire for wealth on the part of their rulers. The system which required the corregidors to collect the tribute, and gave them the exclusive right to trade with the Indians within their several districts, furnished these officers an opportunity to make burdensome exactions. The chiefs as well as the Indian governors were exempt from the tribute, as were also those Indians under a certain age, and those over a certain other age; but these limits were not respected, and what was collected from persons legally exempt from the tribute the *corregidor* might hold without being detected, since it was over and above what was required of him under the law. The mita Indians, those subjected to forced labor, did not pay in person directly to the *corregidor*, but the tribute required of them was paid by the masters, who collected it from the Indians in their service; and those living in small villages paid their cacique, who turned over the whole amount collected to the *corregidor*. Besides the exemptions intended by the law, it was further provided that Indians who had been absent from their district for short periods, one or two years, on returning should pay only one third of the regular contribution for the time of their absence. This provision of the law was, however, not observed, and the returning

Indians were made to pay the full amount that would have been due if they had not been absent; and two thirds of this amount might be held by the *corregidor* as not legally required from him for the public treasury. When it is remembered that the *corregidors* collected tribute from Indians temporarily in their districts, it will be seen that, under this practice, such as were temporarily absent from their homes were obliged to pay double tribute for the years of their absence.

The monopoly of trade held by the *corregidor* in his district enabled him to prevent the Indians from continuing in their accustomed occupation. He took them into his service, with barely sufficient payment for their support, and thus received the profits which the Indians themselves had received before this interference. Where the Indians were weavers, the *corregidor* gave them the materials and very reduced wages, and received the profits of their labor as if they were slaves. But while keeping them constantly employed under conditions where gains on their part were practically out of the question, he still exacted from them the tribute money; and as long as this was not paid they might not leave his service. Inasmuch as the *corregidor* exercised almost absolute power in his district, the Indians had no redress. If they appealed to the courts, they were ruined. To meet the costs of the suit, they were obliged to give up a mule or a cow, which furnished their principal means of support. "These acts of extortion, which have no limit, have reduced them to a condition so deplorable that the state of the most poor and miserable beings that can be imagined is not to be compared with that of the Indians."[1]

The Indians were also under the oppressive system of *repartimientos*, which made the office of *corregidor* a district commissariat. In organizing this system it was thought that an intelligent European would be able to supply the Indians with those things which they might need, but which they would not be likely to have on hand when needed, on account of their lack of foresight; therefore,

"it was ordered that the corregidors might introduce a quantity of such articles as were suited to each district and distribute them among the Indians at moderate prices, in order that, having implements for labor, they might shake off the apathy which is innate in their constitution, and make the exertion requisite for paying their tribute and supporting themselves."[2]

The principal error of the system was that it required for successful execution *corregidors* content with moderate profits. It presumed, moreover, that they would be sufficiently intelligent to discern the real needs of the Indians.

[1] Juan and Ulloa, *Noticias Secretas*, 239.
[2] *Ibid.*, 239.

The tyrannical application of this system is described in the report:

" The articles of distribution are chiefly mules, foreign and domestic goods, and produce. The corregidors who are attached to the viceroyalty of Lima must necessarily go to that city to take out a license, and to receive their despatch from the viceroy, in order to be inducted into office; and as Lima is the principal depot of the trade of Peru, it is in that city that an assortment of articles for distribution is to be made, and for this purpose they take the goods required from the shop of some merchant or trader on credit, at an exorbitant price; for, as the traders are aware of the enormous profits the corregidors make in the sale, they raise the prices of the goods, in order to have a share in the speculation. The corregidors have no money before they come into office, and, being unable to purchase for cash, they are obliged to submit to any terms which the creditor may prescribe, since they are under great obligations, on account of the money which the merchant is to lend them for the purchase of the mules required for transportation.

" As soon as the corregidor comes within his jurisdiction, the first act of his administration is to take a census of the Indians according to their towns and villages. Proceeding to this duty in person, and taking with him the articles of merchandise to be distributed, he goes on, apportioning the quantity and kind he selects for every Indian, and affixing to each article its price, just as suits his caprice, the poor Indians being wholly ignorant of what is to fall to their lot, or how much it is to cost them. As soon as he has finished distributing in one village, he transfers the whole assortment to the cacique, with an exact inventory of the articles belonging to each individual, from the cacique himself to the most humble of all those who are to pay tribute; and the corregidor proceeds to another village, in order to continue the distribution. It is a time of anguish, both to the cacique and the Indians, when they look at the quantity, quality, and prices of these goods. In vain does the cacique remonstrate and to no purpose do the Indians raise their clamors; on the one hand, they maintain that their means are not adequate to such a quantity of merchandise as is assigned to them, being absolutely unable to pay for it; again, they urge that goods of such a description are utterly useless to them, and that the prices are so exorbitant as to exceed anything they had ever paid before. The corregidor remains inexorable, and the Indians are obliged to take whatever has been allotted them, however repugnant it may be to their wishes, and however straitened they are for want of means to make the payments; for these payments become due simultaneously with the tribute money, and the same penalty is imposed for failure to meet one as the other. All the payments of the first distribution must be made within two years and a half, to make way then for the second, which usually does not contain as many wares as the first."[1]

Whenever the *corregidor* goes to collect debts

[1] Juan and Ulloa, *Noticias Secretas*, 240, 241.

he takes with him other goods, and those Indians who have made their payments most promptly are now required to receive another allotment. The least useful wares are given out in the first distribution, in order that the Indians may be more ready to receive those of the second, and in the second distribution they are permitted to select the articles they will take, but the prices are fixed. The Indians are not allowed to get the desired articles elsewhere, and no shop is permitted in the village but that of the *corregidor*.

A large item in the *corregidor's* trade is the distribution of mules. They are allotted to the Indians not in accordance with their need of them, but in accordance with their ability to pay for them. They are bought, five or six hundred at a time, at from fourteen to sixteen dollars, and the Indians are obliged to receive them at from forty to forty-four dollars a head. The gains made by the *corregidor* in purchasing and distributing goods often amount to more than four hundred per cent. of the cost. If the Indian would hire out the mules, he must first obtain the consent of the *corregidor*, which means that the *corregidor* must be permitted to have part of the earnings. When hired out for transporting goods

" the corregidor himself collects the amount of the freight charges, keeps back one half on account of the debt, delivers a quarter part to the owner of

the mules to pay what may be needed for the purchase of hay to feed the animals on the road, and
with the remaining fourth part he pays the peons,
whose office is to drive and lade the mules; so that,
in consequence of this arbitrary distribution, the
owner is left not only without any profit, but even
without the means of making his expenses on the
journey."[1]

Of the quarter part held for the peons, one half
is deducted as part payment of what the peon
owes the *corregidor*. Even if there were no
recorded proof of the avarice and injustice of the
corregidors, they

" might be inferred from the consideration that all of
them go from Spain to the Indies so destitute that,
instead of carrying anything thither, they are in debt
on account of obligations contracted from the time
they leave Spain until they reach the district allotted
to them; and that, during their brief term of office,
which is limited to five years, they make a gain of
at least sixty thousand dollars, and many accumulate
even more than two hundred thousand. This is to
be understood as the net profits, after having paid
their previous debts and fees of settlement, and
after having spent and squandered beyond all bounds
during the whole term of their administration; for
the salary and emoluments of their office are so
scanty as to be almost inadequate for their current
expenses."[2]

[1] Juan and Ulloa, *Noticias Secretas*, 243.
[2] *Ibid.*, 253.

Protests made by the Indians did not bring them relief from these abuses, but sometimes resulted in their punishment as seditious persons. Yet in being compelled to purchase goods which they could not use, they had abundant reasons for protesting, and as the courts furnished no way of escape, the Indians' only hope lay in armed revolt, and such revolts in the eighteenth century begun or threatened kept the government in a state of anxiety and alarm.

The *residencia*, or official investigation, of the *corregidor*, at the close of his administration, failed to attain the end designed, by reason of collusion among the officers concerned.

" When the judge appointed to make the investigation arrives at the principal town of the corregidor's district, he gives public notice of his business, goes through the usual forms, receiving testimony from the friends and domestics of the corregidor that he has ruled well, that he has injured no man, that he has treated the Indians kindly, and in this way he collects all the evidence which may redound to the interest of the corregidor. But lest such a degree of rectitude and benevolence might excite surprise, three or four persons are employed to present trivial charges against him, which are substantiated by summoning witnesses to testify to their truth, and the accused, being brought in guilty, is fined in an amount proportioned to the offence. In the course of these proceedings, an immense mass of writs and documents is collected, and the time prescribed for auditing the accounts gradually slips away, when they are closed and presented to the audiencia for approval, and the corregidor is as legally innocent of the charges as he was at the time his administration began, and the judge who conducted the *residencia* is a gainer to the amount of what the settlement has been worth to him."[1]

In some cases the new officer investigated his predecessor, and reported a clean record in consideration of a certain amount of money paid. If Indians who had suffered at the hands of the *corregidors* presented charges they were made to withdraw them by such means as might be employed by the accused or the judge.

" If charges are made by Spaniards relative to other matters, the judge acts as umpire, and urges them to settle their differences amicably, and forget injuries that are past; but if this method fails, the suit goes on, and, as the judge is biassed in favor of the corregidor, he always labors to acquit him; and if he cannot do it by himself, he appeals to the audiencia; and as all his investigations are so arranged as to present the best evidence in his favor, a little exertion on his part is quite sufficient to have the corregidor acquitted, and his accounts settled agreeably to his wishes."[2]

The wealth yielded by the American colonies,

---

[1] Juan and Ulloa, *Noticias Secretas*, 255.
[2] *Ibid.*, 257.

from the mines, the plantations, or the cattle ranges, came through the labor of the Indians, yet their state was not improved nor their enjoyment increased by the production. On the estates their work was required for three hundred days in the year, for which they were paid as a maximum annual salary eighteen dollars. The tribute of eight dollars, paid by the owner of the estate, was deducted from this amount, leaving ten dollars as the effective annual income.

" From this sum, two dollars and two reals are to be deducted, to buy three yards of cloth, at six reals a yard, that he may make a shirt for himself, as decency requires, and he will have the remaining seven dollars six reals, to maintain himself and his wife and children, if he have any, besides clothing them and paying such contributions as the curate may levy upon him. Nor is this all, for the piece of ground allowed him is so confined that it becomes impossible for him to raise all the corn required for the scanty support of his family, and he is obliged to receive from the owner of the estate half a bushel of corn monthly, which is charged to him at six reals (more than double the usual price), because the Indian cannot purchase of any one else; thus twelve times six reals make nine dollars, which is one dollar and two reals more than the Indian can earn; so that the wretched serf, after toiling three hundred days in the year, besides cultivating a garden of vegetables in the remaining sixty-five, having received only a shirt of coarse cloth and six bushels of corn, becomes indebted to his master one dollar and two reals, on account of the labor he has to perform the following year. Were it no more than this, the patient Indian would endure it all; but his sufferings are yet greater. It frequently happens (as we have witnessed) that an animal dies in the *paramo*, or heath; the master has it brought to the farm, and, in order not to lose its value, has it cut to pieces, and distributes it to the Indians at so much a pound—a price which, however reasonable, an Indian cannot pay, and hence his debt is augmented by being forced to receive meat which is unfit to be eaten, owing to its bad condition, and which he is consequently obliged to throw to the dogs.

" If, as the climax of misfortune, the unfortunate *mitayo* should lose his wife, or one of his children, the cup of his anguish is full when he reflects how he shall pay the inexorable fee of interment, and he is driven to enter into a new contract with the owner of the estate, to furnish him the money extorted by the Church. If he escapes the anguish of losing any of his family, the curate orders him to celebrate a church festival in honor of the Virgin, or one of the saints, and he is obliged on this account to contract a new debt; so that, at the close of the year, his debts exceed his earnings, while he has neither handled money nor got in his possession any articles of value whatever. His master claims the right of his person, obliges him to continue in his service until the debt is paid; and as payment can never be made by the poor Indian, he becomes a slave for life; and, in defiance of all natural and national law, children are required to pay, by their personal services, the un-avoidable debts of their parents."[1]

When the price of corn rose in an unfruitful season, and the prices of all other products rose also, the wages of the *mitayo* remained unchanged. The high price induced the master to sell where he had a prospect of immediate payment, and thus the Indians were left without even the usual oppor-tunities of procuring food. But whatever hard-ships the Indians endured on the plantations, the cattle ranges, and the wool-growing estates, it was in the factories that their lot was hardest. In the factories cloths and woollen stuffs were woven by hand.

" In former years, the woollen manufactory was con-fined to the province of Quito; but it has been re-cently introduced into other districts, although the articles manufactured in the provinces south of Quito are nothing but coarse cloths of very ordinary texture.   In Cajamarca, there are looms for the manufacture of cotton goods."[2]

" The labor of the *obraje*, or factory, begins before the day dawns, at which time every Indian takes his place at the piece which is in process of weaving and the tasks of the day are distributed as may be expedient; and when this process is concluded, the owner of the house closes the door, and leaves them immured as in a prison. At midday the door is

---

[1] Juan and Ulloa, *Noticias Secretas*, 268–270.
[2] *Ibid.*, 275.

opened for the women to go in with their scanty allowance of food, which is soon partaken, and they are
again locked in. When the darkness of the night no
longer permits them to work, the owner goes round
to gather up the stints; those who have not been
able to finish, in spite of apologies or reasonings,
are punished with indescribable cruelty: and those
unfeeling men, as if transformed into merciless
savages, inflict upon the wretched Indians lashes by
hundreds, for they use no other method of counting;
and to complete the punishment, they remand them
again to the workshop, and although the whole
building is a prison-house, a portion of it is reserved
for fetters and instruments of torture, where they
are punished with greater indignity than could be
practised towards the most delinquent slaves." [1]

Those found delinquent during the day by the
overseer were chastised with a whip at once, and
also reserved for punishment later. All the
delinquencies were noted and charged to the
account of the laborer. From year to year they
became more and more deeply in debt, "until,
finding it impossible to make up their arrears,
the master acquired a right, however unfounded,
to reduce to slavery not only the mita Indian, but
all his sons." [2] Those sentenced to the factories
by the *corregidors* for failing to pay the tribute
underwent even greater cruelties. The food they
were able to get, partly rotten corn and barley

[1] Juan and Ulloa, *Noticias Secretas*, 276.
[2] *Ibid.*, 277.

and the meat of cattle that died, was inadequate for their support. Consequently

" their constitution being exhausted partly for want of nourishment, partly by repeated punishment, as well as by diseases contracted from the bad quality of their food, they die before they have been able to pay the tribute with the avails of their labor.   Such is the spectacle exhibited, when they are taken out dead, that it would excite compassion in the most unfeeling heart.   Only a skeleton remains of them to publish the cause which doomed them to perish; and the greater part of these die in the very factories with their tasks in their hands."[1]

The practice of condemning the Indians to the workshop, for slight offences, became very general.

" We frequently meet Indians on the highway, tied by the hair to the tail of a horse, on which a mestizo is mounted, who is conveying them to the workshops, and perhaps for the trivial offence of having evaded the tyranny of the overseer, from fear of punishment. Let what will be said of the cruelty practised by the patrons (*encomenderos*) towards the Indians at the commencement of the conquest, we cannot persuade ourselves, after what we have witnessed, that it could ever have been carried to the extent it now is by the Spaniards and mestizos."[2]

The statement that, without the forced labor

[1] Juan and Ulloa, *Noticias Secretas*, 277, 278.
[2] *Ibid.*, 279.

of the mita, the Indians would have remained idle and the plantations have fallen into ruin, is sufficiently answered by the flourishing condition of those estates where the mita was not observed, and where a slight advance of wages over those paid under the mita gave to such plantations all the labor desired. If the Indians were reluctant to labor, this was no doubt in part due to the treatment which they received at the hands of their employers. Of what they accomplished by their work under other conditions sufficient remains to excite our admiration, and to furnish evidence of extraordinary activity. Moreover,

" all the free Indians cultivate the lands belonging to them with so much care, that they leave no portion of them fallow. It is true that their arable lands are circumscribed; but it is because they are not allowed to possess more, and not for want of care and toil to render them productive. The caciques, who have a larger portion assigned them, lay out extensive planting-grounds, rear cattle according to their means and opportunities, and husband all they can, without being compelled by force, and without using compulsion towards those who labor for them." [1]

On the plantations, as well as in the factories, there were three taskmasters who had constant supervision over the workers. These were the overseer, his assistant, and foreman. The last

[1] Juan and Ulloa, *Noticias Secretas*, 288.

was always an Indian, and while, like the rest, he carried a whip, he was not accustomed to strike those under him.

" Each taskmaster holds his own scourge without letting it fall from his hand the whole day long: this instrument of torture resembles a rope's end, about a yard long, and a little less than a finger in thickness, and is made of cow's hide, twisted like a cord. In case the Indian has been guilty of any wrong or neglect, he is required to lie flat on his face, when his thin drawers, which make up his whole dress, are taken off, and he is scourged with the rod, being himself obliged to count the lashes that are inflicted upon him, until the number prescribed in the sentence has been completed. He then gets up, and is required to kneel in presence of the man with the whip, and, kissing his hand, to say to him, 'May God bless you!' the trembling lips of the wretched Indian thus giving thanks in the name of God for the stripes inflicted upon him, almost always unjustly. Nor are men alone subject to punishment, but their wives and children, and even the caciques, whose rank and dignity entitle them to consideration.

" The practice of scourging the Indians so unmerci-fully is not confined to the factories, plantations, and mita Indians, but the priests chastize their parishioners, and exact any service from them what-ever by dint of blows; for if the Indian should not do promptly what is required of him, it is deemed sufficient motive to make him lie down, and to inflict stripes upon him with a whip, or with the reins of the horse, until his strength is exhausted."[1]

But the punishment of the Indians was not confined to floggings of this kind. "The most insatiable spirit of revenge has never been able to invent any species of punishment which the Indian does not receive at the hand of the Spaniards."[2]

The hardships which the Indians suffered were not alone the results of corporal punishments received. Their property was often the spoil of the Spaniard. In laying out the townships certain portions were allotted to the caciques and Indians belonging to the township, but

"avarice has gradually curtailed them to such a degree, that the tracts which remain to them are circumscribed within narrow limits, and the greater part has been wrested from them altogether. Some Indians have been despoiled of their lands by violence; others, because the owners of the neighboring estates have compelled them to sell at any price they may choose to give; and others because they have been induced to surrender them under false pretences."[3]

While the parish priests should have been the protectors of the Indians against the unrighteous extortions of the *corregidors*, they, instead of

[1] Juan and Ulloa, *Noticias Secretas*, 289, 290.
[2] *Ibid.*, 291.   [3] *Ibid.*, 295.

this, went hand in hand with them in wresting from the poor Indian the fruit of his incessant toil.

" As soon as the parish priests are promoted to their cures, they usually bend all their efforts to amassing wealth; and for this purpose they have devised various measures, by which they appropriate to themselves the pittance which may have remained to the Indian, and which has escaped the rapacity of the corregidor." [1]

There were the fees on the occasion of a saint's festival, the four dollars and a half for high mass,

" and an equal amount for the sermon, which consists in merely repeating a few words in praise of the.saint ";
" to this is to be added the customary offering which the overseers are compelled to make to the curate on every saint's festival, which consists of two or three dozen hens, as many chickens, guinea-pigs, eggs, sheep, and a hog if they happen to have any; so that when the saint's day arrives, the curate sweeps off all that the Indian has been able to collect in money during the whole year, and also all the fowls and animals which his wife and children have reared in their huts, so that his family are left wholly destitute of food, or have no other aliment than wild roots or plants which they cultivate in their small gardens. The Indian who has not been able to rear a sufficient number of animals for the customary offering is

[1] Juan and Ulloa, *Noticias Secretas*, 335.

bound of necessity to purchase them, and should he not have the money, as is usually the case, he is to take it upon pledge, or hire it for the time required, in order to obtain it and pay it without delay. As soon as the sermon of the day is concluded, the curate reads a paper on which he has inscribed the names of those who are to be masters of ceremonies for the festival of the following year, and if any one does not accept it of his free will, he is forced to give his consent by dint of blows; and when his day comes, there is no apology that can exonerate him from having the money ready; for, until it is all collected and delivered to the curate, mass is not said, the sermon is not preached, and the whole service is deferred until three or four in the afternoon, if necessary, to allow time to collect the amount, as we have had occasion to observe repeatedly.

" In order to be more thoroughly acquainted with the excess to which this is carried, and the enormous gains made by the curates at these festivals, it seems proper to mention here what a curate of the province of Quito told us as we were passing through his curacy, which was, that, including the festivals and the commemoration of departed souls, he collected every year more than two hundred sheep, six thousand hens and chickens, four thousand guinea-pigs, and fifty thousand eggs; and it should be re-marked that this curacy was not one of the most lucrative.

" We are then forced to the conclusion that such contributions could be sustained in no way but by tasking to the uttermost not only men and women, but the whole family, in order to exact the payment of the sum total of their earnings during the whole year." [1]

When the Indian boys and girls came every afternoon to be taught the Christian doctrine, they were required to bring bundles of sticks or hay, and by this means fuel was provided, as well as feed for the cattle and horses that belonged to the priests.

" By having recourse to such methods, they have no occasion to spend money for anything; and while they are maintained by the Indians, they become rich at their expense, for all the offerings they can accumulate are sent to market in the neighboring cities, hamlets, and mining towns, and are converted into money. By this means, they augment the revenue of a curacy to such a degree, that although the customary fees might not exceed seven or eight hundred dollars, it gives them an income of five or six thousand dollars annually." [2]

But the oppression appears to have been carried to its utmost bounds by the monks who held curacies, and not only by the monk but also by his concubine.

" This woman, who is known as such, and without exciting surprise, because it is everywhere so common, takes under her charge all the Indian women and children, and converting the whole village into a

[1] Juan and Ulloa, *Noticias Secretas*, 336, 337.
[2] *Ibid.*, 338.

manufactory, she assigns to some tasks in spinning wool or cotton, and to others pieces for weaving; and to the aged, and to those who are incapable of performing this service, she gives hens, and imposes on them the obligation of delivering to her, within a definite time, ten or twelve chickens for each one; it being their duty to feed them at their own expense and, if the fowls should die, to replace them with others; and by these means no one is exempted from contributing something to the revenue of the curate.'' [1]

Moreover, the curate's farm was cultivated by the Indians on Sunday; thus

'' the wretched state of the Indian is to be attributed to the vices of the priests, the extortions of the corregidors, and the bad treatment which they generally receive from all Spaniards.   Unable to endure the hardships, and longing to escape from bondage, many of them have risen in rebellion, and found their way to unconquered districts, there to continue in the barbarous practices of their idolatrous neighbors; and in view of the foregoing, what conclusions are they to form from the scandalous lives of their parish priests? especially when we reflect that the Indian is but partially civilized, and taught rather by example than by precept.''[2]

The Indian town of Pimampiro furnished a case in point.   It contained more than five thousand inhabitants.

[1] Juan and Ulloa, *Noticias Secretas*, 340.
[2] *Ibid.*, 343.

"The behavior of the parish priest drove them to desperation. Uniting in one body, they rose in rebellion, and proceeded by night to the Cordilleras, where they merged themselves with the Gentile Indians, with whom they have continued until the present time." [1]

Similar instances were found in the disappearance of the towns of Lograno and Guariboya.

The Laws of the Indies lay much stress on the religious education of the Indians. A glimpse of the system employed and of the results obtained is presented by our report. At the ceremony of instructing the Indians in Christian doctrine on Sundays,

"all the Indians, male and female, great and small, are to present themselves, and, gathering in the cemetery or square in front of the church, they sit upon the ground, arranged according to age and sex, and the catechising or doctrine commences in the following manner: Each curate employs a blind Indian, whose duty is to repeat the *doctrine* to the rest. The blind Indian is stationed in the centre of them all and, with a kind of recitative, which is neither singing nor prayer, he repeats the collects or offices word for word, and the audience responds in the form of a dialogue. The doctrine is sometimes rehearsed in the language of the Inca (which is that of the Indians), and sometimes in Spanish, which is not intelligible to any of them. This saying of prayers

[1] Juan and Ulloa, *Noticias Secretas*, 343.

lasts somewhat more than half an hour, and it comprises all the religious instruction which is given to the Indians—a method from which they derive so little benefit that old men of seventy know no more than the little Indian boys of the age of six, and neither these nor those have any further instruction than parrots would obtain if they were so taught, for they are neither questioned personally, nor are the mysteries of faith explained to them with the needful simplicity, nor are they examined to see if they understand what they say, nor do they endeavor to make it more intelligible to those who are dull of comprehension. As the whole instruction is confined rather to the tone of the recitative than to the sense of the words it is only by singing that they are able to rehearse detached portions; for, when they are questioned upon any distinct point, they cannot join two words together." [1]

" The curate has no other object in view than to make every one bring the little presents required; and when he has collected these, which consist of what they may happen to have, and has taken a note of those who have failed to bring any, in order afterwards to call them to account, he thinks he is discharged from any further obligation." [2]

At the church festivals, which were followed by orgies of intoxication, the priests did not interfere to preserve order, but were apparently interested only in the gain that was derived from them. In view of the conduct of the Indians at these festivals,

[1] Juan and Ulloa, *Noticias Secretas*, 351.
[2] *Ibid.*, 352.

" their religion does not resemble the Christian religion any more than it resembles that which they had while they were in a state of paganism; for, if we examine the subject with care, it will be found that, notwithstanding the nominal conversion of these tribes, the progress they have made in knowledge is so inconsiderable that it will be difficult to discover any difference between the condition in which they now live and that in which they were found at the time of the Conquest." [1]

In the later years of Spanish rule, after genera_ tions of oppression, it was difficult, from what then might be seen, to form a correct idea of the race as it had been; for the Indians of the better sort had largely perished in the Spanish conquest, or had found it for their interest to ally them-selves with the conquerors, so that those who remained free from any foreign intermixture were the inferior classes, and gave no adequate conception of what the whole people was at the period of its greatest prosperity.   In spite of the legislation in their favor the Indians continued to be the victims of the avarice of the Spaniards. Laws established to define their tasks were dis-regarded, and they suffered the wrongs and bore the burdens which civilized nations have seldom hesitated to impose upon the inferior races.   But here the long subdued rage at last found expression.

[1] Juan and Ulloa, *Noticias Secretas*, 353.

CHAPTER IX

THE INDIAN REVOLT UNDER TUPAC AMARU

IN some respects, as already indicated, the
Indians were treated worse than slaves, since
they had no master who was economically interested in their preservation. But the grievances
which they suffered were not due to any action
decreed by the king, but rather to the malevolence
of officials in America, who did not comply with
the king's orders. They were the result of the
tyranny of the *corregidors*, and of the extortions
and other abuses practised by the *curas*, or parish
priests. The *corregidor's* purchases for sale in his
district were not always such as the Indians
would have selected independently. Silk stockings and razors were among the articles they
were obliged to take at extravagant prices; but
silk stockings for men who wore no shoes and
razors for men who had no beards were not
articles of prime necessity.[1]

[1] In the *Memoirs of General Miller*, i., 7, the case is cited
of a "foolish speculator in Europe who had sent out, amongst
other things, a consignment of spectacles, which lay useless
in the stores of a merchant in Lima. After every hope of
disposing of them had failed, in a country in which people

Neither the king nor the viceroy was ignorant of the abuses of the *corregidors*. Circulars and royal orders were issued to prevent them, but they had very little, if any, effect. A report on their abuses issued by authority of the city of Cuzco, in 1768, twenty years after the investigations of Ulloa, showed that during this period the conditions had remained unchanged. The Indian's life was uninterrupted privation and suffering; and he had no hope of a better fate either for his wife or his children. The orders of the supreme government and the decrees of the viceroys brought him no relief, and the infamous conduct of the *corregidors* and the merciless exactions of the priests had become a fixed tradition. The only basis of hope, and that very uncertain, lay in revolt, and this fact furnishes an explanation of the frequent uprisings that appeared in the remote provinces during the colonial period.[1]

The revolt of Tupac Amaru was thus not without its predecessors. He had doubtless long considered his plan, but in 1780 he seized the opportunity for its execution presented by the general dissatis-

---

retain their eyesight unimpaired to a very late period of life, a corregidor was applied to, who, upon issuing an order that no Indian in his district should attend divine service, upon certain festivals, unless ornamented with spectacles, found means to dispose of the whole of them at an enormous profit."

[1] For an account of these uprisings, see Mendiburu, viii., 121-126.

faction and incipient revolutions. Tupac Amaru was born at Tinta in 1742, and was baptized as José Gabriel Condorcanqui. As the son of a chief, more attention was given to his education than to that of most Indian boys. His instructors were two clergymen of Upper Peru, Antonio Lopez, the *cura* of Pampamarca, and Carlos Rodriguez, the *cura* of Yanaoca. While still very young he was admitted to the Jesuit college of San Borja at Cuzco, which had been established to furnish instruction to the sons of Indian chiefs.[1] At the age of eighteen, in 1760, he was married to Micaela Bastides, and before he was twenty he succeeded his father as cacique of Tungasuca, in the province of Tinta, and other villages that overlook the valley of Vilcamayu. His pretension as heir of the Incas was admitted by the Indians, and about 1770 the royal audiencia acknowledged his claim to the marquisate of Oropesa. This honor had been conferred upon his family by Philip II., and now, at the age of twenty-eight, Tupac Amaru was officially declared to be the lineal descendant of the Inca Tupac Amaru who was executed by the viceroy Toledo, in 1571.

The recognition of the young cacique as the representative of the ancient Inca family and as the bearer of a Spanish title of nobility naturally awakened his pride and intensified his sense of the wrongs his people had suffered. The enjoyment

[1] Markham, *Travels in Peru and India*, 135.

by an Indian of the wealth and the dignity
that attached to the marquisate of Oropesa had
been regarded as a source of danger, and it had
been recommended that all claimants to the
marquisate should be obliged to live in Spain.
This recommendation had, however, not been
carried out, and Tupac Amaru remained in his
native district and continued to govern the villages of Tungasuca, Surimani, and Pampamarca.
His administration within this narrow field
showed careful attention to the interests of the
Indians, and made him conspicuous among the
caciques for his practical sense.   He sought to
make the Spaniards of his acquaintance appreciate the unfortunate condition of his countrymen;
and at the same time he did much to relieve their
distresses.   In some cases he paid the tribute of
the poor, and in other cases he supported whole
families that had been reduced to want.[1]   For
several years he tried every available means to
redress the grievances of his people, and when
he finally took up arms against the Spanish
authorities, he did it because no other course
appeared to offer a ray of hope.   He had appealed
to the ecclesiastics and had petitioned the king;
but the opposition of the *corregidors*, in their
immediate control of affairs, was sufficient to
defeat all favorable reforms the king had been
persuaded to order.   The burdens of the Indians

[1] Funes, *Ensayo Historica*, Buenos Aires, 1856, ii., 234.

increased, and hope of peaceful relief disappeared. The resort to arms was a last resort. But even when hostilities had been determined upon, the end sought was not independence from Spain,

" but to obtain some guarantee for the due observance of the laws, and their just administration. His views were certainly confined to these ends when he first drew his sword, although afterwards, when his moderate demands were only answered by cruel taunts and brutal menaces, he saw that independence or death were the only alternatives." [1]

The immediate occasion of active hostilities was the conduct of Don Antonio Aliaga, *corregidor* of Tinta, in oppressing the Indians within his jurisdiction, which included the villages controlled by the Inca. The unjust acts of the *corregidor* had already called forth threats of assassination, and he had yielded in individual cases without modifying his general policy. He had also encroached upon the jurisdiction of the Church, and had been excommunicated by the ecclesiastical authorities at Cuzco. Since the Church had condemned him, it might be supposed that the Inca would hesitate less than under other circumstances in proceeding violently against him.

On the 4th of November, 1780, the *corregidor* and Tupac Amaru dined with Dr. Carlos Rod-

[1] Markham, *Travels in Peru and India*, 139.

riguez, the *cura* of Yanaoca, who by this dinner celebrated his name-day. The Inca found an excuse to withdraw early, and with a few attendants ambushed the *corregidor* when he appeared a little later, and took him as a prisoner to Tungasuca. By compelling the *corregidor* to sign an order for the money in the provincial treasury, Tupac Amaru received twenty-two thousand dollars in money, and, in addition, a certain amount of gold in ingots, seventy-five muskets, and a number of baggage horses and mules. Tupac Amaru determined that the *corregidor* should suffer death as a punishment for the wrongs done the Indians. He gathered a large force of his followers about him, sent for his old teacher, the *cura* of Pampamarca, and ordered him to inform the *corregidor* of his fate. He also instructed him to administer to the *corregidor* the last religious rites. The ceremonies of the execution, on the 10th of November, were calculated to impress the Indians with the idea that a new power had arisen. The armed retainers of the Inca were drawn up in three lines around the scaffold on the plaza of Tungasuca, and the Inca seized the occasion to explain his conduct and policy to those who had assembled to witness the remarkable scene.

The Inca's declaration moved the assembled Indians to affirm their loyalty and willingness to obey his orders, and the work of bringing them together into a military force under properly appointed officers was carried vigorously forward. The first expedition was directed against the *corregidor* of the province of Quispicanchi, in the valley of Vilcamayu. It was led by Tupac Amaru, but before he arrived at Quiquijana, the provincial capital, the *corregidor* had fled to Cuzco, carrying to that city the news of revolt. Disappointed in not being able to capture the *corregidor*, the expedition returned to Tungasuca, having plundered several mills, and taken a large amount of clothing for his followers, eighteen thousand yards of woollen and sixty thousand yards of cotton cloth, together with a quantity of firearms and two pieces of artillery. The special reason for hostility to the owners of these manufacturing establishments was their conduct in a rigid and unmerciful enforcement of the mita, and their cruelties to the women and children employed. Tupac Amaru had already under his command 6000 men, 300 of whom had firearms. After this expedition, the revolt spread rapidly over the region now embraced in the southeastern part of Peru and the northwestern part of Bolivia, and involved practically all of the inhabitants except a few Europeans and creoles.

The news of the revolt brought consternation to Cuzco. The two regiments who garrisoned the city turned the Jesuit college into a citadel, and steps were immediately taken to increase the forces for defence. The Spaniards and creoles in the city were enlisted, and messengers were sent to other towns for assistance. On the 13th of November Don Tiburcio de Landa, the governor of Paucartambo, led a force of about one thousand men up the valley of Vilcamayu to meet the enemy. Several hundred of these were friendly Indians under the command of the cacique of Oropesa. This little army advanced as far as Sangarara, where they found themselves surrounded by a superior force of Indians under the Inca. This fact and the appearance of a severe snowstorm induced Landa to retreat and take refuge in a church. Here negotiations were opened between him and Tupac Amaru. Landa wished to know the Inca's intentions, and to this inquiry Tupac replied with the suggestion that all Americans should pass over to his camp,where they would be treated as patriots, since he was proceeding only against Europeans, *corregidors*, and employees of the customs.[1] These terms having been rejected, the Inca wrote to the *cura*, asking him to take away the women and children, but the Spanish troops prevented this, and in the struggle that ensued the powder on hand was exploded, blowing off the roof and throwing down one of the walls of the church. Immediately

---

[1] A. Ferrer del Rio, *Historia dei Reinado de Carlos III. en España*, iii., 418.

after this calamity the Spaniards charged the
enemy, but in spite of their heroic onslaught they
were nearly all cut down; there remained only
twenty-eight, all of whom were wounded. These,
however, recovered from their wounds in the course
of time, and were set at liberty. Among the
killed were Don Tiburcio de Landa, the chief in
command, his lieutenant Escajadillo, Cabrera,
the *corregidor* of Quispicanchi, who had fled from
his province to Cuzco, and Sahuaraura, the cacique
of Oropesa, who had led the Indian contingent
of the Spanish forces.

Immediately after the overthrow of the Spanish forces at Sangarara, the way to Cuzco was
apparently open to the victor. The city was in
great confusion and only imperfectly defended.
Tupac Amaru still believed, however, that, on
account of the justice of his cause, he could attain
his object by negotiation. With a view, therefore,
of treating with the enemy, he established his
followers in an encampment near Tinta. He then
issued a proclamation, setting forth the grievances
that led to the revolt, and denounced the tyranny
of the Spanish officials as cruel and impious.
At the same time he saw the possibility of failing
by peaceable means, and called upon the Indians
to join his forces.

In the meantime the cabildo of Cuzco prepared
to resist the threatened attack. It collected arms,
repaired six old field-pieces, and began to make

powder. Reinforcements were received from Urubamba, Calca, and other places. Volunteers from the inhabitants were brought into the military force, and the clergy, ordered out by the bishop, were organized into four companies under the command of Dr. Manuel de Mendieta. At the end of November, Cuzco had three thousand men in arms. Still the authorities felt insecure, and in order to ward off the danger of a general uprising of the Indians, they abolished the *repartimientos* and the *alcabala*, and made known by proclamation these and other concessions.

Instead of leading his forces directly against Cuzco, Tupac Amaru visited several towns or villages in the district, where he called the inhabitants together and told them that the object of his campaign was to correct abuses, punish the *corregidors*, and release the people from their burdens. He was everywhere received by the Indians with enthusiasm and greeted by them as their Inca and Redeemer. Mr. Markham refers to a private letter, dated January, 1781, which describes the Inca's entrance into Azangaro. He rode a white horse, with splendidly embroidered trappings; two fair men, like Englishmen, of commanding aspect, accompanied him, one on the right and the other on the left.

"He was armed with a gun, sword, and pistols, and was dressed in blue velvet, richly embroidered with gold, with a three-cornered hat, and an *uncu*, in the shape of a bishop's rochet, over all, with a gold chain round his neck, to which a large golden sun was attached."[1]

News of the military preparations of the Spaniards called Tupac Amaru back from the south, and led him to concentrate his army in the neighborhood of Cuzco. A detachment under Antonio Castelo, proceeding directly to the city, was defeated at Saylla, a place about two leagues from Cuzco, but it finally reached the main body of the Inca's army, which was stationed on the heights of Picchu, overlooking the town. While encamped here, Tupac Amaru wrote to the cabildo and the bishop. These letters were dated January 3, 1781. In the letter to the cabildo, he affirmed his position as the heir of the Incas, and declared that he was moved to try by all possible means to put an end to abuses, and to have men appointed to govern the Indians who would follow the laws laid down by the Spanish authorities. He declared that the punishment of the *corregidor* of Tinta was necessary as an example to others; and proclaimed the object of the rebellion to be the entire abolition of *repartimientos*, the appointment of an *alcalde mayor*, or judge of the Indian nation, in every province, and the establishment of an audiencia, or court of appeal, with a viceroy as president, at Cuzco, within reach of the Indians; but he did not aim to overthrow the authority

[1] Markham, *Travels in Peru and India*, 145.

of the king of Spain. In the letter to the bishop, he announced that he appeared, on behalf of the nation, to put an end to the robberies and outrages of the *corregidors;* and at the same time he promised to respect the priests, all church property, the women, and the inoffensive and unarmed people.

The Spanish forces in Cuzco were unwilling to make terms with the Indians. They had been reinforced by the cacique of Chinchero and his men, and by two hundred mulatto soldiers from Lima. After a period of ineffective skirmishing, a bloody battle was begun, on the 8th of January, in the suburbs of Cuzco and on the heights. It lasted two days, and was so far unfortunate for the Inca that he was obliged to withdraw his forces to Tinta. The force of six thousand men that had been sent to the provinces of Calca and Paucartambo, under the Inca's cousin Diego, was also unsuccessful. Diego was defeated near Calca, and again at Yucay. The Spanish garrison of Paucartambo made a desperate resistance, and after the arrival of reinforcements under Don Pablo Astete, Diego retired to Tinta, on the 18th of January, 1781. Here the Inca reorganized his army, and, in union with Diego, made another attack on Paucartambo, on the 11th of February. This, like the previous attempt, was unsuccessful, and five days later the Inca's army was back again in Tinta.

The force of 60,000 men that Tupac Amaru gathered at Tinta was more notable for its numbers than for its discipline or its arms. Only a few hundreds had muskets. But the multitude assembled showed how strong was the feeling against the abuses of the Spanish administration. The Indian and mestizo inhabitants of the interior of Central and Upper Peru were practically all in revolt. Only sixteen caciques adhered to the Spaniards. The threatening prospect alarmed the Spanish officials in Peru and Buenos Aires. The viceroy of Peru sent to Cuzco Don José Antonio Areche, as *visitador*, supported by a military force commanded by Don José del Valle; and the viceroy of Buenos Aires commissioned General Ignacio Flores to put down the rebellion in the southern provinces, for the inhabitants of the entire region as far south as Oruro were in a state of revolt. Before the arrival of Flores, La Paz, which was under the command of Sebastian de Segurola, had been besieged by the Indians and subjected to almost daily attacks for four months.[1]

At Cuzco General del Valle collected an army

---

[1] The events of this siege are set down in the diary of the commanding officer of the city. This diary was edited several years ago by Vicente de Ballivian y Róxas and was published in Paris in 1872, by A. Franck (F. Vieweg), in the first volume of *Archivo Boliviano*, under the title *Diario de los sucesos del cerco de la Ciudad de La Paz en 1781, hasta la total Pacificación de la rebelión general del Perú.*

of 15,000 men, and prepared to enter upon the campaign. While this army was still at Cuzco, the Inca wrote to Areche, the *visitador*, setting forth the fact that the Spanish officials had repeatedly violated the laws and had cruelly oppressed the Indians, and that he had sought justice for the Indians, and to this end had urged the necessity of certain reforms in the administration. He, moreover, affirmed his willingness to enter into negotiations through which these reforms might be attained without further hostilities. Areche's answer to the Inca's despatch was a refusal to negotiate, accompanied by a brutal declaration of vengeance and an affirmation that if Tupac Amaru would surrender at once the mode of his execution would be less cruel than if further resistance was made.[1]

The attitude assumed by the brutal *visitador* Areche convinced Tupac Amaru that complete independence or death were the only alternatives before him. But he had not hitherto indicated that he was seeking independence; only that he aimed at such reforms in the Spanish administration as would release the Indians from oppression. There exists a paper, however, attributed to him in which he is styled "Don José I., by the grace of God, Inca, King of Peru, Quito, Chile, Buenos Aires, and the continents of the South

[1] Markham, *Travels in Peru and India*, 148; for the fate of the Inca's letter, see p. 149, note.

Sea, Lord of the River of the Amazons, with dominion over the Grand Paytiti." This paper, moreover, affirms that

" the king of Castile had usurped the crown and dominions of Peru, imposing innumerable taxes, tributes, duties, excises, monopolies, tithes, fifths; appointing officers who sold justice, and treated the people like beasts of burden. For these causes, and by reason of the cries which have risen up to heaven, in the name of Almighty God, it is ordered that no man shall henceforward pay money to any Spanish officer, excepting the tithes to priests; but that tribute shall be paid to the Inca, and an oath of allegiance to him be taken in every town and village."

This document is without date, and Markham suggested that it was forged by the Spaniards to be used as written evidence against the Inca.[1]

About the middle of March, 1781, General del Valle moved from Cuzco against the insurgents. His army was composed of 17,116 men. His line of advance led along the mountains west of the Vilcamayu, where his troops suffered from snow-storms, the lack of food and fuel, and the want of all commissariat arrangements. Finding his position here almost unendurable both for himself and for his soldiers, he moved down from the mountains and ascended the valley of Vilcamayu,

[1] Markham, *Travels in Peru and India*, 149, 150. This letter is given by Mendiburu, viii., 137, who endorses Markham's suggestion of forgery.

captured Quiquijana, and near the village of Checacupe encountered the Inca's army drawn up behind a trench and a parapet that stretched across the valley. Flanking the Inca's forces, he made an attack in front and in the rear, and drove them back to another entrenchment at Combapata. The Indians, routed from this position, fell back to Tinta, where they were overthrown by the artillery fire and a bayonet charge of the Spanish troops. Tupac Amaru's plans had failed because of the treachery of Zunuario de Castro, and his final undoing was due to the traitorous action of one of his officers, Ventura Landaeta, who, assisted by the *cura* of Lanqui, delivered him and his family into the hands of the Spaniards, after he had fled to that place from Tinta. With this the Spaniards began their revolting course of outrage and vengeance. On the day of the Inca's capture General del Valle hung sixty-seven Indian prisoners at Tinta, and stuck their heads on poles by the roadside.[1] The chief prisoners were marched into Cuzco. They were the Inca Tupac Amaru, his wife, his two sons, Hipolito and Fernando, his uncle Francisco, his brother-in-law Antonio Bastides, his maternal uncle Patricio Noguera, his cousin, Cecilia Tupac Amaru, with her husband, Pedro Mandagure, and a number of the officers of the Inca's army, and the negro slave, Antonio Oblitas,

[1] Markham, *Travels in Peru and India,* 152.

who had served as executioner for the punishment of Aliaga. They were taken to separate places of confinement, and informed that their next meeting would be on the day of their execution.

The *visitador* Areche pronounced the Inca's sentence on May 15, 1781. He wished to show the Indians that even the high rank of the heir of the Incas could not deter the Spaniards from imposing the extreme punishment when they considered it deserved. The charge against this victim of Spanish barbarity was that he had rebelled against Spain, that he had destroyed the mills, that he had abolished the mita, that he had caused his portrait to be painted dressed in the imperial insignia of the *uncu* and *mascapaicha*, and that he had caused his victory at Sangarara to be represented in pictures. He was condemned to witness the execution of his wife, a son, his uncle, his brother-in-law Antonio Bastides, and his captains; to have his tongue cut out; to be torn in pieces by horses attached to his limbs and driven in different directions; to have his body burnt on the heights of Picchu, and to have his head and arms and legs stuck on poles to be set up in the different towns that had been loyal to him; to have his houses demolished, their sites strewn with salt, his goods confiscated, his relatives declared infamous, and all documents relating to his descent burnt by the hangman. It was also

14

provided that all Inca and cacique dresses should be prohibited, all pictures of the Incas destroyed, the presentation of Quichua dramas forbidden, the musical instruments of the Indians burned; all signs of mourning for the Incas, the use of all national costumes by the Indians, and the use of the Quichua language should be prohibited.[1]

This sentence in all its barbarity was carried out on the 18th of May, 1781.

" With the death of the Inca the insurrection may be considered ended; nevertheless many Indians still remained under arms, whom the bloody drama of Cuzco, far from discouraging, only seemed to have inspired with new fury. Thenceforward it was a war of extermination, so much so that the number of victims of the vengeance of the Spaniards and the Indians may be reckoned at 80,000." [2]

The surviving leaders moved southward, and, enraged by the horrible cruelty of Areche, their line of march became a path of destruction. Diego Cristoval Tupac Amaru, the Inca's cousin, held the chief command. After the siege of Puno, Andres Mandagure and Miguel Bastides overran the east shore of Lake Titicaca and joined the forces that were carrying on the war about Sorata and La Paz. They

[1] *Memoirs of General Miller*, Spanish ed., vol. i., Appendix A; Markham, *Travels in Peru and India*, 153.

[2] Mendiburu, viii., 144.

" laid siege to the town of Sorata, where the Spaniards of the neighboring districts had taken refuge with their families and wealth. The unarmed Indians were unequal to the storming of fortifications, which, although constructed only of earth, were lined with artillery. But their leader surmounted this difficulty by the adoption of a measure that would have done credit to any commander. By the construction of a lengthened mound he collected the waters which flow from the neighboring snowy heights of Ancoma, and, turning them against the earthen ramparts, washed them away. The immediate result was the storming of the town, and the massacre of its inhabitants, with circumstances of horror exceeding the death of Tupac Amaru."[1]

Practically all of the inhabitants, about twenty thousand in number, were killed. The clergy alone escaped.

The siege of La Paz was continued for six months after the death of the Inca. Like Sorata, it was a place of refuge for the Spaniards of the surrounding country. In defending the city the commanding officer had constructed a line of fortifications, but had determined to include only the principal part of the town, leaving outside the suburbs and several Indian villages. During the continuance of the rebellion in the north, the forces supporting the insurrection had been daily increasing in the south, and requests for assistance

[1] *Memoirs of General Miller*, i., 18.

from the towns near-by were sent to La Paz, with which Segurola complied—as far as possible. He had also used all available funds to gather stores of provisions for the city, which were especially needed to support the increasing number of refugees. The story of the progress of the siege and of the resistance offered by the besieged is given in the dairy of the commanding officer, Sebastian de Segurola. The following extracts from this diary show under what disadvantages the Indians fought; and the fact that in the face of these disadvantages and of their great losses they persisted in the conflict for many months indicates to what a degree they had been moved by their intolerable grievances.

"March 27.—This day the Indians attacked with great force all parts of the city, setting fire to the houses that were outside of the trenches, assaulting these and the wall, from which they were repulsed with great vigor. This engagement lasted from 11 o'clock in the morning till 4 in the evening. At this hour the rebels retired with much loss, which was given at more than one hundred and fifty killed, without any loss on our part.

"March 28.—It was recognized to-day that the number of Indians who approached us was considerably increased. At 8 o'clock in the morning they attacked all parts of the city, aided by some guns which they fired, and at the same time they went on burning the houses outside of the fortifications, and we resisted them with great valor. The attack lasted till 5 o'clock in the afternoon, when the enemy retired with more than three hundred and fifty dead, according to our calculation, and on our side we had only two.

"March 29.—The Indians have been coming down from all sides since daybreak, and at 10 o'clock assaulted the city with desperation, and this attack, repulsed by us, lasted till half-past 5 in the afternoon, at which hour they retired with a loss of more than 150 men, and we had the misfortune, by the bursting of a cannon in one of the forts, to have three killed and several severely wounded, and among the killed was Sergeant-major Joseph de Roxas."

After 109 days of siege, in which a besieging force of 40,000 Indians, according to Segurola's statement, took part, the condition of affairs in the city was desperate, but no word of despair appears in the diary of the commander. "By the grace of God," he wrote, "we have defended ourselves in spite of hunger, pest, and the enemies, even from those within, who have caused not less care than those without." In want of other food, they had eaten the horses, mules, and asses, not merely the flesh but the skins as well, and the dogs and cats, the cat having a quoted price of six dollars. Of the 2000 mules in the city at the beginning of the siege, scarcely more than forty remained at the end of it. During these months, moreover, disease made rapid strides; and many persons in their incautious search for food fell into the hands of the enemy, to whose treatment of them ''we may not refer without the greatest horror, grief, and compassion.''

At the end of June, General Flores arrived with the troops from Buenos Aires and brought the desired relief.[1]   He scattered the besieging force, and caused food to be introduced into the city. Under the protection of the military force, many of the inhabitants left their houses in the city and established themselves temporarily near the camp of the soldiers. But hostilities were continued at different points in the surrounding country; and on the withdrawal of a part of the troops to places where they seemed to be imperatively needed, the siege of La Paz was renewed. This time it was continued from the beginning of August until the 17th of October. At noon on this day the troops from Oruro

[1] '' The reinforcements sent to the royal army from Buenos Aires, Tucuman, and Cochabamba were for the most part regular troops; the Buenos Aireans were armed and equipped as European soldiers; the Tucumanos composed the cavalry, and were armed with butcher-knives and lassos; the Cochabambinos used short clubs loaded with lead, and which, by means of a string several yards in length, they could fling from them, and were deadly weapons. The mode of attacking the Indians was first by the fire of musketry, to throw them into confusion, when, if the ground admitted, the Tucuman horsemen rode among them, dragging down whole ranks with their lassos, followed by the Cochabambinos, who despatched them with their clubs.''—Temple, *Travels in Various Parts of Peru*, ii., 175, 176.

arrived under the command of Lieutenant Josef Reseguin,

" and we began to see on the brow of the hill of Púna certain men who it was not doubted were ours, and in a short time the rest appeared, covering in a moment the top of the hill. From this position they saluted the city with their artillery, filling it with the greatest joy and satisfaction imaginable. The commandant, Don Josef Reseguin, sent to me immediately notice of his arrival with 7000 soldiers and a large quantity of provisions which would supply the city.

" Thus ended the second siege of this afflicted and unfortunate city, if it may not be considered the first; since during the period of the other relief the enemies remained always on the heights of Potopóto, Calvario, and even on the others of the environs, when the troops moved their encampment some distance away. In this it is seen that the rebels to the number of 12,000 fighting men, according to all accounts, not only pursued the siege with fire and blood as before, but also turned the waters against us; and although it had not the same outcome as in the town of Sorata, still it caused considerable destruction in the city. Misery made the same inroads as the last time, and want compelled the use of the same unfit food; in sustaining life there was no exemption for the horses, the mules, the asses, the cats, the dogs, and the most despicable hides, not only of the animals killed but also those furnished by the rawhide trunks and the food pouches of the shepherds."[1]

[1] *Archivo Boliviano*, i., 127, 128.

For still two years or more desultory fighting continued in many parts of the country in which the revolt had appeared. Although the Indians were defeated, they were neither crushed nor placated. From their victory the Spaniards derived little profit and less honor. The Indians remained hostile and in a mood to join any enemy of their hated masters that might arise. Outraged by the barbarity of the Spaniards, they espoused the cause of the creoles and became a powerful factor in the struggle for independence.

A recognition of the disastrous results of Spain's treatment of the Indians led the Spaniards at last to make their exactions less burdensome. Under the new order the Indians might be employed in occupations contributing directly to the general well-being of society: in raising grain and cattle; in building roads, bridges, and edifices for public use. They might also be employed in mining; but it was not expected that they would be employed in occupations that contributed merely to the luxurious gratification of the Spanish part of the population. The line of distinction between these occupations was, however, only vaguely drawn, and was only imperfectly observed in practice. Service in the mines was subject to restrictions that were expected to obviate at least some of the evils that had previously existed. Only a certain number of laborers, not to exceed one seventh of the inhabitants, might be taken from any district, and these were retained for a period of six months. They were paid at the rate of four reals a day. The provision that no Indian might be taken more than thirty miles to work in a mine tended to set aside the practice of taking them from the warm climate of the low country to the cold regions of the mountains. But abuses were continued in spite of the good intentions of the law-makers. The execution of the laws was in the hands of officers far removed from the supervision of their legislative superiors. The great distance and the difficulties of communication still left the Indians practically subject to the discretion of the American end of the administration.

CHAPTER X

IT is impossible to derive from existing records an entirely trustworthy statement concerning the number of the inhabitants of Chile in the eighteenth century. A reasonable estimate is that there were 80,000 in 1700, 120,000 in 1740, and 259,646 in 1778. The last number is that given by the returns of the first census. At the close of the colonial period, there were probably somewhat less than half a million. Of these the province, or intendancy, of Santiago had the larger number. The greater part of the inhabitants were engaged in agriculture and lived scattered throughout the country, but later, on account of the danger of attacks by the Indians, many of them were induced to live in towns.

The government in Chile, as elsewhere throughout South America, was continued in the spirit of Spanish absolutism. "The monarchs," to quote the words of the viceroy of Peru in 1796, "are the sacred vicegerents of God himself for the temporal government of his people." [1] The kings

[1] *Memorias de los Vireyes*, vi., 10.

of Spain preserved, not merely in theory but also in practice, their ancient absolute power; and at the close of the century they were even seeking to make this power more effective.

The chief officer in the colonial government was the captain-general. He was appointed by the king of Spain, and he ruled the colony in the spirit of his superior. He was at once the chief of the militia, the head of the civil administration, and president of the royal audiencia. He presided also over the other superior courts, such as the tribunals of the treasury, of the *Cruzada,* of government lands, and of commerce. Like the viceroy, he was the personal representative of the king, and he differed from that officer very little except with respect to the dignity of his office and the political importance of the district, or colony, under his jurisdiction.

Next to the captain-general, the most important arm of the colonial government was the audiencia. By a decree of Charles III. the number of members in the audiencia, not only in Chile but elsewhere in Spanish America, was increased, and for each audiencia there was created a chief with the title of regent. The object of these changes was to make these bodies more efficient in the administration of justice. In case of the death, absence, or inability of the captain-general, the functions of this office were assumed by the regent, or if there was no regent, by the oldest judge. This rule

remained in force until 1806, when it was decreed
that, in case of such vacancy, absence, or inability, the functions of the chief executive should be
performed by the commanding military officer,
provided this officer was not of lower rank than
colonel.

The military department in Chile called for an
annual expenditure of 277,938 dollars. This was
somewhat more than two fifths of the total
expenses of the colony; yet it was not possible to
reduce this amount without making this arm
of the government inadequate for purposes of
defence, particularly in view of the danger of
foreign invasion which was then feared. Of the
soldiers maintained, eight companies of infantry,
or seven hundred men, were stationed at Concepcion to defend the coast and the frontier. Six
companies, or five hundred men, were established
at Valdivia. There were two companies of artillery,
one of fifty men at Concepcion, and the other of
sixty men at Valparaiso. There were also two
bodies of cavalry: one of eight companies, or four
hundred men, occupied various points in the province of Concepcion, while the rest of the force,
consisting of one company of fifty men, were
quartered in Santiago. The mestizo, of Spanish
and Indian blood, in Chile was recognized as an
excellent soldier, ''vigorous, sober, hardy, docile
under discipline, quick to learn to use his weapon
and to understand the evolutions, patient under

the greatest privations, and endowed, moreover, with courage, which, when circumstances demanded, went even to temerity."[1] There seems to have been no regular system of conscription; many enlisted voluntarily, while others were brought into the ranks, with more or less of violence, from among the unemployed both in the city and in the country; and still others were sent into the service as a form of punishment. Towards the end of the century the army was brought under a somewhat stricter organization and discipline. The officers and soldiers were paid with greater promptness and regularity than earlier; and more care was given to their instruction. But the rank and file were still very poorly clothed and only imperfectly armed.

The ecclesiastical power was exercised by two bishops. The jurisdiction of the bishop of Santiago extended from the desert of Atacama to the river Maule; while the authority of the bishop of Concepcion was exercised over the region south of that river, the two dioceses corresponding to the two intendancies. The tithes of the diocese of Santiago amounted to 32,200 dollars in 1700, 59,509 in 1730, 74,700 in 1770, 87,000 in 1780, 102,000 in 1790, 119,000 in 1800, and 177,700 in 1808. In the diocese of Concepcion they were very much less, amounting in 1802 to only 61,500 dollars. Of the ninety-five parishes in Chile,

[1] Barros Arana, *Historia jeneral de Chile*, vii., 342.

fifty-nine belonged to Santiago, and thirty-six to Concepcion. The higher ecclesiastics, the bishops and the canons, lived in opulence, while the parish priests in the smaller towns, in so far as they relied on their stipulated or legitimate stipends, led an existence not far removed from misery. Towards the end of the colonial period the power of the ecclesiastics was diminished and they became less arrogant in their relations with the civil government. At the same time scepticism and the spirit of free inquiry began to be manifest in the colony, carried into the country on the wave of revolutionary political thought proceeding from France.

In the principal centres of population in America, the revolutionary literature of the last decade of the eighteenth century exerted a marked influence, but the Spanish monarch was entirely unaffected by it. He held to his prerogatives and pretensions as if there had been no French revolution, and his power became more than ever immediately effective. The old council of the Indies was often ignored, and the will of the king was projected, by decrees and royal orders, directly into the affairs of the colonies.

The difficulty of governing extensive territories effectively under this system of extreme centralization led to the establishment of intendancies like those that had been, or were to be, established elsewhere in the colonies. In fact, this reform was effected in Chile by applying, with certain modifications, the law that had been framed for the viceroyalty of Rio de la Plata. By this law the *corregidors* were set aside, and the minor divisions of the territory that had been under their authority, and that were called *partidos* after this change, were placed under the immediate control of officials known as subdelegates, appointed by the intendants and confirmed by the king. The territory north of the river Maule was called the intendancy of Santiago; that south of this river was called the intendancy of Concepcion. The intendancy of Santiago was divided in the beginning into twelve *partidos*, while the intendancy of Concepcion had seven *partidos*. The two intendants were subordinated to the captain-general, and were subject to the jurisdiction of the audiencia, or supreme court, that had its seat in Santiago.

In the list of governors of Chile during the last half of the eighteenth century several held only provisional appointments, and performed the duties of the office awaiting the arrival of the king's commission, or the regularly appointed captain-general. The whole list with the periods of their tenure is as follows:

Domingo Ortiz de Rosas . . . 1745 -1755
Manuel de Amat y Junient . . . 1755–1761
Félix de Berroeta 1761–1762

Antonio de Guill y Gonzaga . . 1762–1768
Juan de Balmaseda 1768–1770
Francisco Jávier de Morales . . . 1770–1773
Agustin de Jáuregui 1773–1780
Tomas Álveraz de Acevedo . . . 1780
Ambrosio de Benavides . . . 1780–1787
Tomas Álvarez de Acevedo . . . 1787–1788
Ambrosio O'Higgins 1788–1796
Gabriel de Aviles 1796–1799
Joaquin del Pino. 1799–1801
José de Santiago Concha . . . 1801–1802
Francisco Diez de Medina . . . 1802
Luis Muñoz de Guzman . . . 1802–1808

It is noteworthy that the most distinguished
person named in this list, the man who made the
most profound impression as captain-general of
Chile, entered upon the duties of his office at an
age when public officials are generally supposed
to have outlived the period of their greatest
usefulness. This man was Don Ambrosio O'Higgins, who was born in Ireland in 1720, and became
captain-general of Chile in 1788. Thus at the age
of sixty-eight he began the career which, on
account of the wisdom and energy displayed,
entitled him to the designation of the Great
Captain-General. After a vigorous administration
of eight years he was promoted, in 1796, at the
age of seventy-six, to the office of viceroy of Peru,
which he held five years, until his death in 1801.

In the later years of the colonies the king of

Spain sought to promote to the highest offices persons who had experience in either the civil or military service of the Indies. At the time of his appointment to the office of captain-general, O'Higgins had served many years as an engineer, a military officer, and an intendant, and had become familiar with the character and needs of the different parts of the Chilean territory. While he was captain-general, moreover, he did not hesitate to undertake the most difficult journeys in order to attend personally to the affairs of the remote districts.

The northern part of the country had not been visited by any of the previous governors or captains-general, while the southern districts, lying between the Araucanian frontier and the capital, had been constantly within the range of the captain-general's observation. The expeditions against the Araucanians had crossed these districts, and, through the numerous conferences with the Indians, they had been kept in mind by both parties. But the northern end of the territory had remained in isolation, and both the economical affairs and the affairs of the administration needed the supervision and stimulus of the central government. The fact that the captain-general made this northern journey of hundreds of leagues over a region with few roads, studying the needs of the inhabitants and seeking to promote their material interests in all possible

ways, is a sufficient indication of the zeal and
force which he brought to the task of government.

The southern districts had not suffered the
same neglect as the northern. Through all the
decades of their occupation the Spaniards had
appreciated the necessity of making a special
effort to confirm their hold on this region, and
they had, moreover, persistently striven to en-
croach upon the territory claimed by the Araucanians. At every point they had met with
vigorous resistance. The government had been
compelled to have thorough information of this
part of the country.

In the long course of the Araucanian war treat-
ies had been made from time to time, but they
were rarely more than temporary interruptions
of hostilities. They permitted the belligerents
to recover from their losses and make ready for
an attack with renewed force. In the conflict
the rules of warfare that prevail among civilized
nations were disregarded. Both parties kept
forces on the frontier, made raids at every opportunity into the enemy's territory, and committed
all kinds of depredations. Neither party trusted
the promises of the other, and time seemed only
to increase the bitterness of their hostility. In
this state of affairs the southern districts might
not be neglected. Moreover, the almost continuous warfare had a very marked influence on the
military arm of the colony. It made the militia

a vital and active force. Imminent war made military discipline possible.

As a means of establishing peace between the two races, Jáuregui, when he became captain-general, in 1773, caused four Araucanian chiefs to be brought to Santiago as ambassadors representing the various Indian tribes. It was intended that these chiefs should be witnesses to the disposition of the Spaniards to deal fairly with their neighbors, that they should be employed as mediators or interpreters in future negotiations, and that through them the complaints of the Indians might be carried to the Spanish authorities. They should be clothed and supported at the expense of the government. They arrived in Santiago in April, 1774, and were placed under the protection of the local authorities, and the public was solemnly ordered, under severe penalties, not to show them any disrespect. This plan received the endorsement of the viceroy of Peru, but there were not wanting persons who saw that it involved an overestimate of the civilization of the Indians and was consequently visionary. It was, nevertheless, confirmed by an agreement between the Indians and the Spaniards made at the conference in 1774. In this agreement it was stipulated that peace should be maintained among the various Indian tribes, and that the Indians should send their sons to be educated in a school to be opened in Santiago for this purpose. The

Araucanians, however, hesitated to comply with the provision respecting the education of their sons. The few who were sent to Santiago acquired a certain amount of elementary knowledge; but difficulties arose when attempts were made to give them more advanced instruction. It was found that the barbarian was only a good beginner in learning. In 1780 the Santiago school for Indians was transferred to Chillan.

With respect to agricultural reform, O'Higgins entertained certain ideas and plans that, under the prevailing natural conditions, could not be fully carried out. He seems to have exaggerated the possibilities of governmental influence in economic affairs. His effort to foster the production of sugar was a case in point. In some of the northern valleys where it was planted on a small scale, the enterprise was in a measure successful, but the attempt to create larger plantations in other districts encountered difficulties, and the cultivation was abandoned after three or four years of experiment. The effort to extend the production of rice had no better result, and the attempt to introduce the cultivation of tobacco met with an insurmountable obstacle in a royal decree of prohibition issued in the interest of the existing monopoly. The motive in these and other proposed agricultural reforms was the betterment of the condition of the people; and, although some of the specific undertakings were unsuccessful, attention was called to the need of more careful cultivation.

But more important for the social well-being of the colony was the effort of the captain-general to set aside the abuses of the encomiendas, and even to abolish the system itself. In the beginning this system was thought to be necessary in order to provide laborers for the fields and the mines; for it was understood that the Indians, like all savages, lacked the habit of consecutive work, and that compulsion would be necessary to make them persistent laborers. The power to compel the Indians to work having been granted to the encomenedros, there remained no practical obstacle to making them slaves; and to this position they were reduced with all the attendant miseries that have become historic. But after two hundred years and more, a class of persons had come into existence who were accustomed to obtain their livelihood by more or less regular work. The reason for compulsory labor originally advanced was no longer valid, and it is to the credit of the captain-general as an administrator that he gave a powerful impulse to the movement for abolishing this system.

While the captain-general was engaged in these and other internal reforms, the coming of foreign vessels to participate in the trade of the colony provoked the opposition of the officials both in Chile and Peru. Even the presence of foreign vessels excited alarm, whether they came to trade or merely halted at a Spanish-American port on their way to another destination. In 1788 an American vessel named *Columbia*, battered by storms, put into the port of the island of Juan Fernandez. The governor of the island, Blas Gonzalez, permitted repairs to be made. Although the vessel was bound for Alaska, and had no design to trade at the ports of South America, Governor Gonzalez was deposed and tried for having furnished succor to the distressed vessel. The viceroy had no warships with which to pursue strange vessels, but a ship furnished by a merchant of Lima was armed and sent to Juan Fernandez; it failed to find any offenders. The coming of foreign vessels, particularly vessels from the United States, was opposed by the authorities not merely because they would tend to overthrow the ancient trade régime, but also because they would help to propagate the political ideas of the young republic, and thus contribute to the destruction of the Spanish colonial system.

While the colonists of Chile were anticipating evils that might proceed from the encroachment of foreigners, it was announced in Santiago, April 2, 1789, that King Charles III. was dead, and that his death had occurred on the fourteenth of the preceding December. After elaborate funeral ceremonies had been had in the Cathedral of Santiago, preparations were made to celebrate the accession of Charles IV. The portraits of the new king and queen were placed over the entrance of the captain-general's palace.

"At five o'clock in the afternoon the captain-general left his palace carrying in his hands the royal standard, accompanied by all the corporations and notable inhabitants of the city; and having mounted a large platform which had been constructed in the principal plaza, the secretary of the cabildo read in a loud voice the royal proclamation which announced the accession of Charles IV. to the throne of his ancestors."

In the company attending the captain-general there were four Indian chiefs, who had been brought from the frontier to render homage to the king for themselves and their people. They were made to kneel and take an oath of obedience and vassalage. Then the captain-general advanced to the edge of the platform, and, dipping the royal standard, cried three times in a loud voice: "Spain and the Indies for King Charles IV. and may God protect him." With this utterance the bells of the twenty-six churches in the city sent forth a prolonged peal, a royal salute was fired from the hill of Santa Lucia, and the populace replied with a shout, "Long live the king." Medals that had been struck in commemoration of the occasion were distributed, and one was hung about the neck of each of the Indian chiefs.

This part of the ceremony was followed by a procession of the participants to another part of the city, where the reading of the proclamation was repeated. The procession passed between two lines of soldiers, while the balconies and doors on either side of the street were brilliantly decorated. On the return to the plaza the captain-general and his attendants listened to a poetic eulogy delivered by a woman gorgeously attired and standing on "a lofty and majestic triumphal arch erected at the entrance of the palace, under which the procession passed." The chronicler of this ceremony, and of the banquets, the mass of thanksgiving, and the *Te Deum*, which followed, affirmed that persons familiar with the grandeur of the most important courts and cities of both worlds maintained that nowhere else had they seen such magnificence as was here displayed.[1] This was the last occasion of this kind on which public enthusiasm was especially manifest; for when Ferdinand VII., the son and successor of Charles IV., ascended the throne, in 1808, the Spanish monarchy was already falling under the shadow of Napoleon's expanding empire, and the loyalty of the people was undermined by the spread of revolutionary doctrines.

Even during the presidency of Benavides the fear of foreign encroachment had led the authorities of Chile to ask the king to send them arms

[1] Barros Arana, *Historia jeneral de Chile*, vii., 39-41.

and ammunition. O'Higgins repeated this request, and with the material received he proceeded, acting on orders from Spain, to put the forts of Chile in a state of defence. Active hostilities appeared to be imminent in 1789 as the result of a dispute between England and Spain concerning the possession of a certain part of the island of Vancouver. The Spaniards having taken two English ships in this controversy, the English government prepared for war. Fearing the consequences of a war with England, in view of its limited resources, the Spanish government withdrew its pretensions and formed a treaty that recognized the sovereignty of England over the territory in dispute, and the right of the English to fish in the Pacific and to make use temporarily of certain points on the coast that were not occupied by the Spaniards. In order to prevent this concession from serving as a pretext for unlawful trade with the Spanish colonies, it was expressly stipulated that English subjects should not navigate the Pacific within ten maritime leagues of any point of the coast occupied by the Spanish. This concession gave English vessels recognized rights on the Spanish-American coast, but the Spanish authorities found it difficult to confine them within the limits of these rights; for vessels that came ostensibly to fish were naturally led to engage in the much more profitable business of smuggling, and the government of neither

Chile nor Peru was in a position to prevent them.

In the last part of the eighteenth century, Chile was almost wholly without roads, except in and immediately around the cities. In fact, the inhabitants, like the Spanish colonists everywhere, were generally content to travel or transport their goods on horseback or on the backs of mules or donkeys. Even between Valparaiso and Santiago there was no wagon road before the last decade of the century. O'Higgins had to make this journey three times during the first two years of his rule as captain-general, and these journeys were sufficient to make him appreciate the need of a road suited to vehicles on wheels. The inhabitants of the capital, as the foreign trade of the country increased, recognized the advantage that would accrue to them from better means of transportation; but when it was proposed to begin the construction, the captain-general encountered two obstacles: the lack of funds and the unwillingness of many proprietors to have the road traverse their lands. Finally, however, certain funds were obtained by imposing a slight additional tax on goods imported and exported at Valparaiso, and some of the proprietors were made to see that their prejudices were groundless, and that the road would be a benefit rather than an injury. The work of construction was begun in 1792.

Two years later Captain Vancouver passed over this road going from Valparaiso to Santiago.

"The making of the new road," he wrote, "had doubtless been a work of great labor; and to a people who are not very industriously inclined, and who are all bigoted to former practices and original habits, it is no wonder that the manifest advantages that must result to the inhabitants of the country from his Excellency's wise undertaking, should be over-looked, or rather not be seen by them; and that the execution of his judicious plan should have deprived him, amongst the lower orders of the people, of much of his popularity."[1]

On a certain part of the road Vancouver found laborers at work, but was informed

"that as a sufficient number of people could not be procured to carry the whole of the design into exe-cution at once, his Excellency, the President, had, in order to facilitate the intercourse between these two great towns, ordered the most difficult and dan-gerous parts of the new line of road to be first made passable and commodious."[2]

"There were about fifty men at work with com-mon pick-axes and shovels; and to supply the place of wheelbarrows for the removal of the earth from the higher to the lower side of the road, the hide of an ox was spread on the ground, and when as much earth was thrown upon it as would require the strength of two men to remove, the corners of

[1] Vancouver, *A Voyage of Discovery*, vi., 258.
[2] *Ibid*, 263.

the hide were drawn together by each of them, and in that state dragged to the depressed side of the road, and emptied where requisite, to preserve a gentle slope in the breadth; or else discharged over the brink and sent down the side of the hill."[1]

The laborers engaged in this work received a wage equivalent to fourteen cents a day.[2]

Among other public works begun at the same time with the road to Valparaiso was the wall constructed to prevent the river Mapocho from overflowing its banks and flooding the city of Santiago. This river flows through the city, and by reason of the nearness of the steep mountainsides it is often subject to a rapid rise. In 1783, during a heavy rain which continued for nine consecutive days without interruption, the river rose to an unprecedented height, broke through all barriers, carried down houses, trees, and cattle, and threatened the complete destruction of the city. It became necessary to take steps to prevent a repetition of this calamity, and at that part of the river where coming down from the north it turns sharply towards the west a dam

[1] Vancouver vi., 264.

[2] The country between Valparaiso and Santiago and the dwellings along the road, particularly in Casa Blanca, as they appeared in the last decade of the eighteenth century, are described by Vancouver in his account of his journey from the coast to the capital in 1795. In the same part of his *Voyage of Discovery*, book vi., chap. v., may be found an account of his reception in Santiago by the captain-general, together with a description of the city.

or wall of brick and mortar was constructed to turn the torrent into its channel towards the west.

Prior to 1790 the road over the Andes between Chile and the Argentine country was the only one in this region on which any considerable amount of labor had been expended. Along this road, which had been widened to accommodate the increasing transportation between Buenos Aires and Santiago, cabins of stone or brick had been erected as places of refuge from storms. Under the enlarged freedom of trade introduced by the code of 1778, the increased commerce between Chile and the viceroyalty of Rio de la Plata demanded better facilities for overland transportation. The improvement of this road was undertaken by Captain-General O'Higgins, and it was brought into such a condition that, without great difficulty, it could be traversed by bands of mules or horses. Most of the other lines of traffic were merely trails across the country marked out by the mule trains in seeking the most convenient route to their destination.

The commerce of Chile, even after 1778, was practically confined to trade with Spain and the other Spanish colonies of America. Spain sent to Chile annually articles valued at somewhat more than a million dollars, and in return received chiefly copper, gold, and silver. In carrying on this trade four or five ships a year arrived in Chile from Spain. In Chile the association of capitalists in industrial and commercial corporations was unknown. The colony in this respect was following the lead of the mother country, where economic corporations were rare, and where there existed a strong prejudice against them.

" Down to the last years of the colonial domination, the commerce of Chile embraced only individual persons, who carried on their business separately and for their own account, and there was no other commercial association than that of certain brothers, who, after the death of their fathers, continued together for a certain number of years in the business which their fathers had established."[1]

There were, moreover, no companies for insuring against the risks of transportation by sea, or against losses by fire. In view of this fact and the great risks attending the route around the southern end of the continent, in the course of time more and more of the wares imported from Europe came by way of Buenos Aires and the Andes, while the sea route was almost entirely neglected.

The absence of a system of credit and exchange necessitated the actual transfer of coin for the payment of debts, whether within or without the limits of the colony. The exportation of money required by this method of making payments sometimes threatened to exhaust the supply of

[1] Barros Arana, *Historia jeneral de Chile*, vii., 401 .

currency, although the mint of Santiago annually sent out coins to the value of a million dollars. This difficulty was in a measure set aside by the circulation, in Chile and also in other colonies, of clipped coins that passed for their nominal value but could not be exported without loss. The coins of circulation were of the same system as those used in Spain and the other colonies but the copper coins that circulated in Spain were not employed. The attempt made in 1781 to introduce them met with vigorous opposition and was abandoned; and it was not until after the establishment of the republic that the project to circulate copper coins was resumed with success. Traders sometimes issued marked pieces of copper for change, but the obligation to redeem them rested only on the persons who issued them.

The original Spanish settlers in Chile, like their countrymen in other parts of America, expected to find their most fruitful sources of wealth in mines of the precious metals. But the fitness of the soil and climate for agriculture made this branch of production important; and its development was limited only by the demand for the products. The early tendency to distribute the lands among many proprietors was checked later, and a large number of the estates fell into the hands of the religious orders. The Jesuits became the owners of about seventy estates, some of them as large as a modern province.

Those that remained in private hands were continued from generation to generation in the same family. This direct descent was furthered by the law upholding primogeniture. There were, however, no estates to which this procedure had been applied prior to the middle of the seventeenth century. In the eighteenth century they were more numerous than at any other time, but at the end of the colonial period there were only eighteen important estates with reference to which this practice obtained. There were others subject to certain restrictions as to transmission, although they were not properly under the law of primogeniture. The heads of some of the families holding estates under this law bore titles of nobility.[1]

The system of inheritance under the law of primogeniture contributed to maintain the prestige of certain families, but it came to be regarded as a cause of the backwardness of Chilean agriculture, and, in 1789, it was decreed that no more foundations of this kind should be made without the express permission of the king. The titles of nobility that were eagerly sought, particularly by the creoles, were conferred by the crown on the

[1] Some of these titles were the following: Marques de la Pica, Conde de Sierra Bella, Marques de Piedra Blanca de Huana, Marques de Cañada Hermosa, Marques de Villapalma, Marques de Casa Real, Marques de Montepio, Conde de Quinta Alegre, Conde de la Conquista, and Marques de Casa Larrain.

presentation of a nobiliary, a statement of services rendered, and the payment of a certain
amount of money, ordinarily not less than twenty
thousand dollars. As might very well be expected,
many persons not worthy to be made especially
prominent in the communities where they lived,
received titles of nobility; and this abuse led
the king, in 1790, to seek to make such regulations
as would set it aside. But the action taken was not
effective; still in the last years of the colonial
period no new titles were granted in Chile. The
large payment of money required was not without
influence in producing this result. Persons seeking some mark of distinction limited their aspirations to the possession of a decoration in the
orders of Santiago, Calatrava, Alcántara, Montera,
or, later, in the order of Charles III.

For a long period the post-office in Spain was a
monopoly conferred by a decree of the king on a
private person; and when it appeared to be
advisable to organize this branch of the administration in the Indies the same plan was followed.
But this system was set aside in the reign of
Charles III. and the postal service was brought
directly under the crown and extended so as to
embrace places that hitherto had not been
reached. During the last quarter of the century
a vessel left Coruña, in Spain, every two months
carrying the mail to Montevideo for the viceroyalty
of Rio de la Plata, Chile, and the southern part

of the viceroyalty of Peru, as far as Lima. The voyage required ordinarily two months, and the journey from Buenos Aires across the pampas and over the mountains to Chile took another month.

Within the limits of Chile there was at first one post a month between Santiago and Concepcion, but this service was doubled under the administration of Captain-General O'Higgins, and at the same time a semi-weekly post was established between Santiago and Valparaiso. The people in general were slow in accustoming themselves to the use of these public means of communication. They continued to send letters by travellers and by muleteers in charge of freight transportation. In order to set aside this practice and make the government monopoly effective a heavy fine was imposed upon the unauthorized carrying of letters between points where the government had established postal communication. But this prohibition was not immediately successful in spite of the fact that the private carrying of letters was irregular, insecure, and illegal.

The manufactures of Chile in the later decades of the century were chiefly such as were auxiliary to agriculture: the making of wine, brandy, jerked beef, drying fruits, preparing the fat of animals for exportation, and tanning hides. As long as the restrictions on trade existed there were certain rude textile fabrics produced, but when foreign nations were able to introduce their wares there was a marked diminution in the production of these things in Chile. In the production of coarse pottery in the form of plates, jugs, and jars, the Chileans encountered no foreign competition, and manufactures of these articles sprang up in many parts of the country. But the lack of knowledge and skill on the part of artisans of all classes was an effective hindrance to industrial progress. This state of things was, however, somewhat relieved by the introduction of foreign workmen, and by the coming of other persons who, in order to carry out their enterprises, undertook to instruct their employees. The Jesuits brought numbers of men to work on their churches, and the example of these workmen furnished a certain stimulus to others. Near the end of the century the distinguished architect Toesca came to direct the construction of important public buildings, and he was obliged to instruct the masons and carpenters who worked on them.

There existed here as elsewhere in the dominions of Spain industrial guilds, and before a person was permitted to work at a trade he was required to give proof of his competence and obtain permission from the proper public authority. This system was carried out rigorously in Europe, but it was maintained with great laxity in the colonies, particularly in Chile. By a decree issued by

Charles IV., in 1789, industry was freed from the tyrannical restraints exercised through the guilds, but the guilds were not abolished.

In spite of the effort that had been made to cause the inhabitants of Chile to live in cities, particularly those that might be subject to incursions by the Indians, at the end of the colonial period two thirds of them were still living scattered about the country, on the estates or at the mines. Except Santiago, no city had more than six thousand inhabitants. Concepcion had about five thousand. The cities next in size were Valparaiso and Serena. After these came Chillan and Talca. Each of the last two had about four thousand inhabitants, and the other cities were still smaller. In general the dwellers in the cities had few opportunities for getting information of events in other countries, and at the same time very little interest in such events. They were, however, intensely interested in local factions and feuds. These arose naturally where the towns were isolated, and where large numbers of persons were idle and without incentives to higher aspirations. There were no amusements but card-playing, bowling, cock-fighting, and horse-racing.

Santiago was the capital of the colony, the residence of the governor, or the captain-general, the seat of the audiencia, and the centre of the most pretentious society of Chile. It had about thirty thousand inhabitants. With respect to its public buildings, it was not below the standard of Lima or Mexico. But the private houses were generally simple, one-story structures, and the interior furnishings were necessarily plain, on account of the expensiveness of European wares and the rudeness of nearly all colonial products. The streets were usually dirty, but this feature of the city's affairs was greatly improved under the republic. The practice of burying large numbers of bodies in the churches led to "the propagation of epidemics that made great ravages among the inhabitants. The churches in which the soil was constantly removed for new burials emitted an unhealthy and pestiferous odor, which made it necessary to open and ventilate them every morning before the faithful assembled." [1]

In Santiago, as in the other important Spanish-American capitals, there was a limited class of men who had acquired titles of nobility, and whose wealth enabled them to live in luxury as compared with the bulk of the inhabitants. Corvallo, describing them, said: "They use costly carriages and fine liveries, and show themselves on the public drives, and visiting and at balls with rich costumes and valuable jewels." [2] The city had no public market, but the plaza in front of the cathedral was used for this purpose. The streets were not lighted, except as those who went out at night or

[1] Barros Arana, *Historia jeneral de Chile*, vii., 459.
[2] *Descripcion histórico-geográfica*, part ii., chap. 4.

their servants carried lanterns. The state of the city in this respect was an incentive to vice and disorder. But the character of many of the lower class made any incentive of this kind superfluous, for "drunkenness was a vice much more common than in our day, as were also robbery, brawls, and assassinations."[1] Begging had attained such alarming proportions that many persons were inclined to seek a remedy, and hoped to find it in the development of industries; and to this end they sought to suppress the obstacles that had stood in the way of industrial progress.

While life in the cities was without doubt unattractive, the country presented much less favorable conditions. On the estates of even the more wealthy families, there were few conveniences for comfortable living. The houses of the proprietors were in some cases large, but they contained only a few rooms. They had very little furniture, and this was usually in the last stages of its usefulness. The windows were without glass. A few plates and other dishes, which often gave evidence of rough usage, made up the table service, and everywhere there was a lack of cleanliness. The food was only such as was produced on the estate. Fresh meat was available only at the annual period of slaughtering, for it was found to be too expensive to kill an ox or

[1] Barros Arana, vii., 463.

other animal in order to provide fresh meat for half a dozen persons for four or five days. Each house had an oratory, where the missionaries arriving from time to time were expected to celebrate mass; but this apartment was often kept in such a filthy and neglected state that the priests refused to use it for religious services.

In the last years of the colonial period a few of the more wealthy owners, particularly those in the neighborhood of Santiago, showed a disposition to increase the conveniences of living in the country. The proprietors, who lived on their estates for only a few months in the year, constituted only a small part of the country population. The large majority was composed of tenants, who were nominally free, but whose condition was not greatly different from that of the vassals of a medieval landlord. Each of them received a certain plot of ground, which he cultivated and on which he might keep a certain number of animals; and in return for this he was required to work for the owner.

"There were without doubt," as Barros Arana says, "kind and charitable proprietors who treated their tenants humanely, who helped them in their times of need, and who were interested in their well-being; but the greater number maintained with respect to their dependents a regimen which was very little different from that to which the Indians of the encomienda were subjected."[1]

[1] *Historia jeneral de Chile*, vii., 466.

The great proprietors frequently exercised the power of public officials, either as agents of the subdelegates or as merely owners of the soil, and their orders had practically the authority of law. They arrogated to themselves the right to administer justice and even to impose punishments. Although the tenant might legitimately leave the estate on which he lived, few of them did it voluntarily, for they either acquired a sentimental attachment to the places where they had spent many years, or they saw nothing to be gained in going from one estate to another. Like the very poor everywhere, who have some permanent abiding-place, they hesitated to move lest they should lose the very small advantage of their actual state, and fall into the more miserable condition of the floating population that wandered over the country seeking work wherever they fancied it might be found. The feudal relations that thus came into existence were generally characteristic of the later colonial society, especially of that portion of it outside of the cities, in the southern part of the continent.

The filth, the vice, the ignorance, the burial of the dead in the churches, and the lack of proper medicinal remedies, both in the country and in the cities, in spite of the general healthfulness of the climate, made it possible for diseases to become epidemic and to carry off large numbers of the inhabitants, not only of the Indians but also of the Spaniards and mestizos. In the records of the municipal council of Santiago, the presence of the epidemics was carefully noted, as was also the action taken to provide prayers, offerings, and processions to allay the evil. But the records give no pathological indications sufficient to inform us of the character of the diseases in question. From other sources, however, it is known that syphilis and smallpox were two of the diseases that spread their ravages through the colony. Smallpox was first introduced into Chile in 1561, and from time to time throughout the colonial period it appeared and carried off its victims by thousands. In 1765 the municipal council recorded the fact that, in the few preceding months, smallpox had caused the death of more than five thousand persons. In 1788–1789 the city of Concepcion, having a population of not more than six thousand, lost fifteen hundred by smallpox. The ravages of the disease, as it swept through the cities and over the country, left horror and desolation in its path. Those persons who escaped death were often greatly disfigured, and many of them were left blind. Its appearance in one province, Santiago or Concepcion, led the other province to establish a quarantine line along the river Maule, but the precautions were always ineffective. In the last half of the century successful vaccination was introduced, but it could not be made general.

Except among the cultivated classes, it met with insurmountable opposition.

In the society of Chile where a small minority of the inhabitants—the Spaniards and the creoles—sought to preserve the lines of class separation, the mestizo constituted a large lower class, the members of which found it difficult to keep above the line of positive misery. They inherited vices as well as virtues from both of the races from which they were descended. The mestizos, like their ancestors on the side of the Indians, were both physically and mentally strong; yet they were rough, malicious, superstitious, given to gambling, intoxicating drinks, and robbery, and they were easily drawn into bloody quarrels. They might have become a powerful factor in the material progress of the country, if the political authorities and the upper class had known how to provide the conditions in which their labor would have been demanded. But in the isolation imposed by nature and under the restrictive legislation imposed by Spain, there was only a limited market for the wares which the country might most readily produce, and as a consequence those persons who might have become most effective laborers were wasted, without employment, in recklessness and poverty.

"Nothing is more common," said Manuel de Salus,

"than, in the same fields which have just produced a rich harvest, to see the very hands that have gathered the crop stretched out begging bread, and sometimes in the place itself where wheat has just been sold at a very low price. Persons who at first observe this state of affairs are disposed to solve the enigma by concluding that the cause is the innate indolence which they have believed to be characteristic of the Indians, and that this has contaminated all persons born on the continent; and, moreover, that this indolence has been encouraged and increased by abundance. Or, more indulgent persons, seeking occult and mysterious causes, attribute this state of things to the climate; but no one takes the trouble to examine the matter carefully, or stoops to seek more simple and probable reasons. To attribute laziness and inefficiency to the people is an error which I have appreciated many times and have shown it to be such to unprejudiced persons. Every day robust laborers may be seen in the plazas and streets offering their extensive services in exchange for wares, many of them useless and very high in price. They may be seen appearing at the doors of houses in the country begging for work, while the proprietors are under the sad necessity of turning them away. I am a constant spectator of this same thing in connection with the public works of the capital, where crowds of these unhappy persons present themselves soliciting work, and praying with such effectiveness that it may be given them, that in order not to augment their misery by a rebuff, or in order to put them off without harshness, I

offered them a silver real for a day's work, and a half a real to the boys,"[1]
and the applications under these conditions exhausted the funds. There was, moreover, no lack of laborers to complete promptly the wheat harvest in spite of its abundance, or to perform the work of the vintage. The market was inadequate to receive the wares that would have been produced if all the laborers had been employed, and the circumstances made the increase of vagrancy inevitable.

Negroes formed only a small part of the colonial population of Chile. The first colonists, instead of buying negroes, availed themselves of the labor of the Indians, with little or no cost. There were, however, three or four thousand African slaves in Chile before the middle of the seventeenth century, but a later rise in their price caused many to be transported to Peru and there sold, and, but for the prohibition of the governor, all of them would probably have been taken away. Valparaiso was the port from which the slaves were shipped; and with this beginning, it became a somewhat important market for slaves brought from Africa by way of Buenos Aires. Many negroes and mulattoes born in Chile were also sold here for transportation to Peru. The low wages of free laborers in Chile made it unprofitable to keep slaves, particularly since the price

[1] Quoted by Barros Arana, *Historia jeneral de Chile*, vii., 442.

had risen from 250 to 600 dollars. Yet at the close of the eighteenth century, there were in Chile ten or twelve thousand negroes and mulattoes, including both sexes. Of this number only four or five thousand were slaves, and these were almost all in domestic service. They were kept by the wealthy families largely for ostentation. They were generally dressed well, sometimes in showy livery, and were treated with kindness. Some of them who appeared to be sufficiently intelligent and trustworthy were made superintendents on estates in the country, while others were taught trades. They became tailors and shoemakers, and made the clothing and shoes for the family of their masters. Among the negroes and mulattoes who were free, there were tailors, shoemakers, carpenters, silversmiths, and some who followed other trades. Those living in Santiago formed a small battalion, under officers of the white race; and in the struggle for independence they rendered important service in the battle of Maipo.

CHAPTER XI

THE battle of Trafalgar, in 1805, against the allied fleets of France and Spain left Great Britain the mistress of the seas. The loss of her thirteen colonies in North America had naturally awakened a desire for compensation in some other part of the world. The limitation of her trade, caused by the French Revolution and the Napoleonic wars, made acceptable the opportunity to bring under her control markets outside of the field of the great European conflict. Not less urgent was the plan to prevent the loss of her power and prestige in the East Indies, which were menaced by the Dutch in possession of Cape Colony. The British determined to take this colony, and sent thither an expedition under Sir Home Popham, in command of the naval forces, and General David Baird, in command of a land force of 6600 men.

The government of Mr. Pitt had had in contemplation as early as 1796 action that would bring South America, or some part of it, under English control to be made available as a market for

England. It was for this purpose that Sir Home Popham was appointed to the ship *Diadem* in 1804.

" He was appointed to that ship," to quote Lord Melville, then at the head of the Board of Admiralty, " with a view of co-operating with General Miranda, to the extent of taking advantage of any of his proceedings, which might lead to our obtaining a position on the continent of South America, favorable to the trade of this country." [1]

In giving his testimony at the trial of Popham, Lord Melville said:

" At all times and in every conversation that I had with Mr. Pitt on the subject, I make no doubt Buenos Aires was often the subject of discussion. My reason for being confident in that opinion is, that in all the considerations I ever gave to the subject of South America, whether the attack was to be made on a smaller or larger scale, I always considered the Rio de la Plata as the most important position for the interest of Great Britain upon that side of South America." [2]

The expedition to the Cape, under General Baird with Brigadier-General Beresford second in command, sailed from Cork in August, 1805; touched at Madeira, then at the Bay of All

---

[1] *Minutes of a Court-martial for the Trial of Sir Home Popham*, London, 1807, 139.
[2] *Ibid.*, 140.

Saints, and arrived at its destination on January 4, 1806. The Cape fell into the hands of the English without great cost, and soon afterwards it was determined to make an attempt on Buenos Aires. Sir Home Popham and Brigadier-General Beresford commanded the expedition to the Rio de la Plata, which consisted of three frigates, three corvettes, and five transports, carrying in all one hundred and seventy-eight guns. The Board of Admiralty took the view that this expedition to Buenos Aires was undertaken by the officers at the Cape without any superior "direction or authority whatever," leaving the Cape, "which it was Sir Home Popham's duty to guard, not only exposed to attack and insult, but even without the means of affording protection to the trade of his Majesty's subjects, or of taking possession of any ships of the enemy, which might have put into any of the bays or harbors of the Cape or ports adjacent." [1]

Sir Home Popham had been directed, however, by the Lords Commissioners of the Admiralty to send a frigate to cruise on the east coast of South America between Rio de Janeiro and Rio de la Plata, as soon as he should have accomplished the object of the expedition on which he was about to proceed, for the purpose of procuring intelligence of the enemy's motions, in order that he might be prepared against any attack they

[1] Admiralty Order in *Trial of Sir Home Popham*, 4.

might be disposed to make on the settlement.[1] And in September he was directed from the Admiralty Office to retain all the transports under his command at the Cape of Good Hope, after the reduction of that settlement, until he should receive further orders.[2]

This expedition against the Cape of Good Hope was undertaken on information furnished the government by Sir Home Popham. While at Portsmouth in 1805, he received information of the weak state of the garrison at the Cape of Good Hope.

"This intelligence," he said, "appeared to me so important, not only from the advantage to be derived from the capture of the Cape of Good Hope itself, but from the facility which the possession of that settlement would afford to the projected conquest of the dependencies on the east coast of South America, that I lost no time in coming up to town and communicating it to Mr. Pitt."

The communication was made through Mr. Sturges Bourne, then one of the Secretaries of the Treasury, whom "Mr. Pitt immediately authorized to make further inquiries on the subject in the quarter from which the communication was stated to be derived." The result of the information obtained by this means "was a complete

---

[1] John Barrow to Sir Home Popham, Aug. 2, 1805 see *Trial*, p. 17.

[2] *Ibid.*, 18.

17

confirmation of the statement made by Sir Home
Popham, and Mr. Pitt instantly determined to
take the necessary measures for the execution of
an expedition against the Cape."[1] The suggestion
by Sir Home Popham appears thus to have been
the origin of Pitt's plan; for Sturges Bourne said
before the court-martial: "I am quite sure that
Mr. Pitt had no such expedition in his contemplation at the time Sir Home Popham made his
proposal, and I have no reason to believe that any
other of the king's ministers had such an object
in view."

Giving testimony at the trial of Popham, Mr.
Huskisson said:

" Mr. Pitt stated to me generally, as he had frequently
stated before, the views he entertained with respect
to South America; that he conceived it a most essential object for this country to use its naval superiority,
and the facility that superiority afforded in extensive
operations against South America, in case we should
be obliged to continue the war, as he apprehended
we should if the success of the confederacy then
forming on the continent did not correspond with
his wishes on that subject; that he thought his plan
of operations most essential not only to the interests
of this country separately considered, but also with a
view to prevent the French themselves from doing
that which he did not doubt they would do in case of
any neglect, namely, getting possession of the princi-

[1] Lord Melville in *Trial of Sir Home Popham*, 142.

pal positions and revenues to that extensive empire; that he therefore gave general credit to the person who furnished that plan and the information but hoped we should be beforehand with the enemy, as our naval means were so much superior to theirs."[1]

It is evident the views of Mr. Pitt with respect to South America were not confined to introducing British manufactures, but took a wider range.

The origin of the plan to take Buenos Aires which was carried out at this time may be seen in the correspondence produced at the trial of Popham. In a letter written by him to William Marsden, of the Admiralty Office, and dated April 9, 1806, he announced that, on account of the unsettled weather, he proposed to remove his squadron from its position in Table Bay, and that he considered the coming of Admiral Willeaumez very improbable. As it was expected that the French fleet would be obliged to resort to Rio de la Plata or the coast of Brazil for supplies, he thought "employing the squadron in cruising a short time off that coast, instead of remaining idle, will be a disposition fraught with some advantages, and which I hope will appear so evident to their Lordships as to induce them to approve of the measure." Starting on the 10th, the lack of the requisite breeze led him to anchor in the outer bay, and here he received "intelligence respecting the weak state of defence which

[1] *Trial of Sir Home Popham*, 146.

Montevideo and Buenos Aires were in." With this information, confirming what he had already learned from other sources, he "suggested the expediency of sparing a few troops for a short time, to enable us to bring a question of such importance to an immediate issue."[1] Popham urged this undertaking, "from a conviction of the great and splendid benefit which the country would derive by a conquest of such a nature at this moment." Sir David Baird after considering the subject seriously and consulting with General Beresford acceded to the proposition and ordered that the 71st regiment should be embarked under the direction of General Beresford. The main advantage of the conquest suggested at this time was the opportunity "to supply several millions of inhabitants with the manufactures of the United Kingdom."[2]

The conquest, moreover, was not expected to be difficult, for Popham was convinced as the

[1] Popham to William Marsden, April 13, 1806.

[2] Sir Home Popham, writing in 1806, finds "that Buenos Aires is the best commercial situation in South America. It is the grand centre and emporium of the trade of all its provinces, and is the channel through which a great proportion of the wealth of the kingdom of Chile and Peru annually passes." "About six hundred coasters enter inwards annually at Montevideo, and one hundred and thirty European ships; and about the same number clear outwards; but in this commercial intercourse the exactions, duties, and restrictions are so arbitrary, that the natives are in a state not many removes from open revolt."—Popham to William Marsden, April 30, 1806.

result of his examinations that there were "not above five hundred regular troops at the two places, some provincial cavalry and militia; that the walls of Montevideo are in a very ruinous state; and the inhabitants disaffected beyond any calculation." In his letter of April 13, 1806, Popham expressed the hope that his superiors in London would consider the undertaking "as far preferable to the alternative of allowing the squadron to moulder away its native energy, by wintering in False Bay, and eventually become paralyzed, after remaining so long as it has done in a state of cold defensive inactivity."[1]

While still at the Cape Sir Home Popham's views were confirmed by a letter received from Mr. Waine, the master of an American ship. The letter was dated March 28, 1806, and was in the following form:

"I beg leave to represent to you, that I have been three times to Buenos Aires and Montevideo; that both places have the greatest abundance of wheat, flour, and indeed every sort of provision. From my knowledge of the minds and dispositions of the inhabitants, I can assure you that his Majesty's squadron, under your command, would, with ease, take possession of either of those places; and if permanent possession could be effected, there is not the slightest doubt of procuring any quantity of flour; and to prove to you that it is not an idle sug-

[1] *Trial of Sir Home Popham*, London, 1807, 46.

gestion to mislead the British, I could have no objection to be one of five hundred men to attack either
place. I am sure the inhabitants are so ridden by
their government, that to prevent a shot being
fired at Montevideo, if they had any threat from
the men of war, they would send out any quantity
of flour or buscuit, to prevent mischief; but the
places may be taken as I describe; and if the trade
is thrown open, all the inhabitants would willingly
acquire and keep the place for the British nation
without troops, which would be a mine of wealth;
I hope you will not make mention of my name im-
properly, as it may injure me greatly. I myself,
with my ship *Elizabeth*, are at your service to do
what you please to get possession of Buenos Aires."[1]

While on the voyage Popham had a plan to take
Montevideo as soon as he reached the coast, and
then to pass on to Buenos Aires. But information
received from an English pilot who fell into his
hands as he entered the river persuaded him that
it would be expedient to move immediately
against the latter city. Of his approach to
Buenos Aires he gave the following account in a
dispatch dated July 6, 1806.

"On the 8th of June we anchored near the island
of Flores; and, after passing Montevideo the following
day, we detained a Portuguese schooner, by whom
the intelligence we had formerly received was generally
confirmed. On the 11th we fell in with the *Encounter*

[1] *Trial of Sir Home Popham*, 43.

and *Ocean* transport,[1] near the south coast of the river; and on the thirteenth we joined the squadron.

"It was immediately determined to attack the capital; and no time was lost in removing the marine battalion to the *Narcissus*, the *Encounter*, and the transports, for the purpose of proceeding to Buenos Aires, while the *Diadem* blockaded the port of Montevideo, and the *Raisonable*, the *Diomede*, by way of demonstration, cruised near Maldonado and other assailable points.

"Our progress up the river was very much retarded by the shoalness of the water, adverse winds, and currents, continual fogs, and the great inaccuracy of the charts; but by the unremitting and laborious exertions of the officers and men I had the honor to command, these difficulties were surmounted, and the squadron anchored on the afternoon of the 25th off point Quelmes, about twelve miles from Buenos Aires.

"As it was impossible for the *Narcissus* to approach the shore, on account of the shoalness of the water, the *Encounter* was run in so close as to take the ground, the more effectually to cover the debarkation of the army in case of necessity: the whole, however, was landed in the course of the evening without the least opposition; consisting of the detachment of his Majesty's troops from the Cape, and that from St. Helena, with the marine battalion under the orders of Captain King, of his Majesty's ship the *Diadem*, which was composed of the Marines of the squadron, augmented by the incorporation of some seamen,

[1] These vessels had parted from the fleet previous to its arrival at St. Helena.

and three companies of royal blues from the same source of enterprise, which had been regularly trained for that duty, and dressed in an appropriate uniform."

A dispatch from General Beresford, who led the landing forces, dated July 2, 1806, gives an account of the movements by land against the city. The extract dealing with this advance is as follows:

"It was eleven o'clock in the morning of the 26th before I could move off my ground, and the enemy could, from his position, have counted every man I had. He was drawn up along the brow of a hill, on which was the village of Reduction, which covered his right flank, and his force consisted principally of cavalry (I have been since informed two thousand), with eight field-pieces. The nature of the ground was such, that I was under the necessity of going directly to his front; and to make my line, as much as I could, equal to his, I formed all the troops into one line, except the St. Helena infantry, of one hundred and twenty yards in the rear, with two field-pieces, with orders to make face to the right or left, as either of our flanks should be threatened by his cavalry; I had two six-pounders on each flank, and two howitzers in the centre of the first line. In this order I advanced against the enemy, and after we had got within range of his guns, a tongue of swamp crossed our front, and obliged me to halt while the guns took a small circuit to cross, and which was scarcely performed when the enemy opened their field-pieces on us, at first well pointed, but as we advanced at a very quick rate, in spite of the boggy ground, that very soon obliged us to leave all our guns behind, his fire did us but little injury. The 71st regiment reaching the bottom of the heights in a pretty good line, seconded by the marine battalion, the enemy would not wait their nearer approach but retired from the brow of the hill, which our troops gaining, and commencing a fire of small arms, he fled with precipitation, leaving to us four field-pieces and one tumbril, and we saw nothing more of him that day.

"I halted two hours on the field to rest the troops, and to make arrangements for taking with us the enemy's guns and our own, which had now, by the exertions of Captain Donnelly, of his Majesty's ship *Narcissus*, been extricated from the bog. He had accidentally landed and accompanied the troops, on seeing them advance to the enemy, and I am much indebted to him for his voluntary assistance.

"I then marched in hopes of preventing the destruction of the bridge over the Riachuelo, a river at this season of the year not fordable and which lay between us and the city; distant from it about three miles, and eight from our then situation; and though I used every diligence, I had the mortification to see it in flames long before I could reach it. I halted the troops for the night a mile from it, and pushed on three companies of the 71st, under Lieutenant-Colonel Pack, with two howitzers, to the bridge, to endeavor to prevent its total destruction. I accompanied this detachment, but on reaching the bridge

found it entirely consumed; and as the enemy during
the night was heard bringing down guns, I withdrew
the detachment before light, as their position was
thought too open and exposed to the enemy's fire,
who had at nine o'clock, on hearing some of our
soldiers go to the river to get water, opened a fire
from their guns, and a considerable line of infantry.

"As soon as it was light I sent Captain Kennet of
the engineers to reconnoitre the sides of the river,
and found that on our side we had little or no cover
to protect us, whilst the enemy were drawn up behind
hedges, houses, and in the shipping on the opposite
bank, the river not thirty yards wide. As our situation
and circumstances could not admit of the least delay,
I determined to force the passage, and for that purpose
ordered down the field-pieces, which with the addition of those taken from the enemy the day before,
were eleven (one I had spiked and left, not being
able to bring it off), to the water's edge, and ordered
the infantry to remain in the rear, under cover,
except the light company and grenadiers of the 71st.
As our guns approached, the enemy opened a very
ill-directed fire from great guns and musketry; the
former soon ceased after our fire opened, the latter
was kept up for more than half an hour, but though
close to us, did us but little or no injury, so ill was it
directed. We then found means, by boats and
rafts, to cross a few men over the Riachuelo, and on
ordering all fire to cease, the little of them that
remained ceased also.

"The troops which had opposed us during these
two days appear to have been almost entirely pro-

vincial, with a considerable proportion of veteran officers. The numbers that were assembled to dispute our passage of the river, I have been since informed, were about two thousand infantry. I had no reason from their fire to suppose their numbers so great; their opposition was very feeble; the only difficulty was the crossing the river to get at them.

"By eleven o'clock A.M. I had got some guns and the greatest part of the troops across the river, and seeing no symptoms of further opposition, and learning that the troops in general had deserted the city, motives of humanity induced me to send, by the honorable ensign Gordon, a summons to the governor to deliver to me the city and fortress, that the excesses and calamities which would most probably occur if the troops entered in a hostile manner might be avoided; informing him that the British character would insure to them the exercise of their religion, and protection to their persons and all private property. He returned to me an officer to ask some hours to draw up conditions; but I could not consent to delay my march, which I commenced as soon as the whole had crossed the Riachuelo; and, on arriving near the city, an officer from the governor again met me with a number of conditions to which I had not then time to attend; but said I would confirm by writing what I had promised, when in possession of the city; and the terms granted and signed by Sir Home Popham and myself I have the honor to annex."

Major-General Baird in his instructions to Brigadier-General Beresford directed him to assume the office of lieutenant-governor, "and to draw whatever salary and allowances may have been enjoyed by the Spanish Governor, his immediate predecessor, until his Majesty shall be graciously pleased to make known his pleasure."[1]

During the advance of the English the city was in confusion, and the authorities displayed only weakness and indecision. After the vessels had been observed entering the river, José de la Pena, the chief pilot of the royal fleet, went along the coast in search of definite information concerning these vessels. On the night of the 23d of June, 1806, in accordance with Sobremonte's orders, he reported to the viceroy at Buenos Aires. But the viceroy refused to adopt Pena's advice, and held that the vessels were only cruising, and had not come to attack the colony. On the 24th, Pena returned to Ensenada to await the viceroy's orders. At daybreak, on the 25th, English vessels appeared off Buenos Aires. The viceroy now caused a call to arms to be sounded, and between seven and nine o'clock the inhabitants gathered at the fort. "But in spite of all this, still no preparations were made; on the contrary, the viceroy remained inactive, notwithstanding the fact that the ships of the enemy were seen approaching Quilmes, three or four leagues from the city, and disembarking in boats and

[1] Major-General Baird to Right Hon. Lord Castlereagh, April 14, 1806, *Trial of Sir Home Popham*, 59.

launches."[1]   Finally as a result of persistent
urging the viceroy caused arms to be distributed
to the militia of Buenos Aires.   This force, having been joined by 800 lancers under the command of Nicolas de la Quintana, was sent to
Quilmes to attack the enemy, and was to be under
the command of Sub-Inspector Pedro de Arce.   In
the meantime 1000 citizens had been given arms
at the fort, but they had no cartridges and their
guns had no flints.   These things they were to
get from their respective captains in the afternoon.   On the 26th, at eleven o'clock in the
morning, 600 of the provincial militia with their
officers marched to Barracas, with the viceroy
as their rear-guard.[2]   In the meantime the English had landed; the Argentinos after firing from
a distance fled, leaving three cannon and a how-
itzer which were immediately taken possession of
by their enemy.

During this skirmish a second call to arms was
sounded in the city, announcing to the rest of the
inhabitants who remained in the town that their
compatriots found themselves in great need of
assistance.

During these operations the alarm had spread
through all parts of the city.   The inhabitants
were terrified by the news of the arrival of the
British forces.   The panic was moreover intensified by the ringing of the bells; and the viceroy,

[1] Calvo, *Tratados*, iv., 387.   [2] *Ibid.*, iv., 388.

abandoning all hope of effective resistance, was
fully occupied in contemplating the possibility of
successful flight. But before his departure he
published, June 26, 1806, the following manifesto:

"I make known to all the inhabitants and faithful
vassals of our master the King in all this country and
frontier, that our enemies the English are disembarking in Quilmes, where many persons of the
neighborhood, full of valor and patriotism, have
gathered manifesting a desire to conquer and destroy
them, and to the end that all others, without distinction of persons, may unite with them as soon as
possible, with as many horses and arms as they may
have or the officers be able to collect, and march to
the bridge of Galvez, where there is another body of
troops; and for all this I authorize Lieutenant of
Blandengues D. José Ruiz, of the Lancers, to proceed
instantly, sending men as well as horses, in order that
the arms of the King may triumph, and the faithful
inhabitants of this country may have the glory of
having conquered the enemy of their sacred religion,
of their property and families, as this superior government hopes, placing its confidence in the God of
armies and in the love of these vassals for the welfare of the sovereign."

There were in the city no disciplined troops, and
no competent leaders to command. In the companies that were formed to ward off the impending
invasion, the officers were as ignorant as the rank
and file. On the 27th of June the British troops,

numbering fifteen hundred and sixty men, entered Buenos Aires. The population of the city at this time was about 45,000, and the more spirited of the inhabitants felt deeply the humiliation of their subjugation, particularly when they saw how small was the body of the conquerors who took possession of the streets and squares, and proceeded to make their power effective in the government.[1]

Having taken possession of the city, and raised the British flag, with much firing of cannon both by the fleet and the artillery on shore, Beresford ordered the public treasure to be put into his hands. Under the circumstances compliance with this demand was inevitable. The money was surrendered and transferred to London. A large amount of merchandise also fell into the hands of the British. It consisted principally of cinchona and quicksilver, and was estimated to be worth between one million and two million

---

[1] In his *Autobiography* Belgrano makes the following statement respecting the taking of the city by the British:

"Confieso que me indigné, y que nunca sentí más haber ignorado, como ya dije anteriormente, hasta los rudimentos de la milicia; todavía fué mayor mi incomodidad cuando ví entrar las tropas enemigas, y su despreciable número para una población como la de Buenos Aires: esta idea no se apartó de mi imaginación, y poco faltó para que me hubiese hecho perder la cabeza:—me era muy doloroso ver á mi patria bajo otra dominación, y sobre todo en tal estado de degradación que hubiese sido subyugada por una empresa aventurera, cual era la del bravo y honrado Beresford, cuyo valor admiro y admiraré siempre en esta peligrosa empresa."

dollars, namely, $1,438,514. The arrival of the spoils in London aroused general joy, and filled the British nation with extravagant expectations of commercial gains. The government of England had not authorized this conquest, but now it approved and confirmed it.

The effect of the fall of Buenos Aires and of the plan of the English to invade Chile was to stimulate the government in Peru to undertake preparations for the defence of the western coast of South America. The viceroy Abascal sent forces and supplies to Chiloé, aroused the Peruvians to enlist in the militia, and proposed to lead a body of troops to Chile, and, if necessary, to Buenos Aires. The struggle of the inhabitants of Buenos Aires to drive out the English and regain the city moved the Peruvians under the leadership of Abascal to lend assistance. They sent 100,000 pesos by way of Cuzco and 200,000 from the treasuries of Arequipa and Puno. From Chile were sent 1800 quintals of powder, 200,000 cartridges and 200 quintals of balls, and other munitions and supplies.

After the surrender of the funds, the intentions of the British government were made known to the inhabitants through proclamations, dated June 28th, and June 30th, and issued by the commanding officers. These proclamations affirmed, among other things, that a free trade should be opened and permitted to South America, similar to that enjoyed by all others of his Majesty's colonies, particularly the island of Trinidad, the inhabitants of which had felt peculiar benefits from being under the government of a sovereign powerful enough to protect them from any insult, and generous enough to give them such commercial advantages as they could not enjoy under the administration of any other country.

The terms granted to the inhabitants of Buenos Aires by Popham and Beresford were published on the second of July. They provided that the troops belonging to the king of Spain, who were in the town at the time of the entry of the British troops, should be allowed to meet in the fortress of Buenos Aires, to march out of the fort with all the honors of war, and should then lay down their arms and become prisoners of war; but such officers as were natives of the country, or legally domiciled, should be at liberty to continue in the province as long as they behaved themselves properly, taking the oath of allegiance to his Britannic Majesty; or they might proceed to Great Britain with regular passports, having previously passed their parole of honor not to serve until they should be regularly exchanged. Moreover, all *bona fide* private property, whether belonging to individual persons, the churches, or public institutions, should be unmolested; all the inhabitants should receive protection; the different taxes should be collected by the

18

magistrates, as usual, until his Majesty's pleasure
should be known; every protection should be
afforded to the exercise of the Roman Catholic
religion; the coasting vessels in the river should
be delivered to their owners; and all public
property should be surrendered to the captors.[1]

[1] The document setting forth these terms, dated July
2, 1806, is printed in Wilcocke, *History of Buenos Aires*,
352; see *Annual Register*, 1806, 599; the original, printed in
Spanish and English, is found in *Colec. Carranza: Invasiones
Inglesas, 1806–1807*, i., Biblioteca Nacional, Buenos Aires;
the English version being in the following form:

"Terms granted to the Inhabitants of Buenos Ayres and
its dependencies by the Commanders in Chief of His Britannick Majesty's Forces by Land and Sea.

1.

"The troops belonging to his Catholic Majesty, who were in
the town at the time of the entry of the British troops, shall
be allowed to meet in the Fortress of Buenos Aires, march
out of the fort with all the honors of war, and shall then
lay down their arms, and become prisoners of war; but such
officers as are natives of the country, or regularly domiciliated,
shall be at liberty to continue here so long as they behave
themselves as becometh good subjects and citizens, taking
the oath of allegiance to his Britannick Majesty, or proceed
to Great Britain with regular passports, having previously
passed their parole of honor, not to serve until they are
regularly exchanged.

2.

"All bona fide private property, either belonging to the
civil or military servants of the late government, to the
magistrates, burghers, and inhabitants of the town of Buenos
Aires, and its dependencies, to the illustrious the bishop, the
clergy; to the churches, monasteries, colleges, foundations,

By proclamation, dated August 4, 1806, Major-
General Beresford made known the conditions

and other public institutions of that kind, shall remain free
and unmolested.

3.

"All persons of every description belonging to this city
and its dependencies shall receive every protection from the
British government, and they shall not be obliged to bear
arms against his most Catholic Majesty, nor shall any person
whatever in the city, or its dependencies, take up arms, or
otherwise act inimicably against his Majesty's troops or
government.

4.

"The cabildo, magistrates, burghers, and inhabitants
shall preserve all their rights and privileges which they
have enjoyed hitherto, and shall continue in full and free exercise of their legal functions, both civil and criminal, under
all the respect and protection that can be afforded them
by his Majesty's government until his Majesty's pleasure
is known.

5.

"The publick archives of the town shall receive every protection from his Britannick Majesty's government.

6.

"The different taxes and duties levied by the magistrates
to remain for the present, and to be collected by them in
the same manner and applied to the same purpose as heretofore for the general good of the city, until his Majesty's
pleasure is known.

7.

"Every protection shall be given to the full and free

under which trade with Buenos Aires and its
dependencies might be carried on. He informed
the people

"that the system of monopoly, restriction, and oppression has already come to an end; that the people
will be able to enjoy the products of other countries
at a moderate price; that the manufactures and
productions of their country are free from the hindrance and oppression that has burdened them, and
prevented the country from becoming what it is

---

exercise of the Holy Catholic religion, and all respect shown
to the most illustrious bishop and all the holy clergy.

8.

"The ecclesiastical court shall continue in the full and
free exercise of all its functions and be precisely on the same
footing as it was heretofore.

9.

"The coasting vessels in the river will be given up to their
owners according to the proclamation issued the 30 ultimo.

10.

"All publick property of every description belonging to
the enemies of his Britannick Majesty shall be faithfully
delivered up to the captors; and as the commanders in chief
bind themselves to see the fulfilment of all the preceding
articles for the benefit of South America, so do the cabildo
and magistrates bind themselves to see that this last article
is faithfully and honorably complied with.

"Given under our hands and seals in the Fortress of
Buenos Aires this second day of July 1806—W. C. BERES-
FORD. Major General—[seal] HOME POPHAM, Commodore
Commanding in Chief. [seal]."

capable of being, the most flourishing in the world; and that the object of Great Britain is the happiness and prosperity of these countries."

The regulations announced by this proclamation[1] provided that a lawful trade in all merchandise, fruits, manufactured articles, and products from

[1] The original proclamation is found in *Colec. Carranza; Invasiones Inglesas, 1806–1807.* The order of the king in council affirming possession of the conquered city and territory and confirming the terms of Beresford's proclamation made it clear that the British government had adopted the results of the conquest, and held the city and the territory as a part of the dominions of the British sovereign. The order of the king in council was issued September 17, 1806, and was as follows:

"Whereas the Capital city, town, and fortress, of Buenos Aires, and its dependencies, have been conquered by his Majesty's forces, and the territory and forts of the same are delivered up to his Majesty; and the same are now in his Majesty's possession; his Majesty is thereupon pleased to order and declare and it is hereby ordered and declared, that all his loving subjects may lawfully trade to and from the said capital city, town, and fortress, of Buenos Aires, and its dependencies, including therein all and every the territories belonging to or forming a part of the government of the same, in British ships, owned by his Majesty's subjects, and navigated according to law, or in ships *bona fide* belonging to any of the subjects, or native inhabitants, of the said city, town, or territories, such native inhabitants being peaceably resident within the same, and under the obedience of his Majesty's government there; and that such trade shall be subject to the same duties, rules, regulations, conditions, restrictions, penalties, and forfeitures, to which the trade to and from his Majesty's Colonies, plantations, and islands, in the West Indies and South America, is or shall be subject by law except as hereinafter specified.

Great Britain, Ireland, and her colonies might be carried on with Buenos Aires and its dependencies, in British ships owned by his Majesty's subjects, or by inhabitants of that country, upon paying, in general, a duty of twelve and

"And his Majesty is further pleased to order and declare, and it is hereby ordered and declared, that all commodities being the growth, produce, or manufacture of the said city, town, and fortress, of Buenos Aires, and its dependencies, including therein all and every the territories belonging to or forming a part of the government of the same, or which have been usually exported therefrom, shall be permitted to be imported into any of the ports of the United Kingdom, in British ships, owned by his Majesty's subjects, and navigated according to law, or in ships *bona fide* belonging to any of the inhabitants of the said city, town, or territories, such native inhabitants being peaceably resident within the same, and under the obedience of his Majesty's government there; and that such commodities shall be subject to the same duties, orders, regulations, restrictions, conditions, penalties, and forfeitures, as articles of the like sort are subject to, coming from his Majesty's colonies, plantations, or islands, in the West Indies or South America.

"And whereas information has been received that the commander of his Majesty's forces, to whom the said city, town, and fortress, have surrendered, has reduced the duties on importation into the same from about thirty four and a half per cent., *ad valorem*, to ten per cent. *ad valorem*, and two and a half per cent. for the consulate or municipal duties, making in the whole twelve and one-half per cent., on all articles imported into the said place and its dependencies, in British ships, owned by his Majesty's subjects, and navigated according to law, or in ships *bona fide* belonging to any of the subjects or native inhabitants of the said city, town, or territories, such native inhabitants being peaceably resident within the same, and under the obedience of his Majesty's government there:—

one half per cent. *ad valorem*, on entering any
port of Rio de la Plata; and that all commodities produced in that country should be permitted to be imported into the United Kingdom,
in the ships already mentioned, under the same
terms as from the West India Islands.

"His Majesty is thereupon pleased to order and declare,
that the said reduced duties shall be continued to be levied,
and no other, on all articles so imported with the exception of
German linens, which are to continue to be subject to the same
duties as were paid thereon before the conquest of the said
place by his Majesty's arms, until his Majesty's pleasure shall
be further signified. And it is hereby further ordered that it
shall not be lawful for any slave or slaves to be landed, imported, or brought into the said city, town, and fortress, of
Buenos Aires, and its dependencies, including therein all and
every the territories belonging to or forming a part of the
government of the same, as aforesaid; upon pain that all
slaves so landed, imported, or brought, together with the
vessels bringing the same, or from which the same shall be
landed, and their cargoes shall become forfeited to his Majesty, his heirs and successors. Provided always that this
prohibition shall not extend to the several cases of slaves
bona fide employed in navigating any ship trading to or from
the said place; or of slaves *bona fide* employed as domestic
slaves, and coming into the said place with their masters; or
of slaves in any manner employed in his Majesty's naval or
military service. And the Right Honorable the Lords Commissioners of the Admiralty are to give the necessary directions herein, as to them may respectively appertain."

CHAPTER XII

BERESFORD was not ignorant of the preparations a part of the inhabitants were making to resist the invaders and to drive them out of the city. Through his spies he was kept informed of the steps taken to organize a patriotic force at Perdriel, a place about fifteen miles from the city. Against these patriots, who had raised their standard of blue and red, Beresford led a body of five hundred men, with six pieces of artillery. In spite of the brave resistance of Pueyrredon and his followers Beresford was victorious. The killed and wounded on both sides, however, did not amount to more than a dozen persons. Although those who had determined on the reconquest of the city were temporarily scattered, they were not discouraged nor were their plans changed. They were almost immediately united with certain forces under Liniers, that had been collected at Colonia, and had left that town for the southern shore on the third of August.

On the eve of his departure from Colonia,

Liniers issued a proclamation to his troops, in which he expressed his confidence in their zeal and patriotism, but affirmed "that if, contrary to his expectations, some forgetting their principles should turn their face from the enemy, they should know that there will be a cannon in the rear charged with grape-shot, with orders to fire on fugitive cowards."

"Valor without discipline," this proclamation continues, "only leads to immediate ruin; forces united and subordinated to the voice of those who direct them furnish the most secure means of attaining victory; therefore I order and command that the most scrupulous obedience be observed, under the most severe penalties of the ordinances for such cases."[1]

In crossing from Colonia the Spanish forces took advantage of a gale that swelled the waters on the bank of Palmas permitting their ships to pass over in safety. They were favored, moreover, by the violent rains that set in, making the roads practically impassable by any force but cavalry; and they were abundantly supplied with horses, while the English had only a few they were able to obtain in the city. Recognizing his disadvantageous position, Beresford deemed

[1] This proclamation was dated August 1st, and the forces left Colonia on the 3d. (Liniers to the Prince of Peace, August 16, 1806); for this and other documents relating to the English invasion, see Calvo, *Tratados de la America Latina*, v., 1–118.

it advisable to withdraw from the centre of the town to the right bank of the Riachuelo. He sent over the wounded and the treasure, but here the Spaniards intervened and prevented his retreat.

General Beresford had expected to be able to keep Liniers's forces at a distance from the town, but his inadequate means of communication and the condition of the roads prevented the execution of his plan. On the 10th of August the Spaniards had closed in upon the town, and occupied the principal avenues, while the inhabitants had armed themselves and taken possession of the housetops and the churches, prepared to carry on guerilla warfare from their posts of advantage. Only a part of the force that had been collected under Liniers was armed; and as it entered the city it continued to be attended by a large number of persons who had neither the arms nor the discipline of soldiers. The people were aroused to do what they might, either with or without arms, to further the cause of their emancipation; and the unarmed were especially helpful in assisting to bring up the artillery.

Liniers's success in life had hitherto been limited by his personal character. He was a man, according to General Mitre's description, of

"high spirit, sensitive imagination, reckless temperament, with more good-nature than energy, and with more zeal in taking up projects than perseverance in carrying them out; he was intelligent, active, and brave, uniting to an heroic yet vacillating ambition the frivolous passions of a superficial man; although he was not wanting in moral elevation and had the characteristics of a gentleman, he was guided rather by his emotions than his judgment."[1]

On the 10th of August Liniers demanded from Beresford the surrender of the city. To his request the British General replied that he would defend it as long as it might be done without overwhelming the inhabitants in calamity. Liniers received this answer at eleven o'clock at night, and three hours later his forces began the march; at five o'clock in the morning they occupied the square, Retiro, and here the contest for the possession of the city began. The result of the fighting which followed in the streets and from the housetops was the unconditional surrender of Beresford and his troops, on the 12th of August. The lost in killed and wounded was three hundred; twelve hundred laid down their arms and became prisoners of war. The victors lost two hundred in killed and wounded.[2]

After the overthrow of the English the fate of Buenos Aires was in the hands of the popular army. The viceroy, the representative of the

[1] Mitre, *Historia de Belgrano,* i., 128.

[2] Liniers to the Prince of Peace, August 16, 1806; Sir Home Popham to W. Marsden, August 25, 1806.

sovereign, had fled before the invaders, and was hopelessly discredited. Under the circumstances it devolved upon the municipality to initiate a movement to effect an organization. This was done by calling a congress of one hundred persons known as notables. This congress was opened, according to Mitre, "in the presence of more than four thousand spectators resolved to intervene in the discussion if it was necessary."[1] Under the strong pressure of a clamorous public, the chief military command was formally conferred upon Liniers, and a committee carrying a notification of this appointment was sent to Sobremonte. The viceroy was found about forty leagues from Buenos Aires at the head of a force of three thousand men, and he professed to be advancing to reconquer the city which had already been reconquered by the citizens themselves. At first he refused to assent to the appointment of Liniers, but was soon convinced by the attitude of the municipality that opposition was useless. He was also convinced that the period of his service as viceroy was ended.

This change left the civil and military power distributed among the audiencia, the cabildo, or municipal corporation, and Liniers, as the military chief. Under this new order, two of the authorities, the cabildo and the military chief, had a popular basis for their power. It was the

[1] *Historia de Belgrano*, i., 141.

voice of the populace which had insisted that Liniers should be formally recognized as the leader of the armed forces; and the cabildo was the representative body of the municipal republic. In the process of colonial emancipation the audiencia, whose members were appointed by the king, and represented absolute power, appeared destined to diminish relatively in influence as the people grew in power.

After the surrender of the troops in the city under Beresford, the fleet remained in the river blockading the ports of both shores. The first reinforcements to arrive were 1400 men from Cape Colony; the next were 4300 men sent from England under the command of General Samuel Auchmuty. Admiral Stirling, who was in command of the convoying fleet from England, was ordered to relieve Sir Home Popham. Both of these expeditions were dispatched before it was known in London that Beresford had been defeated; and they were originally designed to assist him in holding the position he had won. Another expedition of 4400 men had been prepared to invade Chile, but was ordered to the Rio de la Plata when the result of the popular uprising in Buenos Aires had become known to the English government. A little later still another body of 1630 men was sent, under the immediate command of Major-General Lewison Gower. In the beginning of the year 1807, the English had assembled

near Buenos Aires an army of about 12,000 men,
a fleet of eighteen war vessels, and more than
eighty transports. The chief command over all
the land forces serving in this region was conferred
upon Lieutenant-General Whitelocke.[1] General
Whitelocke was commanded, in case the English
succeeded in establishing their authority in the
southern provinces of South America, to assume
and exercise the civil government of the conquered territory, and to pay himself a salary of
four thousand pounds sterling per annum out of
any revenues that might be collected in these
provinces.[2]

Before the news of the disaster reached London
an order was issued for the recall of Sir Home
Popham. The Lords Commissioners of the Admiralty had before them Popham's letter of July
6th, containing information that the city of Buenos
Aires and its dependencies had surrendered to
his Majesty's arms: and they found it advisable
to take note of the irregularity of the conquest.
On September 25th, their secretary, William
Marsden, wrote to Popham:

"I have received their Lordships' commands to
acquaint you, that although they have judged it
necessary to mark their disapproval of a measure
of such importance being undertaken without the

---

[1] Whitelock's military commission was dated February 24,
1807; see *Trial of Lieut.-Gen. Whitelocke*, Appendix i., p. v.

[2] *Trial of Lieut.-Gen. Whitelocke*, Appendix i., p. v.

sanction of his Majesty's government, and of your having left the station which it was your duty to guard without any naval defence, they are nevertheless pleased to express their entire approbation of the judicious, able, and spirited conduct manifested by yourself, the officers, seamen, and mariners employed under your orders on the above occasion."

Rear-Admiral Stirling, appointed to succeed Popham, was authorized to determine in which ship Popham should return to England and, in performing this duty, he indicated the *Sampson* which had a convoy in charge for the Cape of Good Hope; and was then to proceed to Saint Helena on the way to Europe. In protesting against this order Sir Home Popham wrote:

"It is natural, Sir, for me to feel mortified at the idea of having, by any act of mine, given their Lordships cause to supersede me in this country; but when, in addition to this, I learn that it is proposed that I should be subject to all the aggravation of a voyage lengthened by proceeding from South America to South Africa, thence to Saint Helena for convoy, on my way to England, I cannot but say it is the severest punishment that could be inflicted on me. To a mind sensible, as I trust mine is, to every reproach— to any man of proper feeling—it is that sort of punishment which I consider secondary to scarcely any but death: it is carrying me in a situation humbled in the extreme to the place which, in conjunction with Sir David Baird, I had the honor to capture.

There are also reasons, too evident to need any explanation, which would make a visit to Saint Helena, situated as I am, equally galling to my feelings."[1]

The subsequent correspondence on this subject showed Stirling's meanness of spirit under circumstances where he could have afforded to be generous.

After his arrival in England Sir Home Popham was tried by a court-martial, held on the *Gladiator;* and at the conclusion of the trial the following verdict was rendered:

"The Court is of opinion, that the charges have been proved against the said Captain Sir Home Popham. That the withdrawing, without orders so to do, the whole of any naval force from the place where it is directed to be employed, and the employing it in distant operations against the enemy; more especially if the success of such operations should be likely to prevent its speedy return, may be attended with the most serious inconvenience to the public service, as the success of any plan formed by his Majesty's Ministers for operations against the enemy, in which such naval force might be included, may by such removal be entirely prevented. And the Court is further of opinion, that the conduct of the said Captain Sir Home Popham, in the withdrawing the whole of the naval force under his command

---

[1] Sir Home Popham to Rear-Admiral Stirling, December 7, 1806.

from the Cape of Good Hope, and the proceeding with it to the Rio de la Plata, was highly censurable; but in consideration of circumstances doth adjudge him to be *only severely reprimanded;* and the said Captain Sir Home Popham is hereby severely reprimanded accordingly."[1]

The English forces took possession of Montevideo, Maldonado, and Colonia, and appeared to have established their authority firmly on the left bank of the river.

"Merchant vessels had followed in the wake of the ships of war, and the river, lately so deserted, was encumbered with vessels having on board more merchandise than the country would be able to consume in five years. Montevideo had all the appearance of an English city; English placards covered the walls; in all the streets English shops were opened, where English cloth was sold at half the price which had hitherto been paid for it, on account of the thousand hindrances of the Spanish customs, and the unreasonable demands of the smugglers. Finally a Spanish-English journal, *The Star of the South*, was established under the patronage and with the assistance of the English administration, with the purpose of undermining the authority of Spain, whose decadence and weakness it was pleased to expose."[2]

About three months after the taking of Monte-

[1] *Trial of Sir Home Popham*, 179, 180.
[2] Arcos, *La Plata*, 214.

19

video, Whitelocke and Crawford arrived. In view of the firm footing that had been gained on the left bank of the river, and the fact that 1600 men had previously taken the city, the task of the commander-in-chief, at the head of an army of twelve thousand men, did not appear difficult. On the 28th of June, 1807, the English forces landed at Ensenada, a little port about sixteen leagues southeast of Buenos Aires. Since Beresford's easy victory the spirit of the inhabitants of Buenos Aires had undergone a great change, which was in a measure manifest in their expulsion of the invaders, and they now found themselves directed by leaders of energy and foresight. Alzaga stood at the head of the municipality, and the national battalions were commanded by Saavedra, Belgrano, Esteban Romero, Balcarce, Viamont, and Martin Rodriguez. The bulk of the inhabitants, in view of the force and skill that were brought against them, appreciated the difficulties of the situation; but at the same time they felt confident of success.

The English, advancing towards the city, crossed the Riachuelo, and inflicted upon the Spaniards a partial defeat. This defeat destroyed the hopeful expectations of the people and spread a pall of evil foreboding over the city. In the night which followed, Alzaga caused the city to be placed in a condition of defence. The streets around the plaza were cut by deep trenches;

the troops were distributed on the roofs of the churches and other buildings; and the artillery was placed behind street barricades, and where it might command the trenches. Confidence returned to the defenders of the city. The leader of the attacking party appeared also to be confident of victory, for in summoning the city to surrender he offered the following conditions:

"1. All British subjects detained in South America must be delivered up, and sufficient hostages placed in the power of the British commander till their arrival at Buenos Aires.

"2. That all persons holding civil offices dependent on the government of Buenos Aires, and all military officers and soldiers become prisoners of war.

"3. That all cannon, stores, arms, and ammunition be delivered up uninjured.

"4. That all public property of every description be delivered up to the British commanders.

"5. That free and unrestrained exercise of the Roman Catholic religion be granted to the inhabitants of Buenos Aires.

"6. That all private property on shore shall be respected and secured to its owners."

In replying to this proposition, the Spaniards refused to consider any terms which involved the laying down of their arms. The day following the date of this reply, namely, the fourth of July, General Whitelocke wrote to Liniers, stating that he had another column of troops awaiting his orders within little more than a league of the capital; that he had considerable reinforcements on board ship; and that the navy was ready to support such military operations as might be adopted. But Liniers appears not to have been profoundly impressed by the assurance of the invader, and replied, on the same day, that whilst he had ammunition and whilst the spirit which animated the garrison and the people continued to exist, he would not think of delivering up the post which had been confided to him, convinced that he had more than sufficient means to resist all the forces that were ready to be brought against him. Active hostilities began in the city on the fifth of July; and as the result of this day for the English there were 1130 killed and wounded, including 70 officers, and 120 officers and 1500 private soldiers made prisoners. It was now the Spaniard's turn to assume a tone of confidence. At five o'clock on the evening of the conflict, Liniers wrote the following letter to General Whitelocke:

" The same sentiments of humanity which induced your Excellency to propose to me to capitulate, lead me, now that I am fully acquainted with your force, that I have taken 80 officers and upwards of 1000 men, and killed more than double that number, without your having reached the centre of my position; the same sentiments I say, lead me in order to avoid a greater effusion of blood, and to give your

Excellency a fresh proof of Spanish generosity, to offer to your Excellency, that if you choose to re-embark with the remainder of your army, to evacuate Montevideo, and the whole of the River Plate, leaving me hostages for the execution of the treaty, I will not only return all the prisoners which I have now made, but also all those which were taken from General Beresford: at the same time I think it necessary to state, that if your Excellency does not admit this offer, I cannot answer for the safety of the prisoners, as my troops are so infinitely exasperated against them, and the more so, as three of my Aids-de-Camp have been wounded bearing flags of truce; and for this reason I send your Excellency this letter by an English Officer, and shall wait your answer one hour."[1]

Whitelocke's reply was dated July 6th, and in it he affirmed that the idea of surrendering the advantage which the army had gained was quite inadmissible; but the tone of this communication did not suggest a boasting spirit on the part of the writer, and in the treaty which was signed on the following day, he acceded to virtually all of the demands made by Liniers. What the conditions of the final agreement were, can hardly be more succinctly stated than in the language of the treaty itself:

"I.   There shall be from this time a cessation of hostilities on both sides of the River Plata.

---

[1] *Trial of Lieut.-Gen. Whitelocke*, Appendix, vol. i., p. xxxviii.

"II.   The troops of his Britannic Majesty shall retain for the period of two months the fortress and place of Montevideo, and as a neutral country there shall be considered a line drawn from San Carlos on the west to Pando on the east, and there shall not be on any part of that line hostilities committed on any side, the neutrality being understood only that the individuals of both nations may live freely under their respective laws, the Spanish subjects being judged by theirs, as the English by those of their nation.

"III.   There shall be on both sides a mutual restitution of prisoners, including not only those which have been taken since the arrival of the troops under Lieutenant-General Whitelocke, but also all those his Britannic Majesty's subjects captured in South America since the commencement of the war.

"IV.   That for the promptest dispatch of the vessels and troops of his Britannic Majesty, there shall be no impediment thrown in the way of the supplies of provisions which may be requested for Montevideo.

"V.   A period of ten days from this time is given for the reembarkation of his Britannic Majesty's troops to pass to the north side of the River La Plata, with the arms which may actually be in their power, stores, equipage, at the most convenient points which may be selected, and during this time provisions may be sold to them.

"VI.   That at the time of the delivery of the place and fortress of Montevideo, which shall take place at the end of the two months fixed in the second article, the delivery will be made in the terms it was found, and with the artillery it had when it was taken.

"VII. Three officers of rank shall be delivered for and until the fulfilment of the above articles by both parties, being well understood that his Britannic Majesty's officers who have been on their parole cannot serve against South America until their arrival in Europe."[1]

This treaty was signed by Lieutenant-General Whitelocke and Rear-Admiral George Murray, on the part of the English, and by Santiago Liniers, Cesar Balbiani, and Bernardo Velasco for Spain. The English were required to evacuate Buenos Aires within forty-eight hours, and Montevideo within two months, and they complied strictly with these requirements. At the expiration of the term fixed, the posts which they had held on the Plata were abandoned.

The complete victory won by the inhabitants of Buenos Aires had come after brief periods during the conflict when it was feared that all was lost; and the announcement of peace, with these extraordinary and unexpected conditions, was received with many signs of public joy. The patriots owed their deliverance not merely to their own bravery, but also, in large part, to the stupidity of the English leader. Their loss during the days of fighting was 302 killed and 514 wounded, of whom 37 were officers.

[1] *Trial of Lieut.-Gen. Whitelocke*, Appendix, vol. i., p. **xxv.**

Concerning the attitude of the Spanish towards the English in Montevideo, an English resident of that city made the following statement in a volume published in 1808:

"The intercourse which subsisted between the Spaniards and English in Montevideo, gave them an idea of our character, conduct, and liberal intentions, so different from what they had been taught to expect, that could they have followed their own wishes, and what they knew to be their own interest, by far the greater part of them would have rejoiced at our continuance among them. They confessed that they had never before seen such commerce, that they had never enjoyed under their former government such security and happiness, or known such strict impartiality in the administration of justice.

"It indeed seemed, without exaggeration, that the inhabitants of Montevideo, on the news of our repulse at Buenos Aires, felt even more severely than ourselves, and lamented, instead of rejoicing, at the successes of their countrymen. As the period of our departure approached, and when they found by our preparations that the place was really to be abandoned, which was a circumstance that they for a long time thought incredible, a gloom seemed to pervade every countenance. Not the most distant appearance of exultation could anywhere be discovered. They took leave of us with regret, and seemed by the tears that were shed, to be parting from their friends and relations, rather than from enemies."[1]

---

[1] *Notes on the Viceroyalty of La Plata in South America*, London, 1808, 104–106.

Whitelocke returned to England, and was there tried by a court-martial on four distinct charges. The essential points of these charges were as follows:

1. That Whitelocke had sent a message to the Spanish commander, demanding, among other things, "the surrender of all persons holding civil offices in the government of Buenos Aires as prisoners of war."

2. That during the march from Ensenada to Buenos Aires he "did not make the military arrangements best calculated to ensure the success of his operations against the town," and ordered the forces to enter the city with arms unloaded, and on no account to fire, thus unnecessarily exposing the troops to destruction, without the possibility of making effectual opposition.

3. That he "did not make, although it was in his power, any effectual attempt, by his own personal exertion or otherwise, to co-operate with or support the different divisions of the army under his command, when engaged with the enemy in the streets of Buenos Aires, on the 5th of July."

4. That he, subsequently to the attack on the town of Buenos Aires, and at a time when the troops under his command were in possession of posts on each flank of the town, and of the principal arsenal, with a communication open to the fleet, and having an effective force of about five

thousand men, did enter into, and finally conclude a treaty with the enemy, whereby he acknowledged in the public dispatch of the 10th July, 1807, that he resolved to forego the advantages which the bravery of his troops had obtained, and which advantages had cost him about two thousand five hundred men in killed, wounded, and prisoners, and by such treaty he unnecessarily and shamefully surrendered all such advantages, totally evacuated the town of Buenos Aires, and consented to deliver, and did shamefully abandon and deliver up to the enemy the strong fortress of Montevideo, which had been committed to his charge, and which, at the period of the treaty and abandonment, was well and sufficiently garrisoned and provided against attack, and which was not, at such period, in a state of blockade or siege.[1]

General Whitelocke was found guilty of these charges, with the exception of that part of the second charge which relates to the order prohibiting firing on entering the city. He was in consequence "cashiered and declared totally unfit and unworthy to serve his Majesty in any military capacity whatsoever."

The city of Buenos Aires, by its heroic achievements in expelling Beresford and resisting the assault of Whitelocke, won marked distinction. By the king it was ennobled and permitted to

[1] *Trial of Lieut.-Gen. Whitelocke*, Appendix, vol i., i–iv.

employ the title of *Excellency;* and all the other cities of the viceroyalty sent deputations congratulating it on its heroism.[1]

Although this episode cost Buenos Aires many lives and not a little destruction of property, by it the inhabitants acquired a valuable experience. It showed that the authority of Spain in this part of America might be easily overthrown; at the same time it made manifest the fact that a new society already stood prepared to assert itself. By this struggle the inhabitants of these provinces had moved forward to a new position. They had been deserted by their official ruler, and, in the presence of a powerful enemy, they had been obliged to take up the reins of public power which the cowardly viceroy had thrown down in his flight. By their experience, gained in successfully defending themselves, they had been politically transformed. They had acquired the spirit of an independent commonwealth. They had the power to be free, and wanted only the will to be free. The revolt against Spain was therefore destined to come whenever the community should become conscious of its real position. The events of the two years past had tended to arouse their self-consciousness. The English carried off the spoils of the colony, but they contributed to the development of a nation.

[1] See *Trial of Lieut.-Gen. Whitelocke;* also Watson, *Spanish and Portuguese South America,* ii., chap. xviii., and Appendix.

CHAPTER XIII

COLONIAL INDUSTRY AND COMMERCE

THE affirmation that the Spanish colonies in America were governed under a protective and restrictive policy is a commonplace of political discussion. This affirmation is, however, little more than a statement that the Spanish colonies were governed in accordance with ideas which were generally accepted at the time. The Spanish system of colonial administration was not an entirely isolated instance of commercial restriction. England, in dealing with her foreign possessions, reserved to herself monopolies, limited the industrial and commercial freedom of her dependencies, and aimed to have her will and not the normal laws of social activity determine the economic destiny of the colonists. She expected, by monopolizing the raw material produced in her colonies, to cheapen the cost of her manufactures, to dominate the foreign markets, and thus to establish her economic supremacy at the expense of her dependencies. Like England, Spain aimed to prevent the industrial independence of her colonies. But she went a step farther than England. England sought from her colonies the greatest possible amount of raw material, the products of agriculture. Spain's action even tended to discourage rather than to promote agriculture. Whatever extension was made in the number of articles cultivated in the Spanish colonies, or whatever improvement was effected in the method of production was due to individual initiative instead of governmental encouragement; and whatever laws were formed respecting this subject contributed to restrict rather than to advance production.

In 1618, the viceroy, Don Francisco de Borja, issued an order prohibiting the establishment of sugar mills within six leagues of Lima. At the same time he commanded the immediate closing of those already established.[1] Down to 1792 the introduction of material for the equipment of such mills was prohibited, and prior to 1794 the construction of sugar refineries in Peru was not permitted. The cultivation of cane was further discouraged by preventing the making of brandy from cane in Peru. This order not proving effective, a tax of twelve per cent. was imposed upon this article, and later it was definitely decreed that the Indians might not work in the sugar mills, and they might not be employed in cutting and carting the cane without express

[1] Mendiburu, ii., 58.

governmental authorization.[1] "If in forming this law the well-being of the Indian was had in view, there is no doubt that the principal object of it was to suppress the sugar mills of Peru."[2]

The cultivation of the grape was also discouraged, and the kings of Spain and the viceroys gave various reasons for their hostile attitude towards this form of agriculture. Philip II. prohibited the use of Indian labor in cultivating the vine "on account of the great inconveniences which have been encountered in employing Indians in this work"; and the viceroy Don Francisco de Toledo was instructed not to consent to the establishment of vineyards for many reasons of great importance, and principally in order not to "diminish the trade and commerce with these kingdoms." The viceroy Don Luis de Velasco was also instructed not to grant licenses for planting vineyards nor for restoring those that had already been planted. The Peruvian wines, moreover, might not be sold in the American markets. The market of Guatemala was closed to them in order to favor Spanish wines. But the reason given for this action was that "being strong and new, they would injure the Indians."[3] They might not be introduced into Panama, and after 1620 they might not be exported from Peru to

[1] *Leyes de Indias*, lib. 6, tit. 13, ley 11.
[2] Oliveira, *La Politica Economica de la Metrópoli*, 34.
[3] *Leyes de Indias*, lib. 4, tit. 18, ley 18; Oliveira, 37

Mexico.[1] All these acts of prohibition had one general purpose, namely, to prevent the production and consumption of Peruvian wines, and to leave the markets of America open to Spanish wines. It was, however, seen in the course of time that these restrictions were disadvantageous to Spain as well as to the colonies, and they were relaxed; yet even while the laws existed without modification they were not completely effective, they frequently were not obeyed. But as long as they stood unrepealed the production of wine was necessarily a precarious business, for it could not with entire safety be presumed that the policy of one viceroy to allow planters to ignore the law would be followed by his successor.[2]

This was practically a general prohibition, and later the action of the king left no doubt as to his design. In the thirteenth article of his instructions to the new viceroy, the previous injunctions to the viceroys were repeated, that the colonists should not manufacture cloth or plant vines or olives. Yet, in spite of this prohibition, the vineyards had greatly increased; and, in the thirty-first article of the instructions, the king recommended that in the future such increase should be prevented, and that no permission should be given to plant vines or olives, or to renew the fields that had already

[1] *Leyes de Indias*, lib. 4, tit. 18, ley 15.
[2] Oliveira, 41.

been planted, without special application to the
king.[1]

This prohibitive action of the government,
provoked by the complaints of Spaniards in
Spain, ran directly counter to the purpose of the
Spaniards settled in America, whose attention,
in the beginning, was directed to the cultivation
of the various grains and other food products
with which they had become familiar in Spain.
The lack of frequent communication with any
civilized country made such cultivation necessary
to their existence; and already in 1501 "there
were cultivated on this continent wheat, rice, and
all the nutritious grains of Spain; there had been
introduced the Spanish domestic fowls, sheep,
hogs, goats; the ox and the ass and the horse
aided man in the cultivation of the fields, where
before he had worked alone"; sugar cane flourished, and among the other products which had
been introduced from Spain were the fruit of the
vine, the olive, silk, and linen.[2]

Not less decisive was the governmental opposition to the cultivation and use of the coca plant.
This was the sacred tree of the Incas, and was
employed in their religious ceremonies. To it was
ascribed

"the magical virtue of placating the anger of the
tutelary gods. In order that the sacrifices offered

---

[1] Quesada, *Vineinato del Rio de la Plata*, 139, 140.

[2] Benzoni, *History of the New World*, 91.

to the Peruvian divinities might be agreeable to them, it was necessary that the coca should be converted into spirals of smoke before the altars; and the priest could not hear the voice of the gods in consulting the oracles if he did not chew the sacred leaf. The Inca, son of the Sun, Supreme King and Supreme Priest, was the only one who might plant, on his estate, the sacred tree.

"The Indians, preserving their tradition, made of the coca, during the colonial period, the same use as their ancestors; and on account of this the Spaniards regarded it with disfavor. A law affirmed, that the Indians used coca 'for their superstitions, ceremonies of witchcraft, and other evil and depraved ends.' And Toledo, himself, maintained that the coca plantations ought to be extirpated, since this product, by devilish practices, promoted the superstition of the infidels.

"The legislation concerning coca was not merely the child of religious fanaticism, but also of Christian piety. The plant grew in unhealthy regions, and experience had taught that the Indians who went to the coca plantations, if they did not lose their lives, came back to their homes with weakened bodies. To seek to abolish the coca plantations was, therefore, in a certain way, to spare the sufferings of the oppressed race."[1]

The public action at first taken with respect to coca was thus taken under the influence of ideas of religion and charity. By an ordinance issued by viceroy Toledo under royal authority, it was

[1] Oliveira, 42, 43.

provided that no person might plant coca. As penalty in case of violation of this ordinance, it was ordered that the plants should be pulled up and burned, a fine of two thousand dollars should be paid, and the culprit should be banished for four years. And it is noteworthy that while the Indians were prevented from working on the coca plantations, they were permitted to work under the much more destructive conditions of the mines. The reason of this discrimination is found in the fact that the mines contributed one fifth of their product to the king, while, in the view of the authorities, "coca was the diabolical instrument of superstition." [1] Working in the mines might kill the body, but the use of coca tended to demoralize the spirit. The absurdity of this legislation appears to have been perceived at last by the viceroy himself, for he subsequently issued an ordinance permitting the establishment of new coca plantations. [2]

If the government of the viceroys of Peru sought to discourage the cultivation of wine and coca, it was equally active in promoting the cultivation of wheat. During the earlier decades of the Spanish occupation the amount of wheat produced in Peru increased to such an extent as not only to supply the domestic demand, but also to provide a surplus which was exported to Guayaquil and Panama. But by the earthquake of 1687

1 Oliveira, 45.   2 Ibid., 46.

an important change was effected in the coast
lands of Peru. Much of their productiveness was
destroyed, and the inhabitants became dependent
on Chile for their required supply of wheat. This
state of things continued until 1722, after which
wheat was again extensively produced in the valleys of Peru. With this revival of production
arose the policy of protecting the Peruvian
wheat market from the more abundant and
cheaper production of Chile. The first step
towards this end was to reduce the tax burden
on Peruvian farmers who raised wheat. Then
it was ordered that dealers should sell Chilean
and Peruvian wheat in equal quantities, and,
later, that Chilean wheat should be sold only
after the Peruvian wheat had been exhausted.
These measures, however, appear not to have
been entirely satisfactory, for it was found that
in 1815 a tax of a dollar per "fanega" was imposed on wheat from Chile. Finally, under viceroy O'Higgins, action was taken that suggests
one phase of the culture system of Java. The
farmers of central and western Peru were required
to devote a part of their estate to wheat cultivation, the amount to be sown to vary with the size
of the estate.[1]

Yet in spite of these protective measures, Peru
had not great expectations regarding her agriculture. A large part of her territory was com-

[1] Oliveira, 47–49.

posed of mountains, and another large part was made up of deserts. More might have been done if systematic and persistent efforts had been devoted to irrigation. But with profitable mines at hand and with an energetic part of the population in eager search for others, it was not to be expected that large sums would be invested in carrying out elaborate plans for irrigation, when the profits of such undertakings would be realized only after some years. There was wanting both an adequate local demand for the products and also the requisite labor to stimulate and develop agricultural production. The devastating scourge of smallpox, the violent and unaccustomed efforts of the Indians taken to work in the mines under the oppressive system of the mita, and the introduction and immoderate use of spirituous liquors destroyed a large part of the original inhabitants, and the immigration was not sufficient to compensate for the loss. A savage people unused to the regular tasks which civilized man imposes upon himself appears to be unable to maintain itself when subjected to the conditions of civilized life. The mere fact, therefore, that savages disappear when brought into contact with civilized society does not necessarily involve a condemnation of the superior race. Unnecessary hardships imposed upon the inferior may hasten the inevitable declines. For imposing such hardships a nation may be justly blamed, and on this point the verdict has been rendered against the Spaniards.

Agricultural production was embarrassed not only by lack of internal consumption but also by the difficulties of transportation. Sugar shipped from Havana to Spain brought the owner a clear profit of fifty cents a quintal. The white sugar of Martinique sold in France brought a profit of sixty-two and a half cents a quintal. On account of the larger freight charges, sugar from Peru sold in Europe in competition with that from Havana caused the owner a very considerable loss. In the same way cotton from Peru could not successfully compete in Holland with that from other parts of the world. In view of these facts, Peru had to rely on gold and silver as exports.

Other causes leading to the decline of agriculture were the diminution of the number of inhabitants, the lack of an organized and effective system of cultivation especially needed in a country where much depended on irrigation, and the general aversion of the natives to work on being released from the authority of their traditional rulers. Under these conditions the support of the population became increasingly difficult.

The importation of the African negro, as an agricultural laborer, did not greatly improve the condition of affairs. As a slave laborer, he had all the economic defects of his class. But the defects of colonial agriculture was not all due to the

laborers.   The proprietors were only interested
in spending their income in ease.   They brought
to their undertakings a minimum of that practical
intelligence which should manifest itself in new
appliances and improved methods of cultivation.
With respect to those who tilled the soil independently on a small scale, the circumstances
were hardly more favorable.   Under the com-
munism of the Inca period, the work of the Indian
was prescribed by a superior authority.   When,
therefore, this authority was removed the Indian
was deprived of his accustomed direction, and
he did not possess sufficient power of initiative to
make his efforts extend much beyond the satisfaction of his immediate wants.   The early gains
in gold and silver and the hope of finding rich
mines made the Spanish and creole population
impatient of the meagre returns from cultivating
the soil, and the presence of slave laborers brought
the work of the agriculturist into disrepute.
Furthermore, the arid lands of the rainless coast
and the broken region of the Sierra offered few
attractions to agricultural undertakings, and the
Spanish government took no steps towards storing
the waters of the mountain streams, or system-
atically utilizing them in irrigation, a work
clearly transcending individual effort.

Although the mines were one of Peru's most
important sources of wealth, this industry was
subject to certain inconveniences.   It could not

be carried on advantageously without the mita, while the continuance of the enforced labor of the mita caused the rapid destruction of the Indians. It was moreover carried on without adequate scientific knowledge. It was burdened with the payment of a fifth of the product to the king. It suffered from lack of credit, or from credit obtained under onerous conditions. Banks for assisting mining enterprises either did not exist, or when created were opposed and discredited. Stock companies that might have brought together the requisite capital were, if formed at all, of little importance. The bank proposed in Arequipa in 1792, with a capital stock of fifty thousand dollars divided into five hundred shares, found that the country was not accustomed to such projects and failed for lack of support. Progress in mining was, moreover, hindered by the Spaniard's lack of initiative; also by the desire of the creole who had a fortune to consume it in ease instead of increasing it by means of work; or, if he invested it, by his search for such investments as would cause him the least trouble. The ill-success that attended the quicksilver mine of Huancavelica at certain periods was due to maladministration and the neglect or hostility of the government favoring the Spanish mine of Almaden.

While prices in Spain were rising as a consequence of the importation of gold and silver from

America, the Spanish government, not knowing the cause of this rise, sought to prevent it in certain cases by diminishing the demand for articles for sale in Spain. The inhabitants of the colonies in America were, therefore, prohibited from purchasing cloth in Spain, and this action, taken by the Cortes in Valladolid, in 1548, furnished protection for the manufacturer of the articles in question in America. Whatever advantage was derived by the American manufacturer was not designed by the Spanish authorities, but accrued as a consequence of an act taken in ignorance of the influences affecting their trade. Later ordinances were issued to further manufactures in different parts of America, and to make the wares produced cheaper.

This direct reversal of the original policy was not maintained subsequently without vacillation. Philip II. sought to encourage trade in wool between Spain and America, "hoping that the textile industry of the colonies would be destroyed in being deprived of one of its most essential materials."[1] The great distance and the difficulties of transportation furnished, however, sufficient protection to keep the industry alive. Yet a little later it was dealt a severe blow by an ordinance issued by Philip II. in 1595, which provided that "in no province or part of the Indies may the Indians work in the mills for

[1] Oliveira, 92, 93.

making woollen, silk, or cotton cloth."[1] But this ordinance did not apply to those manufactories belonging to communities of Indians and worked by them exclusively; it also did not apply to those belonging to the king. It affected only those owned by private persons and those in which Indians and Spaniards were engaged to work together. The motive of these acts of prohibition was revealed in the instructions to the viceroy Velasco, when it was required "that he should prohibit the manufacture in order that the trade and commerce in cloth might not be weakened." The Marquis of Salinas was unwilling to carry out this policy and affirmed

"that the manufactories are so necessary and the cloth made in them is of so great importance and service for the poor people, and that which comes from Spain is so dear, that the Indians, the negroes, and even the Spaniards would go naked if the manufactories were closed; and this could not be done without great resentment from many private persons in this kingdom, who have them and who are supported by them."[2]

With the coming of the Austrian kings in the beginning of the eighteenth century the vacillating policy that had been pursued came to an end, and the textile manufactures of Peru were doomed. The viceroy and audiencia were ordered to destroy

[1] Solórzano, *Politica Indiana*, libre ii., cap. 12.
[2] Mendiburu, viii., 288 ; Oliveira, 95.

all the factories and mills which had not been established by the express permission of the king, and to give an account of those demolished and of those that remained.[1]

The policy here initiated was maintained until permission granted by the crown to the English and the French to trade with the colonies finally brought about the complete destruction of the textile industries in Spanish America. With this permission ruin was inevitable. England, France, and Holland, less hampered by legal restraints, were able to furnish the desired wares at lower prices, if they could only break through the cordon which Spain had undertaken to draw around her American possessions. Here had been a motive for smuggling, and the great gains possible in case of success more than balanced the risks of contraband trade. Santo Domingo was for a time an important emporium, to which traders from Havana, Vera Cruz, Guatemala, Carthagena, and Venezuela resorted to purchase European wares. The colonists preferred French goods, and the French merchants relied on this preference to maintain

[1] On November 4, 1711, the viceroy Ladron de Guevara received a royal order which provided: "Que se demoliesen todos los batanes, obrajes, trapiches y chorrillos que se hubiesen fabricado sin expresa licencia del rey: y que a los que la tuviesen se les prohibiese trabajar con indios. Que los corregidores y curas no pudiesen emplearlos en sus tratos, comercios y tragines" (Mendiburu, iv., 372).

their trade, and required cash payments in all transactions. After the social collapse of Santo Domingo contraband trade carried on through Jamaica received a new impulse. The English, unlike the French, did not insist on cash payments, but allowed their Spanish customers credit, and assisted them in the transportation of their wares, either by carrying their merchandise to the mainland or escorting their vessels, going sometimes to the extent of stationing armed vessels off the coast to protect the contraband traders.

The island of Curaçao fell into the hands of the Dutch in 1634, and immediately became an important trading post. Here the colonists from the mainland found they could get European commodities for their agricultural products, and by this an impetus was given to the cultivation of the soil, which had been neglected in the fruitless search for mines. The principal ports that traded with Curaçao were Coro, Porto Cabello, and La Guayra. The commodities sent to the island were hides, indigo, coffee, and sugar but these amounted rarely to more than six tenths of the value of the articles purchased from the Dutch, and the balance was paid in money.

During the period of contraband trade, the viceroy of Peru maintained a most inhospitable attitude towards foreign ships off the coast of his dominions. This attitude is illustrated by his views respecting the treatment an American ship from Boston had received. This vessel having lost one of her masts, sprung her rudder, and run short of fire-wood and water, touched at the island of Juan Fernandez. The governor of the island discovered her distress, allowed her to get the supplies needed, and to make the necessary repairs. This manifestation of hospitality displeased the viceroy. He was surprised at the ignorance of the governor in not knowing "that every strange vessel which anchored in these seas, without a license from our court, ought to be treated as an enemy, even though the nation to which she belonged should be an ally of Spain." Moved by this event, the viceroy ordered the intendants and all other officers along the whole coast of Peru to allow no foreign vessel whatever to anchor; and if any such vessel should enter a port, "to use every artifice to take possession of her and her crew." The viceroy, moreover, urged that "lest strangers should demand supplies, and threaten to use force, the cattle and other articles in the neighboring farms, which might afford relief to them, are to be carried off to the interior upon these occasions." He also wished sentinels and watchmen placed on all the hills overlooking the coast, who might send him information whenever a vessel was sighted.

The popular awakening in the English colonies of America and in France during the last half of the eighteenth century made the restrictions imposed by Spain on her colonies appear more burdensome than ever before. The colonists became distinctly conscious that Spain's short-sighted policy hindered their prosperity. By withholding adequate opportunities for direct trade with the mother country, the Spanish government had made the inhabitants of some of the colonies largely dependent on contraband trade with members of other nations. The restrictions imposed on shipping to the port of Buenos Aires gave the neighboring Portuguese an opportunity to smuggle their goods over the border, and build up an illicit trade, which not only supplied the Spanish settlement on the Rio de la Plata, but also threatened to diminish the trade of Lima, by way of the Isthmus. The effect of this restrictive policy, except in a few favored places, like Lima and the city of Mexico, was to prevent the use of European wares, and to compel the settlers to accept such substitutes as they were able to produce or obtain from the Indians. In other words, the trade restrictions which were imposed upon the colonists, instead of permitting them to start with the advantages of the achievements of European civilization, in many cases drove them back to the barbarism of the aborigines, and doomed them to go over again the painful way up to civilization which their ancestors had already trod in Europe.

The commercial aggression of the Portuguese
was one of the circumstances that urged the
establishment of the viceroyalty of Buenos Aires.
Under the conditions "contraband trade was a
natural function of the economic organization,
a fact beyond the control of the king of Spain
and of his subordinates in America; and in the
conflict of vital interests, the natural law had necessarily to prevail, and this in effect happened."[1]
It was expected that in making Buenos Aires
a centre of more important political power, a
counterpoise to Portuguese influence would be
created.

Thus the ultimate effect of the commercial
freedom established in the early years of the
viceroyalty was a noteworthy growth of the
trade of Buenos Aires. In the three years from
1792 to 1795 forty-seven vesels left the port of
Buenos Aires, and fifty-three vessels arrived from
Spain. The value of the exportations and importations for this period amounted to somewhat
more than $8,000,000. The internal trade had
also greatly increased. Mendoza, during this
time, sold annually about 7300 barrels of wine;
San Juan more than 3000 barrels of brandy; and
Tucuman great quantities of hides and textile
fabrics. Paraguay's trade was chiefly in yerba-
maté, tobacco, and lumber. This province sent
also large numbers of mules to Peru. Of the

[1] Mitre, *Historia de Belgrano*, i., 50.

maté exported, Chile consumed annually about
4,000,000 pounds and exported in payment gold
and silver.

The mules sent to Peru were driven by easy
stages from the eastern provinces to Salta where
they were kept over the winter; and in the spring
they were taken to Potosi. In the province of
Buenos Aires they cost at that time between
three and four dollars a head, but at Potosi they
brought eight or nine dollars a head. In case
they were taken farther into the country, they
brought a larger price, amounting in some places
to forty or fifty dollars apiece. They were required in Peru for use in the mines, but the hard
conditions under which they worked caused
many of them to be short-lived, thus making
the demand for them greater than it would have
been if they had been employed under more
favorable circumstances.

Tucuman had also an important trade with
Peru. It sent annually to that country 18,000
head of cattle, 4000 horses, and a considerable
number of mules. From Santa Cruz de la Sierra,
Peru derived, moreover, about 20,000 mules a
year.

Cordova, Salta, and Jujui lay on the main
route from Buenos Aires to Peru, and the inhabitants of these towns, by furnishing means of
transportation, derived important advantages
from this overland trade. The goods were gener-

ally carried in carts drawn by four or more oxen, and the freight rate from Buenos Aires to Jujui was four dollars a quintal, or approximately four cents a pound. For transportation beyond Jujui mules were substituted for oxen and carts, and the charges varied according to the season and the abundance or scarcity of mules.

The early policy to make Buenos Aires dependent on Lima for European wares was checked, as has been indicated already, by the rise of contraband trade with the Portuguese, and the emancipation of the eastern provinces was finally completed by the increase of importations at Buenos Aires directly from European ports. In this later trade with Peru, therefore, Buenos Aires, having a cheaper source from which to obtain European wares, received in return for her exportations large quantities of gold and silver, products of the Peruvian mines.

The trade between Buenos Aires and the western coast by sea was inconsiderable. Now and then a vessel arrived at Montevideo from Callao with wares intended for shipment to Spain. Ships were also occasionally sent from Montevideo to Arica with quicksilver for the mines, and they carried at the same time small quantities of yerba-maté and tallow.

The principal trade of Buenos Aires with Chile was with the province of Cuyo, on the eastern side of the Andes. This province having been

settled from the west remained under the captain-
general of Chile until after the establishment of
the viceroyalty of Rio de la Plata. The exports
from Chile and Cuyo to the eastern provinces
were woollen goods, particularly ponchos, wines,
brandy, and oil; raisins and dried peaches;
apples, snuff, and sugar; and copper, gold, and
cordage.

Before the close of the eighteenth century
Talcahuano had become noted for its shipment
of wheat to points in the colonies outside of
Chile. The average annual amount exported
was two thousand four hundred tons. Nearly
all of this was sent to Lima. Of the other articles
exported, the principal were jerked beef, tallow,
and wine. There was also a certain amount of
trade in raw hides, wool, dried fruits, salt fish,
and pulse. The articles imported were European
manufactured goods, sugar, salt, and tobacco.

To what extent the establishment of freedom of
trade in 1778, carried into general effect in 1783,
stimulated shipping to the colonies may be seen
from the fact that in 1785 sixteen vessels arrived
at Callao with cargoes estimated at twenty-four
million dollars. At this time the annual production of gold and silver in the country was only
about four million dollars; and these were the
principal commodities produced that might be
exported to pay for imports. Thus the zeal to
embrace the new opportunities for trade brought

to Peru goods to the value of twenty-four million dollars in a period when four million dollars represented the normal consumption of imports. The result of this oversupply was to glut the market completely and to cause a temporary interruption of trade. In some cases the wares could not find a market at any price, and were committed to the flames. This was a warning to shippers, and caused them to withhold their shipments, thus reducing the imports to the quantities of the various commodities needed.[1]

The enlarged freedom of commerce, moreover, gave an increased value to the products of the herds of Buenos Aires. Hides and salted beef

[1] *The Present State of Peru*, 108–110; at the beginning of the nineteenth century a large part of the wares in use in Lima were English. Writing from his observations made at the time, Stevenson says "the windows were glazed with English glass—the brass furniture and ornaments on the commodes, tables, and chairs were English—the chintz or dimity hangings, the linen and cotton dresses of the females, and the cloth coats and cloaks of the men were all English; the tables were covered either with plates or English earthenware, and English glass, knives, and forks; and even the kitchen utensils, if of iron, were English; in fine, with very few exceptions, all was either of English or South American manufacture. Coarse cottons, nankeens, and a few other articles were supplied by the Philippine company. Spain sent some iron, broadcloth, Barcelona prints, linen, writing paper, silks, and ordinary earthenware. From the Italians they had silks and velvets; from the French, linens (platillas), common cutlery, and glass; everything else was either English or of home manufacture."—*Twenty Years' Residence in South America*, i., 349.

could now be profitably exported in the numerous vessels that brought European wares. The wealth of the inhabitants increased rapidly, and justified the expenditures of large sums on private houses; and the viceroy took advantage of this prosperity to embellish the city with important public buildings. The city hall, the mint, and the buildings of the university were begun in the last quarter of the eighteenth century.

While the original commercial policy of Spain was maintained, it was sometimes found that Spain could not furnish the wares imperatively needed in certain parts of America. Under such circumstances special permission had been given to persons needing the wares in question to procure them from other Spanish colonies. An instance of this may be seen in the permission granted Mexican miners to procure mercury from the mines of Huancavelica in Peru, when the supply from Almaden in Spain was inadequate. The freedom of trade that was established in 1778 removed the need of obtaining special permission for intercolonial trade, and brought the colonies into normal commercial relations with one another. In 1789 there were thirty-two ships of all classes belonging to the port of Callao. The largest of these was the galleon, *San Miguel*, of eighteen hundred tons; the smallest was the packet boat, *San Antonio*, of one hundred and twenty-three tons. The total amount of tonnage was sixteen thousand three hundred and seventy-five tons. The population of Peru at this time was about one million, and of this number four hundred thousand were Indians, who did not increase materially the demand for foreign wares. [1]

Among the exports from Peru were a small

[1] The following is a brief statement of the trade of Peru through Lima with the other colonies in 1789:

Exports to Buenos Aires	$2,034,980
Imports from Buenos Aires	864,790
In favor of Lima	$1,170,190
Exports to Chile	$458,317
Imports from Chile	629,800
Against Lima	$171,483
Exports to Chiloë	$30,000
Imports from Chiloë	51,200
Against Lima	$21,200
Exports to Guatemala	$ 28,350
Imports from Guatemala	124,500
Against Lima	$96,150
Exports to Santa Fé	$128,295
Imports from Santa Fé	284,460
Against Lima	$156,165
Total amount of exports	$2,679,942
Total amount of imports	1,954,750
In favor of Lima, total	$725,192

quantity of vicuña wool and a certain amount of
cinchona, or Peruvian bark. The value of the
wool did not exceed ten thousand dollars, but
the value of the annual export of cinchona was
estimated at fifty thousand dollars. Although
the wool at the place where it was sheared was
worth only about four cents a pound, the expenses
involved in shearing and transporting it, including
commissions and duties, were so great that it could
not compete successfully with the wool of Spain.

As the port of the political and commercial
capital of South America Callao had more shipping
than any other point on the Pacific, except, perhaps, Panama. A pier was constructed at Callao,
in 1779, by running an old ship on shore, and
filling her with stones, and driving piles about
her to prevent the waves from breaking her in
pieces. The town at this time, thirty-three
years after its destruction by the great earthquake and tidal wave of 1746, presented a mean
appearance. The houses were "generally about
twenty feet high, with mud walls, flat roofs, and
divided into two stories; the under one forming
a row of small shops open in front." [1]

Buenos Aires had grown very slowly under the
severe restriction which Spain had placed upon
her trade. In 1608 the town contained 2000
inhabitants. During the following one hundred
and seventy years its population increased from

[1] Stevenson, i., 135.

2000 to 24,205, an average addition of only about 130 persons a year. The progress was more rapid after the organization of the viceroyalty and the establishment of commercial freedom. The last quarter of the eighteenth century added somewhat more than 15,000 persons to the city's population, so that at the beginning of the nineteenth century Buenos Aires contained 40,000 inhabitants, and 46,000 in 1810.

The route from Buenos Aires to Peru was more frequented during the colonial period than any other long route in South America. The fact that Buenos Aires was for a long time a closed port made it necessary for the inhabitants of this region to get many articles of commerce from Peru; and, on the other hand, Portuguese smuggling made it advantageous for the Peruvians to resort to the valley of La Plata for certain articles that could not be procured as cheaply elsewhere. Thus, in the course of time, a line of communication was established across the plains and over the mountains between Buenos Aires and Lima, a distance of somewhat more than two thousand eight hundred geographical miles. In the early decades the journey was made by caravans of explorers or traders over a more or less trackless wilderness, but in 1748 posthouses were established at intervals along the way, at which travellers might obtain horses and carts or carriages. The route passed through Cordova,

Santiago del Estero, Tucuman, Salta, Jujui, Potosi, Oruro, La Paz, Juli, Pucara, Santa Rosa, Cuzco, Abancay, and Huancavelica. The difficulties, the delays, and the expenses of making this journey or transporting goods were very great; and in the last decade of the eighteenth century Don Fernandez Cornejo sought to find some way by which they might be lessened. To this end he explored the river Bermejo. In 1790, taking a small vessel and two canoes, and accompanied by twenty-six persons, he passed in forty-four days, without encountering any obstacles, from the mouth of the tributary Centa to the junction of the Bermejo and the Paraguay, a distance of about a thousand miles. The knowledge of the practicability of this route did not cause it to be used; the communication between Buenos Aires and Lima continued to be maintained by land, notwithstanding the great expense and all the other inconveniences. [1]

[1] The names of all the stations and the distances are given by Wilcocke, *History of Buenos Aires*, 104–118.

CHAPTER XIV

IF we turn to the subject of public reverse, we find that in the Spanish colonies, in the last decades of their dependence, it was derived from many sources, but chiefly from taxes that fell on profits and rent. The most productive of all the taxes was the *alcavala*. This was a tax that had been known in Spain since the middle of the fourteenth century. It was originally imposed to provide funds for carrying on the wars against the Moors. Having been established for a long time, its collection came to be regarded almost as a prerogative of the crown; and when the question arose as to the propriety of introducing it into America, it was assumed that without any new grant it might be extended by the king to all possessions annexed to the Spanish empire. It was thus established in Mexico in 1574, and in Peru in 1591. The rate fixed for the colonies was two per cent., and this rate was maintained for a number of years; but about the middle of the eighteenth century it was raised to five per cent The *alcavala* was a percentage tax on the price of every article sold, and was due at every sale of the article in question, whether this article was a bundle of fagots or a great estate. In the case of a retail dealer it would have been evidently inconvenient to collect the tax on the occasion of each sale. An account of such a trader's stock was, therefore, taken annually, and the annual sales estimated. The tax was then collected on the estimated sales for the year. On land or other property that was seldom sold this tax was not burdensome; but it tended to absorb the value of wares that passed from hand to hand many times during the year. Under this system, if trade was dull and few exchanges were made, the annual profits were naturally small; if the trade was brisk, the profits were absorbed by the public treasury.

The import and export duties varied with the articles involved and with the ports where they were landed, the larger ports having a higher rate than the smaller.[1] The impost known as the *armada* was a tax collected for the purpose of maintaining government vessels designed to protect the coast from pirates. In the course of time it was found that smaller vessels than those at first employed were better adapted to this purpose, and an additional impost was established for maintaining them. This tax was called

[1] See the writer's *Establishment of Spanish Rule in America*, 170, 291.

armadilla. Later the pirates ceased to infest the coast, but the tax to provide means for warding them off continued to be collected.

A small special import and export tax was levied to pay the salaries and other expenses connected with the consulate. It amounted to an average duty of one per cent. on all articles brought from Spain and from different parts of Spanish America, or shipped to these regions. The import and export taxes levied for this purpose on trade with foreign countries were much higher, averaging about three per cent. There were some exceptions to these rates; horses and mules paid a specific duty of one dollar a head, while horned cattle paid one per cent.

In the larger cities there was a license for the sale of intoxicating liquors. The amount of this license for saloons, or shops, for this traffic was fixed in proportion to estimated sales; but this payment did not release the dealers from the *alcavala*, which they were obliged to pay, in addition, as retail traders.

The practice of selling titles, which had been resorted to in Spain as a means of increasing the royal revenues, was extended to the colonies. A resident of Spanish America who wished the distinction of a title of nobility paid the king a prescribed sum; or he might even enter into an agreement to pay annually interest on the sum prescribed. The interest on these obligations constituted a source of revenue for the king. Back of this practice lay the desire and purpose of the king to maintain in America social conditions similar to those of Spain.

There was a long list of other sources from which revenues flowed more or less abundantly into the royal treasury. The following were the most important:

1. The *media anata*, which was the half of the salary, or yearly product, of places or offices under the government to which appointments were made. It was paid into the treasury for the first year. In case of increase of salary by promotion or otherwise, the half of the increase was paid for the first year after it was granted.

2. There was the source of revenue known as the royal ninths, which comprised the parts of the tithes not allotted to ecclesiastical or other institutions. The tithes, established in America by an edict of Charles V., October 5, 1501, were at first applied solely to the support of the Church. Forty years later, it was provided that they should be divided into four parts. One part, or one quarter of the whole amount, was given to the bishop of the diocese; and one part to the chapters Of the remaining half of the whole amount collected, two ninths (one ninth of the whole) went to the crown; three ninths were set apart for the foundation of churches and hospitals;

and the remainder, four ninths, was devoted to the support of curates and other officiating ecclesiastics. Later this last amount was increased to seven ninths of the half of the whole amount, absorbing the three ninths previously devoted to founding churches and hospitals.

3. The tribute paid by the civilized Indians constituted an important contribution to the royal revenue. This was the annual tax imposed upon every male Indian between the ages of eighteen and fifty, over whom the Spaniards had acquired jurisdiction. The amount of the tribute varied both with respect to persons and with respect to provinces. It was collected by the *corregidors*, or governors of districts, who were allowed six per cent. of the sums collected in accordance with the assessment as placed in their hands. In the colonial system established by Spain, every Indian was regarded as a vassal either immediately subject to the king or dependent on an encomendero. During the years in which the inhabitants were being brought into subjection to Spanish authority, the king made numerous and extensive grants, and large numbers of Indians were assigned to the various holders of these grants. Making these **grants** was a part of the policy of conquest; for a Spaniard on whom had been bestowed an extensive territory, together with a large number of Indians, would necessarily be disposed to dominate his

possessions and maintain peace among his dependents. In the course of time these grants, which were for only one or two lives, reverted to the crown, and the tribute which had been paid previously to the encomendero was, after this reversion, paid into the king's treasury. The effect of this change was to increase the king's revenue and to make a larger part of the inhabitants dependent immediately on him. This tax caused dissatisfaction; for those who paid it regarded it as a sign of personal subordination, or bondage.

4. The royal treasury received also a large sum from the sale of offices, particularly municipal offices, to which appointments were frequently made after a considerable payment to the crown by the candidate.

5. The income derived from the sale of stamped paper increased with the increase of the population and the growth of official business.

6. The royal treasury received, moreover, a certain increment from lost property and strays, which, having been found and held for a year, belonged to the king.

7. The fifth part of the product of the mines was, perhaps, the most noteworthy element of the royal income. A large part of the income from the mines, though not strictly as a royal fifth, was derived from the quicksilver mine of Huancavelica. This mine was discovered about

1566, but it was not of great importance until after 1571, when Pedro Fernandez Velasco introduced the process of refining silver by the use of mercury. It was purchased by Philip II. from Amador de Cabrera, in 1570, and it continued to be the property of the crown until the beginning of the nineteenth century. The office of governor or superintendent of the mine was sometimes held by a member of the royal audiencia, but in 1790 the duties of this office were added to the functions of the viceroy of Peru. During the two hundred and nineteen years from 1570 to 1789, the mine of Huancavelica produced 1,040,469 quintals of mercury, making an average annual product of 4751 quintals.[1] The price of the metal extracted was sixty dollars per quintal in 1786, and seventy-three dollars in 1791. At a fair average of the prices that prevailed during the whole period in question, the value of the product was 67,629,396 dollars. After deducting the expenses of the mine, there remained a profit for the crown of about 65,000,000 dollars. The prosperity of this undertaking was in part due to the fact that the mine held a monopoly for furnishing mercury to the silver mines of Peru. Sometimes, moreover, when the mines of Almaden in Spain did not provide an adequate supply of mercury for the silver mines of Mexico, a special privilege

[1] Mendiburu, iv., 428-431.

was granted to the Mexicans, as has been seen, permitting them to purchase it from Huancavelica.

It is impossible to make an accurate statement of the output of the other mines of South America, from which the king drew the allotted twenty per cent. It is estimated that the mines of Potosi alone, in their first ninety years, produced 395,619,000 dollars; and that between 1545 and 1800 the king's fifth from the product of these mines amounted to 163,000,000 dollars. On the basis of this estimate the total output of the mines of Potosi for these years would appear to have been 815,000,000 dollars. It has been estimated, moreover, that Spain received from America, during two hundred and forty-eight years ending in 1740, the sum of 9,000,000,000 dollars. These figures are, however, only estimates, as the condition of the accounts of the mines has always made it impossible to derive from them an accurate and trustworthy statistical statement.

8. The proceeds of the salt tax belonged to the crown, but it was one of the less productive sources of income.

9. The king also received the fees paid by ships on entering and clearing at the ports.

10. The royal revenue embraced, moreover, the sums paid for the privilege of maintaining cock pits.

11. The proceeds from the sale of the bull of

Cruzada, although this was apparently an institution of the Church, were gathered into the royal
treasury. The *Cruzada* mentioned here as a source
of revenue was a bull published every two years
which carried absolution from past offences and
contained certain privileges with respect to the
future. By purchasing it one might obtain
ecclesiastical permission to eat certain kinds of
food during Lent that were not ordinarily
allowed on meagre days. The prices paid for
the bulls ranged from a few cents to several
dollars.

12. The crown received an important addition
to its revenues from the tobacco monopoly. The
tobacco crop was received by the government
at a price fixed by itself and was sold from the
general storehouse at a price which secured to the
government a very large profit. But this profit
was in large part consumed in maintaining the
numerous officers who were employed in managing the monopoly and preventing illicit trade.
No one was permitted to cultivate tobacco without
permission from the director of the monopoly;
and "on delivery the planter was obliged to make
oath as to the number of plants which he had
harvested, also that he had not reserved one leaf
for his own use, nor for any other purpose."[1]
The administration of this culture system created

[1] Stevenson, i., 199.

more dissatisfaction among the planters than any of the other forms of taxation to which they were subjected.

There was also a tax on titles of nobility. Each holder of such a title paid annually five hundred dollars to the king. He might be released from the annual payment by a single payment of ten thousand dollars. This tax was, however, of very little importance except in Lima and the city of Mexico. In Lima at the beginning of the nineteenth century there were sixty-three persons who were expected to pay this tax.

These sources of revenue may be grouped in four divisions. The first division embraces the payments to the king as superior, or sovereign, lord of the land, comprising the tax on gold and silver extracted from the mines, the profits of coinage, and the tribute paid by the Indians. The second division comprehends the various taxes on trade: the *alcavala*, the minor excise taxes, the stamp tax, and the customs duties. The third division consists of the payments made to the king as head of the Church, among which were the first-fruits, the annates, the *Cruzada*, and the other exactions imposed by the Church. The fourth division is made up of the profits of various monopolies reserved to the crown.[1]

---

[1] From these sources the following amounts were derived in Buenos Ayres just before the English invasion of 1806:

22

With respect to the population, it was recognized that in view of the great resources of the new continent, an increasing number of inhabitants, in at least the early stages of social growth, meant an increasing prosperity for the community or the people concerned. When, therefore, it was observed that the population of the Spanish dominions in America was decreasing, the authorities were moved to seek means to prevent the

First Division

Tax on gold and silver . .	$650,000	
Profits of coinage . . .	120,000	
Tribute of the Indians . .	550,000	$1,320,000

Second Division

The *alcavala*	$385,000	
Minor excise taxes . . .	200,000	
Stamp tax	32,000	
Customs duties	750,000	$1,367,000

Third Division

First-fruits and annates . .	$ 30,000	
Royal ninths of the tithes . .	72,000	
Crusada	160,000	$262,000

Fourth Division

Profits on the monopoly of quick-silver, tobacco, gunpowder, and paper	$350,000	
Slave trade	200,000	
Trade in yerba-maté . . .	500,000	
Other monopolies formerly held by Jesuits	400,000	$1,450,000

	$4,399,000

decrease. The Marquis of Castel Fuerte, viceroy of Peru from 1724 to 1736, wrote at the close of his reign, that population is the basis of the state and the vital part of kingdoms; it is the population that produces their wealth and establishes their power. It is of little advantage that there are fertile fields, rich mines, and benignant climates, if people are wanting to cultivate the fields, work the mines, and enjoy the climates. Without population the lands are merely the corpse of an empire, wanting in power to perpetuate itself. The means proposed for preventing this decline were to restore to the central government control over trades; to guard with care the treatment of the Indians by the priests and the *corregidors*; to prohibit the sale of spirits; to transfer to the decadent provinces a sufficient number of families from the more densely inhabited provinces; to prevent too great a number of convents and monasteries; to rehabilitate the arts and trades; and to oppose the increase of luxury.[1]

[1] *Memorias de los Vireyes*, iii., 133.

INDEX

A

Abarca, 67

Abascal, viceroy, sends forces to Chiloé, 272

Absolute power of provincial governor, 65

Absolutism, 49; 218

Accounts, 49

Acevedo urges establishment of viceroyalty, 36, 37

Acosta, Friar, opposes theatre in Buenos Aires, 93

Administration, system of, 33; of Tupac Amaru, 196; colonial, 300

Admiralty, commissioners of, 286

Adrian VI., 138

Advertisements of negroes and mules, 106, 107

Agonizantes in Lima, 12

Agriculture, under O'Higgins in Chile, 228, 239; in Peru, hindrances to, 308-310

Aguirre, Francisco de, governor of Tucuman, 60

Alaska, *Columbia* bound for, 230

Alcalde mayor, 85, 203

Alcaldes, *de corte*, 9; of wards, 6; 78, 81-84

Alcavala, 84, 202, 328, 330

Alexander III., 128

Alexander VI., bull of, 120, 122

Aliaga, corregidor of Tinta, 197

Almaden, mine of, 311, 334

Alzaga, head of municipality, 290

Amalgamation of races, 100

Ambassadors, Indian, in Chile, 227

Amparados de la Purisima Concepcion, 12

Amusements in Chile, 244

Amuzquibar, inquisitor of Lima, 20

Andean road, 237

Andes, 75, 95

Apostolic See, 121

Appeals from bishop, 127

Appointment to ecclesiastical positions, 127

Arab comments on Aristotle, 152

Araciel, Dr., on ecclesiastical status of king, 123

Aranda, Count of, 161, 162, 164

Araucanians, 68; ambassadors of, 225-227

Arce, Pedro de, 269

Archbishop, of Lima, 135; sinecure, 136

Areche, visitador, 205, 206; sentenced Tupac Amaru, 209

Arequipa, 2; sent money to Buenos Aires, 272; bank in, 311

Arespacochega, governor of Tucuman for life, 66

Argentine, 1; plains of, 71; 75, 95

Argentinos fled before the British, 269

341

23